THE TELEVISION
SHERLOCK
HOLMES

THE TELEVISION
SHERLOCK HOLMES

Peter Haining

Virgin

For

THE CASTLEFIELD IRREGULARS
Michael Cox, Jeremy Brett,
David Burke, Edward Hardwicke
and, of course,
June Wyndham Davies
She is 'the' woman

This third revised edition first published in
Great Britain in 1994 by
Virgin Books
A division of Virgin Publishing Ltd
332 Ladbroke Grove
London W10 5AH

Original edition published by W.H. Allen in 1986,
and reprinted in October 1986
Second revised edition published by
Virgin Publishing Ltd in 1991,
and reprinted in 1991

Published in association with Granada Television,
makers of the internationally successful series *The
Adventures of Sherlock Holmes, The Return of Sherlock
Holmes, The Casebook of Sherlock Holmes* and *The
Memoirs of Sherlock Holmes*

Cataloguing in Publication Data available from
the British Library
ISBN 0 86369 793 3

Typeset by Phoenix Photosetting, Chatham, Kent
Printed and bound in Great Britain by
Mackays of Chatham PLC, Chatham, Kent

❧CONTENTS❧

❧FOREWORD❧

by Jeremy Brett

'The best way of acting a part successfully is to be it' wrote Conan Doyle in *The Dying Detective*, which we are shooting as I write.

Trying to be Sherlock Holmes is like trying to catch an arrow in mid-flight. I used to say I would not cross the street to meet him. I now know that I only said that because of my fear of rejection. In the past, I have arranged to meet him at the Savoy for tea, but neither of us turned up. He always seems to be one field ahead of me, forever escaping with speed and grace my endeavours to meet him face to face.

I know Watson is a truly good friend who doesn't report everything that happens; such consideration. Nor does he see the hairline cracks in the marble edifice of my face. Is that, I wonder, why Holmes moves so fast?

I do know that the team at Granada Studios are the finest. To everyone who has worked on our films of Sir Arthur Conan Doyle's stories in the past decade, only one word can express how I feel . . . Bravo!

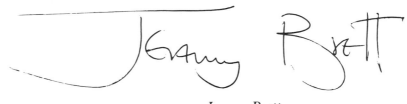

Jeremy Brett
Manchester, October 1993

P.S. November 9th, 1993. I apologise for not being as lean as I should have been in the last twenty films. This has been due sadly to what has only recently been diagnosed as heart failure. I am now living on foxgloves and water pills, and I'm told that in the not-too-distant future I will be lean once more. Yours, J. B.

A DECADE
❦OF THE❦
DEFINITIVE HOLMES

*'Holmes is an upholder of the law, and
he has a magnetism and mental genius
that have always been compulsive for people
throughout the last hundred years.'*
Jeremy Brett

Ten years ago on April 24, 1984 a new Sherlock Holmes made his debut on British television. Since the screening of 'A Scandal in Bohemia', an hour-long adaptation and the first of the series *The Adventures of Sherlock Holmes*, the world-wide success of this Granada production has inspired three further series, *The Return of Sherlock Holmes*, *The Casebook of Sherlock Holmes* and, currently, *The Memoirs of Sherlock Holmes*. During this time, the programme has also been masterminded by two producers and featured two Doctor Watsons. Only Jeremy Brett has remained the ever-constant feature and in so doing he has created a figure regarded by Sherlockians and the general public alike as the quintessential Sherlock Holmes.

The long-running success of the series is a tribute to the vision of the first producer, Michael Cox, who had the courage to attempt a painstakingly faithful transfer of Sir Arthur Conan Doyle's stories to the screen, and also to the imaginative skill and determination of June Wyndham Davies who succeeded him in the producer's chair in 1986 and who has, despite a diminishing number of suitable stories for adaptation, maintained the same authenticity and visual quality. It also owes much to David Burke, the quiet and commanding Shakespearean actor who at last demolished the image of Holmes' faithful accomplice as a bumbling clown; and Edward Hardwicke who, faced with the unenviable task of playing the second, slightly older Watson, made the transition seem virtually seamless and has since developed the Good Doctor into Holmes' best friend and soulmate, as his original creator intended.

Though the importance of all these factors – not to mention the scriptwriters, directors, designers, co-stars and all the rest of the Granada backroom team –

should never be underestimated, the greatest accolade certainly belongs to Jeremy Brett. During his ten years portraying Sherlock Holmes, Jeremy has overcome personal tragedy (the death of his much-loved wife), health problems (a much misrepresented nervous breakdown) and a gruelling production schedule in which the detective was rarely off-screen, to create an enduring success story which is not only unique in the annals of television but is now the focus of a world-wide cult.

This achievement has not gone unrecognized. At the time of writing (prior to the screening of the new six-part series of *The Memoirs*), the series has been seen in a total of 77 countries, with the most enthusiastic viewers (apart from those in the UK, where it attracts audiences of around 12 million) to be found in the USA, Australia, Canada, France, Germany, Italy, Spain and, particularly, Japan. Video sales are also booming in several of these territories (plus Norway). Jeremy Brett has been lauded by Sherlock Holmes societies throughout the world for his performance, and he receives an average of 3,000 fan letters a week from all over the globe. A number of honours have marked his decade in the role, and most recently the *Société Sherlock Holmes de France* has petitioned President Mitterand for him to be awarded a *Légion d'Honneur* – the self-same distinction presented to Holmes a century ago in 1894. Jeremy also featured on a series of stamps issued by the Royal Mail in October 1993.

In the ten years since I first became involved with the making of the Granada series and the writing of this book, I have met Jeremy Brett on several occasions, and have seen him in both the best of spirits and the worst. The way in which he has coped with the personal pressures and first created, then developed and finally maintained the character of Holmes as a sometimes surprising, occasionally perverse but always fascinating and intriguing character who dominates the small screen, has been an acting *tour de force* of the highest order.

For some years Jeremy was loath to talk publicly about his personal problems, but some of the misconceptions which arose as a result now deserve to be laid to rest once and for all. He was understandably devastated when his wife, Joan, an American television producer, died of cancer in 1986 – 'it was as if all the light had gone out of my life,' he says – and this, coupled with the strain of playing the role, resulted in him suffering a nervous breakdown. Granada, Jeremy says, were wonderful, immediately enabling him to enter a psychiatric hospital to regain his health. Rumour and gossip, however, got to work on his enforced absence from the Sherlock Holmes set.

There were stories circulating that he had actually gone mad playing the remote, neurotic, drug-taking Baker Street detective. That he would never be able to work again. Worst of all, that he was suffering from AIDS.

'I was certainly worried at the start about playing this dark, lonely character who never shows any emotion,' Jeremy reflects quietly today. 'I was afraid it might even bring my career to a grinding halt. But actually Holmes and I are alike in some ways. I discovered that he was vulnerable, as I am below the surface. And like me he falls apart when he's not working – though once we are both on a job we are set alight.

'The only way to describe things during those first couple of years was like being on a train that's going too fast. There were the demands of making the series and then suddenly Joan's death. Like that train I ended up off the rails.'

Jeremy's face darkens as he remembers the traumatic build-up of rumour and gossip. 'People were saying I had gone mad, that I was finished as an actor. Then

9

just as I was getting better these journalists from one of the tabloids turned up at my flat. They pretended to have brought a car to take me to the studios. Innocently, I let them in and as soon as one stepped into the room he announced which paper he was from and asked if it was true I had AIDS. I couldn't believe what I was hearing. But I did manage to reply, "Rubbish! I have just had a good old-fashioned nervous breakdown," and threw them out.'

Understandably, both Jeremy and the members of the Granada production team remain deeply resentful of that experience and the subsequent story which was published. All the more so because Jeremy's naturally solid frame showed none of the signs of the cruel and wasting disease. Grim as it was, though, it made Jeremy all the more determined to return to the role.

'It was something of a warning,' he says. 'I became determined not to let myself become suicidal playing Holmes as some actors have done. So I was careful to cast off the character at the end of each day and mix with lots of people. If I had any problems, I prayed or meditated – or just opened a bottle of champagne.'

A naturally gregarious man who is warm, friendly and blessed with a rapier-sharp wit, Jeremy has grown increasingly thoughtful both about the character of Holmes and himself. He believes that he has been able to incorporate some of his own personality into the character, thereby making him a little less cold, a little more vulnerable. However, the demands of keeping the role fresh – 'I'm constantly on a treasure hunt to add new elements to his character,' Jeremy says – mean he needs to keep himself on an even keel when he is not in front of the cameras. For this reason he takes a mood stabiliser, lithium, and has given up the wine and champagne he used to enjoy drinking so much.

'The lithium balances me, it stops me getting depressed,' he explains. 'I'm normally an up person, but the way my illness manifested itself was to make me too high. I would go into restaurants and buy everyone champagne.

'It was a hard decision to give up alcohol, but it counteracts with lithium, so I just knew I had to stop. There are certainly times when I feel resentful that my life is no longer my own and that I can't take a drink. But life must go on and you work and you survive.'

Jeremy's courage is not only admired by his fellow professionals, but stories of his breakdown and determination to overcome it have also inspired viewers of the TV series.

'I have had encouraging letters from fans who have also suffered with mental problems telling me how much I have helped them by being honest about my breakdown. They then see me on television and it gives them hope. I find that deeply heartening.'

Now aged 58, Jeremy believes he is taking better care of his health now than at any time since his teens when he suffered a bout of rheumatic fever which left his heart dangerously enlarged. Eight months of complete rest enabled him to regain his health – though the first time he rode the motorcycle given to him by his parents to 'aid' his recovery, he had an accident and broke one of his legs! Today he gets his exercise from riding, a little jogging and archery, of which he is very fond. His one vice is the cigarettes he takes from his pocket whenever he puts down Sherlock Holmes' pipe.

Jeremy also readily acknowledges the debt he owes both on screen and off to his 'Watson', Edward Hardwicke. He was able to find seclusion and the rest he required by staying with the Hardwicke family in France at the farmhouse which they own in Normandy; and then back on the set, Edward gave him all the support and encouragement he needed to work once more. The two men in fact act so smoothly and seemingly effortlessly together that it is not difficult to see how close their friendship has become.

Indeed, Jeremy believes friendship is the key to the Holmes–Watson partnership.

'To me, the Sherlock Holmes stories are about a great friendship,' he says. 'The two men are interdependent; without Watson, Holmes might well have burnt out on cocaine long ago. And Watson leads a pretty dull life, enlivened only by his adventures with Holmes. I hope the series shows how important friendship is.'

Edward Hardwicke seconds this view and cites it as a reason for trying to inject a little more humour into the screen Watson than is found on the printed page.

'Close friendships need humour and tolerance,' he says. 'Watson needs a sense of humour to survive Holmes' worst excesses. And being a doctor he is also a bit of a detective and can contribute to the investigations in his own way.'

Like Jeremy, Edward is a very different person to his character in real life. Although he is the son of the celebrated British dramatic actor, Sir Cedric Hardwicke, and spent much of his childhood in Hollywood, his main love is for comedy.

'I'm not a straightforward chap at all – I'm nothing like the good doctor,' he says with a wry smile. 'I was actually more interested in comedy and comics as a youngster. My heroes were the comedians Sid Fields and Danny Kaye. Although I am better known for straight roles, I still love making people laugh.'

Making the series has thankfully not been as beset with traumas for Edward as it has been for his friend. Indeed, it was the good fortune of landing the role of Doctor Watson that generated the money which enabled him to purchase the house in Normandy to which Jeremy retreated during his illness. Edward and his actress partner, Prim Cotton, like to escape there whenever possible, and he was somewhat surprised when some French neighbours recognised him recently.

'These neighbours invited us over for a drink one evening when one of the Sherlock Holmes episodes was being screened. Of course it was dubbed in French, so because both Jeremy and I appeared to be speaking rapid French, the locals assumed I spoke the language. In fact, I can only just get by.'

Edward believes that the major reason for the great success of the series both at home and abroad has been the skill with which they capture the period of the adventures.

'The stories are somehow just right for our times,' he says, 'in much the same way that the Basil Rathbone and Nigel Bruce films caught the public imagination half a century ago.'

Edward also enjoyed playing his Watson to Brett's Holmes in a stage version of the adventures entitled *The Secret of Sherlock Holmes* which ran for a year at the Wyndham's Theatre in London (from September 23, 1988) and then toured the provinces for three months. It was a welcome break from the demands of television, although it also involved several members of the Granada team. The script was written by Jeremy Paul, author of several of the series adaptations (including 'The Musgrave Ritual', which won an Edgar Allan Poe award from the Mystery Writers of America), and was directed by Patrick Garland who had directed several of the TV episodes. (Gary Hopkins won the second coveted Edgar award for 'The Devil's Foot').

11

Jeremy Brett explains how the transition from small screen to live stage occurred.

'It all began when I got this urge to put on tape all that I had learned about Holmes. I talked for something like eight hours about his childhood, his isolation, about the cracks in the marble that made him human. I spilled out all the little inventions that I had used to keep my performance alive. In particular I talked about Holmes' friendship with Watson. The play became my attempt to balance the ledger with Watson, to say things to him like "Thanks" and "Without you I would be lost".'

Utilising these tapes, Jeremy Paul created *The Secret of Sherlock Holmes*, with the secret hinging on the infamous Professor Moriarty's identity. Neither Jeremy Brett nor Edward Hardwicke was quite prepared for the success of the production.

'I thought it might run six weeks in London,' Jeremy reflects. 'But it just took off and we had full houses for a year. We must have done over five hundred performances by the end of the tour, and at times it was a struggle to keep the performances fresh. It was almost a relief to get back to the television studios.'

What also surprised Jeremy about the success of the stage presentation was the number of children he noticed in the audience. 'They were young children,' he remembers. 'I could just see their little faces over the tops of the seats. And when I talked to some of them after the performances I realized that Holmes was a heroic figure to them. I had never thought of him in that way before.'

Jeremy was even more amazed to learn that Sherlock Holmes is a sex symbol to a large number of women. During the run of the stage show, he says, there were several women who saw the production more than a hundred times; others who flew over specially from America and Japan; and even a dozen-strong band of young girls aged between 17 and 21 who called themselves the Regulars and acted as bodyguards, escorting him to his car after each performance.

'I was astounded when I realised how attractive he is to them. You'd never suspect it for one moment from the books. Girls long to seduce him. I know from experience that quite simply he is the man who has power over women. They lust after him because he's a challenge. Holmes is unattainable and that acts as a great turn-on.

'Holmes treats women as objects of interest, not as objects of desire, and that gets to them. Women throughout the world identify with what's going on and see me as Holmes. It's all very flattering and frightening at times. I just have to realise I'm in the fantasy business, but I do feel responsible and I get very concerned about the power this character wields.'

One of Holmes' greatest female admirers also happens to be the producer in charge of the series, June Wyndham Davies – masterminding the development of the scripts, overseeing the production, and coping with the hundred and one problems which are part and parcel of the producer's job. In the person of June, the programme is headed by a consummate professional with an outstanding track record for handling period drama with precise attention to authentic detail.

Throughout her tenure as producer, June has maintained close links with Dame Jean Conan Doyle, the author's daughter, and sought her approval for the changes that have been necessary in some of the more recent adaptations of her father's stories.

'She understands the weakness in some of the later stories as far as TV drama is concerned,' June says, 'and has been sympathetic to many of our ideas. We have always tried to observe her father's original intentions and only taken dramatic licence where it has been essential. What Dame Jean does *not* like is pastiches of the Holmes stories.'

June is particularly proud of the three two-hour specials which were screened in 1992–3. The first was *The Master Blackmailer*, with Robert Hardy as the evil and unscrupulous Charles Augustus Milverton, which was presented as a Christmas special – and which made world-wide headlines with a sequence in which Holmes kissed a serving maid.

'It was so well received that Granada asked me to produce two more,' June explains. 'The first was the case of the conniving *Eligible Bachelor* with Simon Williams, and the second was *The Last Vampyre*, starring Roy Marsden. This was based on 'The Sussex Vampire' which is a story I have always liked. In fact, vampire stories appeal to me, and although Francis Ford Coppola got the lion's share of the publicity with his new version of *Dracula*, we were actually ahead of him with our story.'*

Setting up the new six-part series, *The Memoirs of Sherlock Holmes*, has not been without its problems. Initially, the season was to consist of two more two-hour specials, but the central scheduler reversed this decision in favour of six one-hour episodes. Granada financed the first two hours themselves.

'Despite all the success of the series, money was not easy because period drama is so very expensive to make,' June recalls. 'At one stage I thought we might actually rely on Japan to finance the new series. Holmes is extraordinarily popular there. The suggestion was that Toshiba were interested in sponsoring us – but in the end we have been able to remain on familiar home territory. Although it would be nice to visit Japan!'

Sadly, though, the famous Baker Street set which adjoins the equally famous *Coronation Street* lot is now part of the Granada Studios visitors' tour and cannot feature in any further episodes. As ever, though, the inventive use of Victorian properties throughout Lancashire and, occasionally, further south as far as London, will ensure the authenticity which is the hallmark of the show.

As for the next decade, June Wyndham Davies believes that the episodes will almost certainly have to be two-hour specials based on the remaining short stories, each augmented with new characters and incidents. Jeremy Brett has already indicated his willingness to carry on playing the role he has made so uniquely his own.

'I no longer feel threatened by Holmes,' he says with a contented smile; 'in fact I really enjoy playing him. I have told Granada I'll finish all the stories. It has never been done before and means I have about another dozen or so to go. It would be crazy to have done so many and stop now.'

Such plans would certainly see the television Sherlock Holmes into the 21st century, and the second century of his own 'existence'. A truly remarkable achievement for the greatest detective who never lived.

---

*Author's note: I also have a special affection for *The Last Vampyre* and its original story, having acted as the programme's consultant on vampire history and provided from my own library the copy of the rare Victorian 'penny dreadful' novel, *Varney the Vampire*, which young Jack (Richard Dempsey) was seen reading in one of the crucial scenes.

HOLMES AND WATSON AT HOME IN BAKER STREET –
AN ORIGINAL ILLUSTRATION BY SIDNEY PAGET
FROM *THE STRAND* MAGAZINE.

SHERLOCK ❧HOLMES❧ AT ONE HUNDRED

The Centenary
of the
Master of Detectives

'My name is Sherlock Holmes. It is my business to know what other people don't know.'

It is just over a hundred years since the man who said those words stepped out of a young writer's imagination and onto a sheet of lined writing paper in the inner sanctum of a doctor's surgery. It was perhaps an inauspicious beginning for a character destined for literary immortality, but there is much about the origins of the world's most famous detective that is as fascinating and intriguing as the very stories about him.

The young doctor was, of course, Arthur Conan Doyle, a solidly-built 27-year-old medical practitioner, trying to make the best living he could in a small practice at Southsea, a typical middle-class English resort on the South Coast close to the big naval depot of Portsmouth. Patients were not plentiful at his compact surgery in Bush Villas, on Elm Grove, and it was out of a mixed sense of frustration and a genuine desire to write that Conan Doyle took up his pen while he waited in vain for the surgery bell to ring and let his imagination roam free . . .

Conan Doyle was born in Edinburgh, Scotland, on May 22, 1859, at Picardy Place, situated at the end of the famous Queen Street and right alongside Regent Gardens. His father, Charles Altamont Doyle, was a water-colourist, architect and journalist in the city, and it has been argued that he may well have been the inspiration for Conan Doyle's interest in crime fiction as he *could* have been the anonymous author of a series of 'yellowback' detective stories published in Edinburgh by John Menzies & Co (now famous as newsagents and booksellers) and featuring the cases of a 'City Detective' called James McGovan. These stories were included in a number of volumes such as *Brought To Bay, Hunted Down, Strange Clues,* and *Traced and Tracked* and *Solved Mysteries,* all published between 1856 and 1888, and now of the utmost rarity. Whether this attribution is true or not, Edinburgh was certainly a hotbed of detective-novel publishing when Conan Doyle was a boy, and we have evidence he read the McGovan stories while he was at college.

I actually possess a number of these pioneer Scottish detective stories – including a rather special copy of a book called *Clues, or Leaves From a Chief Constable's Note Book* written by one William Henderson and published by Oliphant, Anderson & Ferrier of Edinburgh. It is special to me because the title page is intriguingly signed 'James Watson, April 4, 1889' – and Doctor Watson did, of course, dip into 'yellowback' novels and was a fan of the great nautical writer of the time, W. Clark Russell!

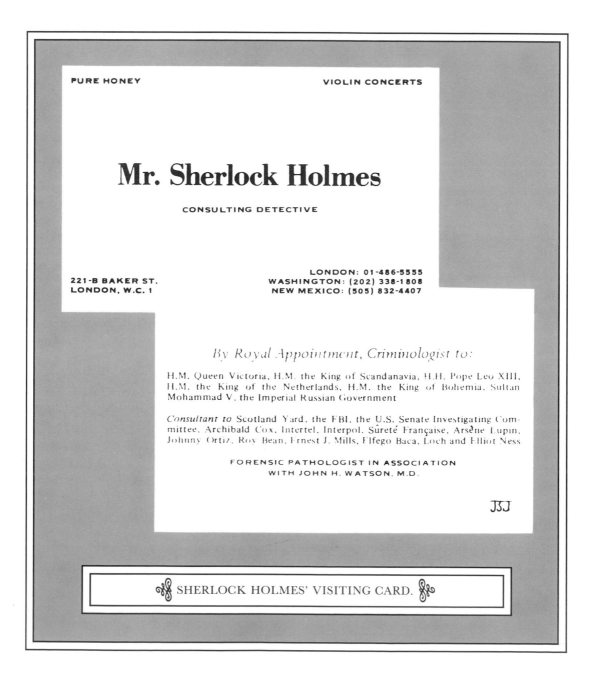

SHERLOCK HOLMES' VISITING CARD.

DOCTOR JOSEPH BELL OF EDINBURGH –
THE INSPIRATION FOR SHERLOCK HOLMES.

There is no doubt, however, that it was Conan Doyle's mother, Mary Foley, a woman of Irish descent, who instilled in him a love of literature and history. The fact that he could also claim relationship to Sir Walter Scott seems to have made his career as a writer almost inevitable.

It was, though, medicine which he studied at Edinburgh University, after his general schooling at Hodder House and Stonyhurst. It was at the University, of course, that he also met Doctor Joseph Bell the man who was to provide the model for Sherlock Holmes: but these memories were to lie dormant for a while.

After qualifying as an MD, Conan Doyle satisfied his natural bent for adventure by serving as a ship's surgeon on an Arctic whaling cruise. But the harsh conditions and poor pay soon drove him back to dry land. Returning to London in the depths of winter, he spent a memorable night wandering around the fog-bound streets in the vicinity of Regent's Park where he had digs.

The atmosphere of the city, its dank buildings and roads, mysterious little alleyways and gas-lit streets, as well as the hansom cabs merging in and out of the fog and the huddled figures of people going about their business, had a deep, even traumatic, effect upon him. Those sights were to provide the raw backgrounds for many of his stories to come.

It was in Southsea, however, that he put up his shingle as a doctor – and waited in vain for patients. In view of what fate had in store for him it was a most appropriate place to have chosen. The great Charles Dickens had been born the son of a navy Pay Clerk at nearby Mile End Terrace in Portsmouth in 1812. H. G. Wells worked as an unhappy drapery assistant in a city shop at the corner of

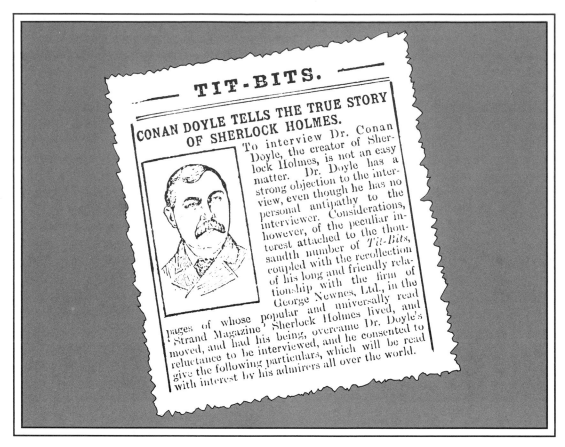

**A FACSIMILE OF A RARE ARTICLE BY ARTHUR CONAN DOYLE
ABOUT THE ORIGINS OF SHERLOCK HOLMES –
AND A FACSIMILE OF HIS SIGNATURE.**

King's Road and St Paul's Road. And Rudyard Kipling also spent six miserable years of his childhood lodging with a woman in Camberwell Road, Southsea while his parents were in India.

Although there was much to inspire the fledgling writer about the area in which he lived – Southsea has a spectacular 2-mile stretch of beach backed by parkland, unrivalled views of Spithead, and history-filled Southsea Castle – it was high adventure stories that first came from his pen and, after several rejections, at last found favour with the editors of magazines, including *Chamber's Journal* (based in his native city, Edinburgh), *Blackwood's Magazine* (another Scottish journal), *London Society* and *All Year Round* which had, of course, been founded by Charles Dickens.

It was early in the year 1886 that he had the sudden flash of inspiration which was to change his life – and write his name large in the history of literature. Though not *so* large that he could even come close to the stature that was to be accorded the creation of this inspiration, Sherlock Holmes.

On a gramophone record that Conan Doyle made shortly before his death entitled, *The Actual Voices of Kipling, Conan Doyle and Shaw* (1930) he speaks on the second side about how he created Holmes. His voice, echoing sonorously down the years, sounds uncannily like several of the actors who have played Holmes – including Arthur Wontner whom Conan Doyle applauded as the best *speaking* Sherlock of the movies. It is also, surely, the most authentic record we have of the 'birth' of the great detective.

'I was educated in a very severe and critical school of medical thought,' Conan Doyle says, 'especially coming under the influence of Doctor Bell of Edinburgh who had the most remarkable powers of observation. He prided himself that when he looked at a patient he could tell not only their disease, but very often their occupation and place of residence. Reading some detective stories I was struck by the fact that their results were obtained in nearly every case by chance. I thought I would try my hand at writing a story in which the hero would treat crime as Doctor Bell treated disease and where science would take the place of chance.'

Interestingly, Conan Doyle had also been interviewed on *film* about Sherlock Holmes the previous year, 1929, although his conversation is predominantly about Spiritualism – which was, of course, his great passion at that time – and it seems probable that he only agreed to mention Holmes as long as he was given ample opportunity to discuss the Spirit World. There is, though, a nice acknowledgement to Holmes in two of the props he uses – one of the collections of Sherlock Holmes' cases and a large dog which lies at his feet. Although he adds nothing to what is said on the record, he does appear as a gentle, well-spoken man with the same kind of fatherly face that has been possessed by generations of screen Watsons.

Having decided on the basic concept of his story, Conan Doyle now needed a name for his hero. Again we have his own words on the matter, in an article he wrote entitled *The Truth About Sherlock Holmes* for the American publication, *Collier's* (which serialized Holmes) in December 1923.

'But what should I call the fellow?' he wrote. 'I still possess the leaf of notebook with various alternative names. One rebelled against the elementary art which gives some inkling of character in the name, and creates Mr Sharps or Mr Ferrets. First it was Sherringford Holmes; then it was Sherlock Holmes. He could not tell his own exploits, so he must have a commonplace comrade as a foil – an educated man of action who could both join in the exploits and narrate them. A drab, quiet name for this unostentatious man. Watson would do. And so I had my purpose and wrote my *Study in Scarlet*.'

Conan Doyle worked on the story – his first attempt at a full-length novel – through the early months of 1886 and was finished by April. He felt it was 'as good as I could make it' and sent it off to James Payn, the editor of *Chamber's Journal*, who had already accepted several of his short stories.

The reaction of the first man to have seen this ground-breaking story was curious. 'I have enjoyed reading your detective novel,' he wrote to Conan Doyle, 'but I found it both too short and too long.'

Among all the remarks of the editors of publishing houses who have turned down books that later became international successes – and I was once among their number myself – this must surely be the strangest!

Conan Doyle was disappointed – and even more so when his second submission, to the firm of Arrowsmith & Co in London – was returned unread in July 1886 after having been in their keeping since May. Would Holmes and Watson *ever* make their bow he must have wondered.

According to Conan Doyle 'two or three others sniffed and turned away' his

A RARE PHOTOGRAPH OF
SIDNEY PAGET, THE MAN WHO DREW
THE CLASSIC VERSION OF THE
GREAT DETECTIVE.

manuscript, and he was on the point of consigning the work to his waste paper basket when he came across the name of Ward, Lock & Co who made a speciality of publishing cheap and often sensational literature.

On October 31, 1886 – and all Sherlockians mark that date – Conan Doyle received a letter dated the previous day which brightened his heart – though not the financial ambitions with which he had set out.

'Dear Sir,' the letter said. 'We have read your story and are pleased with it. We could not publish it this year, as the market is flooded at present with cheap fiction, but if you do not object to its being held over till next year, we will give you £25 for the copyright.'

Although Conan Doyle was obviously far from happy with the meagre offer, he felt there was no alternative but to accept. And so Sherlock Holmes and Doctor Watson remained in manuscript for another year, until *A Study in Scarlet* appeared in *Beeton's Christmas Annual* of 1887.

The rest of the story of Sherlock Holmes is, of course, history. The story was read and enjoyed by the Editor of the American journal, *Lippincott's Magazine*, who commissioned Conan Doyle to write another story of Sherlock Holmes and *The Sign of Four* appeared in 1889. Then, in 1891, Greenhough Smith, the Editor of a new English magazine, *The Strand*, asked for six short stories featuring the ingenious detective – and on their appearance Holmes rapidly became a national favourite.

There is no doubt that the illustrations of the stories heightened their appeal and their impact. Curiously, by one of those strange twists of fate that dot the history of Sherlock Holmes, the magazine had intended to commission the artist Walter Paget to illustrate Holmes – but by mistake the letter went to his brother, Sidney, and a legend was born. For generations, enthusiasts have wondered just *how* Holmes might have first appeared if it had been Walter and not Sidney Paget who had given him form and features.

As it was, Conan Doyle's own vision of the detective did not quite match what he later saw on the printed page. Again in the article for *Collier's* he wrote, 'I may say that the drawings are very unlike my own original idea of the man. I saw him as very tall – "over six feet, but so excessively lean that he seemed considerably taller" said *A Study in Scarlet*.

'He had, as I imagined him, a thin, razor-like face, with a great hawk's-bill of a nose, and two small eyes, set close together on either side of it. Such was my conception.

'It chanced, however, that poor Arthur (sic) Paget who, before his premature death, drew all the original pictures, had a younger brother, whose name, I think, was Harold, who served him as a model. The handsome Harold took the place of the more powerful but uglier Sherlock, and, perhaps from the view of my lady readers, it was as well.'

It is also recorded that having written two series of short stories, Conan Doyle tired of his creation because he was interfering with his more serious work. (He had, by now, abandoned his medical practice, and was also married.) He determined to put a stop to what he regarded as a 'lower stratum of literary achievement'.

'Therefore, as a sign of my resolution,' he wrote later, 'I intended to end the life of my hero. The idea was in my mind when I went with my wife for a short holiday in Switzerland, in the course of which we walked down the Lauterbrunnen Valley.

I saw there the wonderful falls of Reichenbach, a terrible place, and that, I thought, would make a worthy tomb for poor Sherlock – even if I buried my banking account along with him. So there I laid him, fully determined that he should stay there – as indeed for some years he did.'

The public outcry which greeted *The Final Problem* is also a legend. As is Conan Doyle's final capitulation to public demand and the 'resurrection' of Holmes in 1901 in the novel, *The Hound of the Baskervilles*, and then the new short stories which restarted in *The Strand* with *The Empty House* in 1903 and continued thereafter until shortly before the author's death.

The public delight at the return of Holmes was unbounded. The newspapers and magazines of the time publicized the event as little short of a second coming. The humorous magazine *Punch*, for example, carried a specially composed song to mark the occasion in its issue of May 27, 1903, and this is reprinted here for the first time as being typical of the media attention that greeted the reappearance of Holmes.

Though Conan Doyle was by now financially secure as a result of the success of his detective stories, he already felt himself pursued, haunted even, by his creation. His post carried endless requests from readers all over the world seeking the assistance of Mr Sherlock Holmes. Even when Conan Doyle received a knighthood in 1902 ostensibly for his political writings championing the British cause in the Boer War there was no separating them. (There were those who felt the honour had been bestowed for bringing back Holmes!)

In an essay for *The Strand* magazine in December 1917, *Some Personalia About Sherlock Holmes*, he told the following amusing story.

'Shortly after I received my knighthood, I had a bill from a tradesman which was quite correct and businesslike in every detail save that it was made out to "Sir Sherlock Holmes". Now I hope that I can stand a joke as well as my neighbours, but this particular piece of humour seemed rather misapplied, and I wrote sharply upon the subject.

'In response to my letter there arrived at my house a very repentant clerk, who expressed sorrow at the incident, but kept on repeating the phrase, "I assure you, sir, that it was *bona fide*."

'"What do you mean by *bona fide*?" I asked. "Well, sir, my mates in the shop told me that you had been knighted, and that when a man was knighted he changed his name, and that you had taken that one!"

'I need not say that my annoyance vanished, and that I laughed as heartily as his pals were probably doing round the corner.'

Of course, any writer who creates a legend is bound to be compared to that creation to see what, if anything, of himself he has put into it. The comparisons between Conan Doyle and the occupants of 221B Baker Street are, indeed, quite striking.

There are those who maintain that the author saw himself as Watson – for both are doctor-writers, physically similar and of quiet demeanour. But, then, look at the even stronger similarities between Conan Doyle and Holmes.

Conan Doyle loved working in an old dressing-gown, smoked clay pipes, kept voluminous scrapbooks of newspaper cuttings and collected documents. He was keen on detective work, too – keeping a magnifying glass in his desk and a revolver in the drawer – and solved the real-life cases of Oscar Slater and George Edalji in a manner that Holmes himself would have been proud of. (This aspect of his life

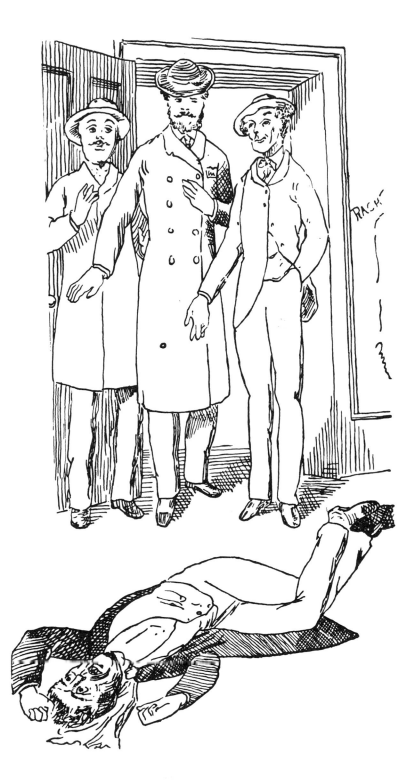

ONE OF THE EARLIEST SKETCHES OF HOLMES AND WATSON
MADE BY CONAN DOYLE'S FATHER, CHARLES ALTAMONT
DOYLE, FOR THE BOOK PUBLICATION OF
A STUDY IN SCARLET IN 1888.

THE CLASSIC AMERICAN INTERPRETATION OF HOLMES
BY FREDERIC DORR STEELE, DRAWN FOR *THE ADVENTURE OF
THE MISSING THREE-QUARTER*.

was, in fact, successfully dramatized in a 1974 TV drama, *Conan Doyle*, one of the episodes in a series called *The Edwardians* and starring Nigel Davenport as Conan Doyle.)

Both Conan Doyle and Holmes had artists in their families (Holmes' was allegedly the French painter Horace Vernet), and both were depreciative of their achievements. (Conan Doyle once claimed to have written one of the Holmes stories during an afternoon watching cricket at Lords, while the historical novels were written with immense concentration over long periods of time.)

Perhaps we are best taking Conan Doyle's own view on the matter, though someone with his ambivalent feelings towards his work is bound to leave question marks.

'I have often been asked,' he said in 1923, 'whether I had myself the qualities which I depicted in Holmes, or whether I was merely the Watson that I look. Of course, I am well aware that it is one thing to grapple with a practical problem and quite another thing when you are allowed to solve it under your own conditions. At the same time a man cannot spin a character out of his own inner consciousness and make it really lifelike until he has some possibilities of that character within him – which is a dangerous admission for one who has drawn so many villains as I!'

While this particular debate is obviously far from finished, Conan Doyle was undoubtedly delighted when Holmes and Watson were transported from the printed page, first onto the stage and then into films and radio. Sadly, he did not live long enough to see his great detective brought into the latest medium of communication and the one which is the primary concern of this book, television.

It was the American actor/playwright William Gillette who, with Conan Doyle's permission, brought Holmes alive in the first major stage production *Sherlock Holmes* in 1899. Gillette was the embodiment of the great detective in both appearance and mannerisms, and this identification was further strengthened, in America at least, when an artist named Frederic Dorr Steele illustrated the stories in *Collier's* magazine in preference to Sidney Paget.

Conan Doyle, though, was completely bowled over by Gillette and his performance, writing later, 'It is not given to every man to see the child of his brain endowed with life through the genius of a sympathetic artist, but that was my good fortune when Mr Gillette turned his mind and his great talents to putting Holmes upon the stage.' He ended his tribute by tendering his thanks to 'the man who changed a creature of thin air into an absolutely convincing human being'.

Though William Gillette was not to be the first man to play Holmes on the screen – that honour belongs to the man who appeared in a 30-second, 1900 movie called *Sherlock Holmes Baffled* and who may or may not have been Walter Huston (we shall return to that little matter later) – in 1930 he *was* the first man to play Holmes on the radio for NBC's half-hour version of *The Adventure of the Speckled Band* with Leigh Lovell as Watson.

This book is not, though, the place to discuss the various actors who have played the great detective on the stage, in films or on the radio – for there are already several books in the Sherlockian library on each of those subjects. The names of the men, too, run off the tongue with familiarity: H. A. Saintsbury, Eille Norwood (who we *shall* be looking at in some detail because of the extraordinary coincidence that he shares the same original name as the latest Holmes, Jeremy Brett), John Barrymore, Clive Brook, Reginald Owen, Raymond Massey, Arthur Wontner,

Basil Rathbone, Peter Cushing and the host of recent impersonators including John Neville, Robert Stephens, George C. Scott and others.

What *is* important to mention, I think, is Conan Doyle's interest in the personification of Holmes on the screen. The medium of the movies evidently fascinated him, and we know he watched Eille Norwood filming scenes for the series of silent movies made in the Twenties.

Not surprisingly, Conan Doyle was not altogether happy with the updating of the stories to a contemporary period, but was full of praise for Norwood's acting which he said was of 'a rare quality'. He was similarly impressed by the actor's 'unrivalled power of disguise'.

Eille Norwood told Conan Doyle when they met on the set that it had always been his greatest wish to play Sherlock Holmes, and that when he died he wanted the epitaph on his grave to read:

'Lies Sherlock Holmes beneath the soil,
His still remains disarmed, destroyed,
But thanks to Stoll and Conan Doyle,
He still remains in celluloid.'

In 1923, Conan Doyle and his wife went to America, and during their stay made a special visit to Hollywood where they were fêted like visiting Royalty. Most of the top stars were as eager to meet the creator of Sherlock Holmes as he was them, and Conan Doyle was pressed for news about further exploits of the Baker Street detective.

Conan Doyle particularly enjoyed meeting the two biggest stars in the film capital, Douglas Fairbanks and Mary Pickford. A rare photograph of this meeting on one of the huge Hollywood sets is reproduced here.

It is said that Conan Doyle was vastly amused to hear from Douglas Fairbanks about the film the actor had made in 1915 called *The Mystery of the Leaping Fish* which was a parody of the Holmes adventures. The author's biggest laugh was reserved for Fairbanks' revelation that the name of the master sleuth he had played had been called 'Coke Ennyday'!

When talking pictures arrived, one of the earliest to be made in Britain with the addition of sound was . . . a Sherlock Holmes adventure. *The Sleeping Cardinal* shot at Twickenham Film Studios in the spring of 1930 was based on *The Final Problem*, *The Empty House* and a little of William Gillette's play. In the starring role was Arthur Wontner, a screen veteran, then 56, who bore an uncanny likeness to the Paget drawings of Holmes.

SIR ARTHUR AND LADY CONAN DOYLE
IN HOLLYWOOD IN 1923,
MEETING MARY PICKFORD
AND DOUGLAS FAIRBANKS.

CONAN DOYLE HIMSELF IMPERSONATED ON TELEVISION IN
THE SERIES, *THE EDWARDIANS*, MADE IN 1974. MARIA AITKEN
PLAYS HIS WIFE, JEAN.

In May of that year – just two months before his death on July 7, 1930 – Conan Doyle was invited to Twickenham and there introduced to this latest man to portray Holmes. The old man was immediately struck by the actor's likeness. 'I doubt if there is another actor in the country more suited to the part than you,' he said, and then with a passing reference to the new technique of sound, added: 'Though I cannot say quite how Sherlock Holmes' voice might sound!'

Wontner opted for his natural rather gentle and reserved tones, which has led some critics to see him as the most understated of all the screen Holmes. He also sought to make him among the most authentic by sticking to the original dialogue as much as possible.

Wontner was the last man Conan Doyle ever saw portraying Holmes, and although television had been demonstrated by John Logie Baird as early as 1926, the first public TV service by the BBC was not started until a decade later in 1936. The creator of Sherlock Holmes died without the slightest knowledge of the impact

ARTHUR WONTNER, THE SCREEN
HOLMES IN 1930, WHOM
CONAN DOYLE THOUGHT IDEAL
TO PLAY THE PART.

that the detective would have on this new medium – though judging by what had already happened on the stage, in the cinema and on radio, he might have had a pretty good idea!

The reason for the enduring popularity of Holmes is one that has exercised the minds of both admirers and detractors for the best part of the last one hundred years. The more so now as we near the end of yet another century and his reputation grows ever stronger.

Two opposing viewpoints will illustrate what I mean. Take Peter Lewis writing in the *Daily Mail* of November 26, 1977, when ITV screened *The Silver Blaze* with Christopher Plummer in the lead role.

'What is it about Sherlock Holmes that will not die?' he asked. 'For when you come to look into him what *is* Holmes? He is a collection of props. He is a deer-stalker hat and an Inverness cape and that curling pipe – the perfect disguise. Once inside them, all actors look very much alike . . .

'Take all the props away and what have you got? The answer is that you have nothing recognisably human at all. In Doctor Watson's words: "He was, I take it, the most perfect reasoning and observing machine that the world has seen". Of all the gallery of immortals of literature – Romeo or Falstaff, Shylock or Scrooge, Robinson Crusoe or Alice, Don Quixote or Sancho Panza, Holmes least deserves to be there, because he is more machine than man.'

On the other hand, Julian Symons, the mystery writer and author of *A Three Pipe Problem*, thinks that a lack of emotion is certainly *not* one of the things missing from the stories. Talking in March 1985 as the latest television series was launched in America he said:

'Three things have ensured their permanence: the period flavour, the quality of the tales, and the central characters. "Period flavour" should really be "flavours" for the stories have been read differently by successive generations.

'For readers of *The Strand*, in the Nineties, Conan Doyle's London was romanticized but recognisable. Move on 30 years to my own childhood, and the blend of past and present in the stories (gas lighting had almost gone, so had hansom cabs, but fogs remained) was what made them enthralling. Move on another 30, and for my children the saga was now altogether a period piece. London fogs had vanished with the Clean Air Act, frock coats and Inverness capes were as strange to them as ruffs and periwigs. But although the trappings had gone, the magic remained.'

Mr Symons says he has no doubt that the magic remains for new readers in the 1980s, although modern crime writers may be more clever and cunning in their plotting. And he adds:

'To say that literary creations are two-dimensional may not sound like much of a recommendation, but Holmes and Watson transcend this kind of criticism. They are not "real people" . . . and we don't require of them that they should have emotional problems or worry about paying the rent. They come freshly to each

IAN FLEMING, WHO MADE
A SYMPATHETIC WATSON TO
ARTHUR WONTNER'S HOLMES IN
THE 1932 FILM,
THE MISSING REMBRANDT.

generation because they are embedded in the world of myth, heroic figures like Don Quixote and Sancho Panza, of whom we wish to know nothing more than their creators have told us, and whose exploits and adventures hold us endlessly fascinated.'

It is just this 'endless fascination' which Michael Cox, the then head of drama series at Granada TV, wanted to tap into when he decided to make the series of Sherlock Holmes adventures which have since been shown in over 50 countries of the world and caused their star, Jeremy Brett, to be hailed as *the* Sherlock Holmes: the actor who has 'wiped the memory clean of all previous portrayals' to quote reviewer Alan Coren in *The Mail on Sunday* of September 15, 1985 – the sister paper, incidentally, to the *Daily Mail* which so swingeingly dismissed Holmes a mere eight years earlier.

Granada have now made five full-length stories (*The Sign of Four*, *The Hound of the Baskervilles*, *The Master Blackmailer*, *The Last Vampyre* and *The Eligible Bachelor*) and four series: the 13-part *Adventures of Sherlock Holmes*, culminating in the drama at the Reichenbach Falls; the 11-part *The Return of Sherlock Holmes*; and two six-part series, *The Casebook of Sherlock Holmes* and *The Memoirs of Sherlock Holmes*. The only change was a new Watson to accompany Brett's Holmes after the first series.

It was the creation of that first series, together with the people who made it, and the impact it has had on our view of Holmes, that inspired the first edition of this book. The screening of the third series – *The Casebook of Sherlock Holmes* – provides a further opportunity to examine in detail the many interpretations of Holmes that have appeared on television over a span of more than half a century since the invention of the medium. Our area of coverage is the world – for Sherlock Holmes knows no boundaries in his appeal. Even the now-lowered Iron Curtain, you will see, allowed his influence to sweep through!

The Television Sherlock Holmes is, I am delighted to say, a 'first' in Sherlockian terms – and that's no mean achievement in a field which has already generated enough books to fill a library. (And *does* fill a number in Britain, America and several other places.) For, prior to this book's first appearance, no single work had dealt with Holmes on TV, which is now clearly another major and constantly developing aspect of the legend of Sherlock Holmes.

One of the features that has characterized the Granada series apart from the brilliant acting and stunning sets, has been the scrupulous attention to canonical detail. Great care has been taken to follow the original plots faithfully and, wherever possible, even use Conan Doyle's original dialogue.

At the very outset of the project, Michael Cox decided to compile a *Baker Street File* into which he and his colleagues poured all the relevant details about Holmes and Watson and their adventures. It was a painstaking and worthwhile exercise involving combing the entire Holmesian *oeuvre* – on a scale which had not previously been attempted by a film-maker.

Michael was well aware that because of the haste with which Conan Doyle wrote many of the cases, discrepancies and even errors had crept in, and he was

THE PARTNERSHIP OF JEREMY BRETT
AND DAVID BURKE WHICH AT LAST
BROKE WITH TRADITION AND
ACCURATELY PORTRAYED THE
RELATIONSHIP BETWEEN HOLMES AND
WATSON IN THE GRANADA SERIES.

DAVID BURKE AND JEREMY BRETT
ON LOCATION IN SWITZERLAND
DURING THE FILMING OF
THE FINAL PROBLEM.

anxious to iron these out wherever possible. Why, didn't he even have the author's *own* confession about his literary lapses?

'Sometimes I have got upon dangerous ground,' Conan Doyle admitted late in his life, 'where I have taken risks through my own want of knowledge of the correct atmosphere. I have, for example, never been a racing man, and yet I ventured to

34

write *Silver Blaze*, where the mystery depends upon the laws of training and racing.

'The story is all right, and Holmes may have been at the top of his form, but my ignorance cries aloud to Heaven. I read an excellent and very damaging criticism of the story in some sporting paper, clearly written by a man who *did* know, in which he explained the exact penalties which would have come upon all concerned if they had acted as I described. Half would have been in jail and the other half warned off the turf forever.

'However, I have never been nervous about details,' Conan Doyle added, 'and one must be masterful sometimes. When an alarmed Editor wrote to me once: "There is no second line of rails at this point," I answered: "I make one." On the other hand, of course, there are cases where accuracy is essential.'

Granada's decision to pursue accuracy and attention was emphasized by spending some £5 million on creating the 13 episodes of *The Adventures of Sherlock Holmes*, and their reward was popular and critical acclaim on both sides of the Atlantic. The huzzahs from America were particularly gratifying, for there the image of Basil Rathbone as *the* Holmes had remained unchallenged for many years. The reaction to the series was typified in reviews like this by Ed Siegel in the *Boston Globe* of March 14, 1985.

'Thursday night, March 14, 8 pm. Mark it down. History will record it as the date and time where "The Curse of Basil" was lifted from the English speaking world – well, at least the American subdivision.

'In 1939, 20th Century Fox took Hollywood's most notorious villain, Basil Rathbone, and turned him into one of English literature's most notable heroes, Sherlock Holmes. After 14 movies and a radio series, it has been all but impossible to read an Arthur Conan Doyle story about the detective and not hear the late British actor's authoritative baritone or visualise Rathbone's razor-sharp angularity. There were many cinematic Holmeses before and even more since, but none had approached Rathbone's portrayal.

'Until April of 1984. That's when Granada Television, the makers of *Brideshead Revisited* and *Jewel in the Crown*, unveiled Jeremy Brett as the resident detective of 221B Baker Street on British television. It is an astounding, almost awesome, performance.'

The partnership of Holmes and Watson was also seen by other critics as a major triumph. Said *US Today* TV critic, Jack Curry:

'Where the show really breaks ground is in the way it depicts Holmes' relationship with Doctor Watson. It's anything but elementary. Rather than the traditional mentor-appreciation interpretation, there is a complex inter-dependence – a bond of respect and friendship other portrayals have missed. It turns the well known tales into buddy adventures.'

In reading the piles of clippings that reviewers have showered on a delighted Granada, I was struck once again as I have been before, in my years of association with Holmes, how strongly the belief that the great detective actually *exists* still persists. Scott Bond and Sherry Rose Bond, reviewing the early stories, were just two of the many who commented on this factor.

'To over four generations of people around the world,' they wrote in *Applause* magazine, 'Holmes is more than a fictitious character. He is a real criminal investigator, in retirement now, but always there if he should be needed to solve the problem of a missing heiress or to recover a national treasure.'

The British critic, Benny Green, also said much the same thing. 'That Mr

Sherlock Holmes really exists is a truism which no intelligent man would deny, except possibly Moriarty, that scoundrel who has done so much to confound the fundamental issues of right and wrong . . . Even the most detached observer finds himself utterly convinced of the corporeal reality of Holmes. For he simply exists in too great a variety of guises for him not to be real. Too many men have impersonated him, too many nations have paid him court, too many alien syntaxes have wrestled with the nightmare of disguising him as the flower of some other culture, too many subtle minds have discussed affairs with him. But as to *where* Holmes exists, that is not so easy to answer . . .'

How Sir Arthur Conan Doyle, wherever he may be, must smile at this! For he saw it all coming before his death as this remark in the early Twenties shows:

'I do not think that I ever realized what a living actual personality Holmes had become to the more guileless readers until I heard the very pleasing story of the *char-a-bancs* of French schoolboys who, when asked what they wanted to see first in London, replied unanimously that they wanted to see Mr Holmes's lodgings in Baker Street . . .'

In this statement, in fact, lies the answer to Benny Green's question. For Holmes exists in the nostalgic hearts of all of us – with a little help from the groups of Sherlockian enthusiasts all over the world, and that London thoroughfare which is still the Mecca of all admirers.

At the Abbey National building in Baker Street which widespread opinion pinpoints as the location where 221B once stood – for it extends from 219 to 233 – they have a department kept busy answering the mail which still floods in from all over the world for Holmes, seeking his aid. More than 400 letters a year, in fact.

'Dear Mr Holmes,' a typical letter, extracted for my interest and postmarked New York, read, 'I would like to secure your services. My aunt and uncle have had a robbery at their home. We think it was an inside job . . .'

Or this from a London teenager, 'Perhaps you wonder why a sensible and quite sane school girl should attempt to write to you? It is because to me you are immortal.'

There are also on file letters inviting Holmes to be guest speaker at a dinner in Toronto; a request from Poland for a signed photograph; and from Tokyo an obviously heart-felt plea from a former cocaine addict urging the great detective to renounce his habit before it is too late . . .

Not wishing to destroy the illusion, a standard reply is sent to all these enquirers: 'You will appreciate that Mr Holmes had to vacate his rooms and unfortunately we do not know his present whereabouts.' Nor are the Abbey National unaware of the allure of their address, for there have been plans mooted to bottle and sell well-water drawn from a spring beneath the premises . . .

Although I hate to spoil such a widespread illusion, I think I have at last discovered where 221B *really* is. If you face south it is not on the right-hand side of the street where the Abbey National building is located at all – but further down beyond Marylebone Road towards Portman Square on the *left-hand* side. The contemporary engraving reproduced here of the area in the 1880's when Conan Doyle decided upon the address will help you locate the spot.*

---

* This conclusion is also one shared by the researchers for the Granada TV series who have located 221B on this same side of the road, as the reader will learn later.

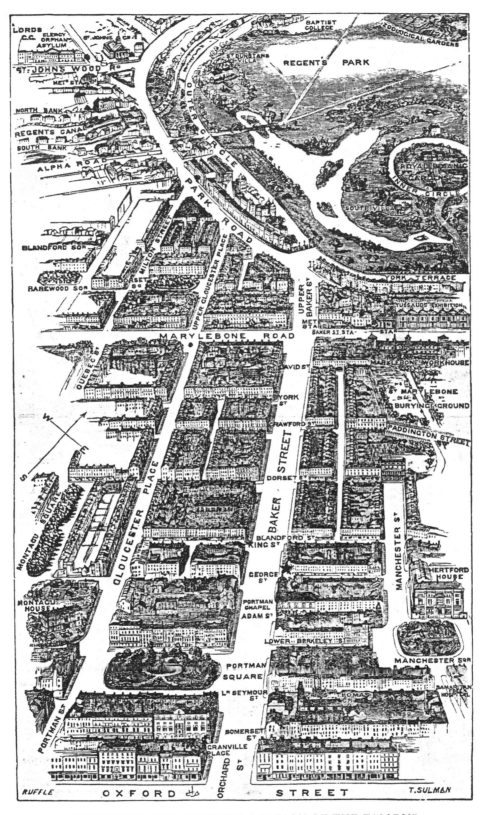

221B FOUND AT LAST! THE LOCATION OF THE FAMOUS
BAKER STREET ADDRESS AS GIVEN BY CONAN DOYLE
AND PIN-POINTED ON A LONDON STREET MAP OF THE 1880'S.

The source of my information is Conan Doyle himself – albeit quoted from a secondary person. And I must immediately hush the Sherlockians who will thrust at me the author's much quoted remark from his 1923 article, *The Truth About Sherlock Holmes* – 'Many have asked me which house it is, but that is a point which, for excellent reasons, I will not decide.'

This, though, was not a resolution to which he held firm, as the man who supplied my information insists. He is Nigel Morland, the British crime novelist and historian, who was also a life-long friend of Edgar Wallace.

Mr Morland, who was born in 1905, was like Wallace in that he only had a basic education and then taught himself in the school of life. Later, he tried various jobs – including printer, door-to-door salesman and mortuary assistant – before discovering his natural ability as a writer. Thereafter he poured out a stream of crime novels as well as screen, radio and television adaptations, encouraged all the time by Wallace. Like his mentor, he was incredibly prolific – writing well over 300 books – and for a time he was also Editor of the *Edgar Wallace Mystery Magazine*.

This is the relevant story which Morland tells of the location of 221B. 'Many years ago, when I was a very young man, I was walking down Baker Street with Edgar Wallace when we ran into Conan Doyle. We were walking towards Portman Square and, eventually, Oxford Street.

'I recall Edgar Wallace asking exactly where 221B was supposed to be. Conan Doyle pointed unhesitatingly to a house on the left-hand side of the street, just after we passed George Street, and said: "It's about there, if anywhere."'

I suppose, though, in the final analysis, we prefer the mysteries of Sherlock Holmes to remain . . . mysteries. It is part of his appeal that we can debate the 'facts' of his life just as freely as we relish going yet again on those adventures which are already so familiar and well-loved.

Television has proved yet another medium to demonstrate the magic of Holmes and Watson and the allure of their cases, as I hope the pages which follow will clearly demonstrate. And I suspect that they will be afoot in this medium for many years to come. For what are a hundred years to a legend?

As the great Orson Welles – who once actually played Moriarty on the radio – so perceptively said of Holmes: 'He is a gentleman who never lived – and who will never die.'

LEFT: A SKETCH BY THE CARTOONIST, THOMAS DERRICK, OF A STATUE OF SHERLOCK HOLMES WHICH IT WAS PROPOSED SHOULD BE ERECTED IN BAKER STREET IN 1933.

OPPOSITE: SCULPTOR GERALD LAING WITH HIS STATUE OF SHERLOCK HOLMES INSTALLED IN EDINBURGH IN 1991, AND BELIEVED TO BE THE ONLY ONE IN BRITAIN.

BACK TO HIS NATIVE STRAND
(Sherlock Holmes is to reappear in *The Strand* Magazine)

HOLMES REAPPEARS IN *THE ADVENTURE OF THE EMPTY HOUSE* AS DEPICTED
BY PAGET FOR *THE STRAND* MAGAZINE IN OCTOBER 1903 –
AND JEREMY BRETT MEETS HIS NEW WATSON, EDWARD HARDWICKE.

Air: *Archie* in *The Toreador*

Oh, Sherlock Holmes lay hidden more than half a dozen years
He left his loving London in a whirl of doubts and fears.
    For we thought a wicked party
    Of the name of MORIARTY
Had despatched him (in a manner fit to freeze one).
They grappled on a cliff-top, on a ledge six inches wide;
We deemed his chances flimsy when he vanished o'er the side.
    But the very latest news is
    That he merely got some bruises.
If there is a man who's hard to kill, why he's one.
    Oh, Sherlock, Sherlock, he's in town again,
    That prince of perspicacity, that monument of brain.
    It seems he wasn't hurt at all
    By tumbling down the waterfall.
That sort of thing is fun to Sherlock.

When Sherlock left his native Strand, such groans were seldom heard;
With sobs the Public's frame was rent: with tears its eye was blurred.
    But the optimists reflected
    That he might be resurrected:
It formed our only theme of conversation.
We asked each other, Would he be? and if so, How and where?
We went about our duties with a less dejected air.
    And they say that a suggestion
    Of a Parliamentary question
Was received with marked approval by the nation.
    And Sherlock, Sherlock, he's in town again.
    Sir Conan has discovered him, and offers to explain.
    The explanation may be thin,
    But bless you! we don't care a pin,
If he'll but give us back our Sherlock.

The burglar groans and lays aside his jemmy, keys, and drill;
The enterprising murderer proceeds to make his will;
    The fraud-promoting jobber
    Feels convinced that those who rob err;
The felon finds no balm in his employment.
The forger and the swindler start up shrieking in their sleep;
No longer on his mother does the coster gaily leap;
    The Mile End sportsman ceases
    To kick passers-by to pieces,
Or does it with diminishing enjoyment.
    For Sherlock, Sherlock, he's in town again,
    That prince of perspicacity, that monument of brain,
    The world of crime has got the blues,
    For Sherlock's out and after clues,
    And everything's a clue to Sherlock.

Punch, May 27, 1903

41

HOLMES MAKES HIS DEBUT ON
TELEVISION – A RARE PHOTOGRAPH ON
THE SET OF THE NBC PRODUCTION
OF *THE THREE GARRIDEBS*
IN NEW YORK IN 1937.

SHERLOCK ❧ON❧ TELEVISION

The World's Longest-Running Series

Despite the longevity of a number of British, American and even European soap operas and serial stories, the adventures of Sherlock Holmes are by far the longest running series on television – some fifty years to be precise! Indeed, even before public television was unveiled in America, Sherlock was being utilized as a character in trial broadcasts – and his popularity has never waned in the years since. This is surely, therefore, an appropriate moment to look back over what is an astonishing half century of achievement at the very moment when the Great Detective has found his most accomplished television portrayer.

When, in fact, Holmes and Watson made their debut on the little screen, it soon proved to be just one further step in the development of the Legend of Sherlock Holmes, because he had already been adapted for the stage, screen and radio and proved hugely popular with audiences on both sides of the Atlantic.

The first of these transitions from the pages of Conan Doyle's books was a full-length play, a five-act drama, *Sherlock Holmes, Private Detective*, which appropriately opened in Scotland, at the Theatre Royal, Glasgow, in May 1894. Adapted by Charles Rogers, it starred John Webb as Holmes and St John Hamund as Doctor Watson. It later toured extensively and successfully throughout the British Isles. Five years later saw the more famous four-act version, *Sherlock Holmes*, written by the distinguished actor William Gillette in conjunction with Conan Doyle. This adaptation, with Bruce McRae as Watson, first introduced Holmes to American audiences before transferring to London.

A year on, in 1900, the first silent film, *Sherlock Holmes Baffled*, was made by the American Mutoscope & Biograph Company. This little drama of Holmes confronting a daring masked burglar who has actually invaded 221B Baker Street and literally disappears into thin air when threatened with arrest, ran for just 30 seconds! It is possible the actor playing Holmes was a young Walter Huston, the famous character actor and father of director, John Huston, but this has never been satisfactorily proved. The distinction of being the first *confirmed* screen Sherlock Holmes therefore belongs to Maurice Costello, another American, who appeared in the Vitagraph Company's 1905 production *The Adventures of Sherlock Holmes* (shown in Britain as *Sherlock Holmes: Held for Ransom*), which was based on *The Sign of Four* and had Kyrle Bellew as Doctor Watson.

It was not until October 1930 that the great detective was adapted for the radio – once again in America with William Gillette being the star of the NBC series which began with Edith Meiser's adaptation of *The Speckled Band*. Curiously, Gillette only made the first broadcast, and was then replaced by Richard Gordon. Leigh Lovell played Watson during the show's run which continued until June 1931. Despite several more successful seasons on the American airwaves, it was not until July 1943 that the BBC brought Holmes to British radio listeners with Arthur Wontner as Holmes and Carleton Hobbs as Doctor Watson in the 'Saturday Night Theatre' adaptation of *The Boscombe Valley Mystery* by Ashley Sampson.

It was in 1937, however, that Sherlock Holmes made his bow on television and began the record-breaking run which shows no sign of coming to an end. The facts about the various productions which I have gathered together here for the first time make fascinating reading.

Although John Logie Baird gave the first practical demonstration of black and white television on January 27, 1926, it was not until ten years later, on November 2, 1936, that the world's first public television service was inaugurated from the BBC Station at Alexandra Palace in North London. (It was also Baird, incidentally, who first demonstrated colour television in 1928, but this was not successfully adapted for broadcasting until December 1953 in America.)

Despite this head-start in Britain – television was not launched in the USA until the New Year – it was to be the Americans who first brought Holmes to the screen. This occurred during the trial broadcasts for television in New York, when the newly-formed National Broadcasting Company decided on producing a Sherlock Holmes tele-play. The evident popularity of the detective was obviously a major reason for this decision – and the company understandably hedged their bet by picking a story in which Americans featured, *The Three Garridebs*. Permission for this adaptation was sought by NBC from Lady Conan Doyle, for Sir Arthur had, of course, been dead for almost seven years.

The script for the production was written by Thomas H. Hutchinson, and two actors with a wealth of stage and radio work were cast in the leading roles, Louis Hector as Holmes, and William Podmore* as Doctor Watson. Two of the Garridebs of the title, John and Nathan, were played by Arthur Maitland and James Spottswood. On the night of November 27, 1937, a little piece of Sherlockian history was made when the resulting production was broadcast for members of the American Radio Relay League. Fortunately for us the *New York*

---

*By another of those curious coincidences which dot the history of Sherlock Holmes, the name of the executive producer of *Coronation Street*, which runs adjacent to Baker Street at Granada's Manchester headquarters, was also William (Bill) Podmore.

THE FIRST HOLMES AND WATSON, LOUIS HECTOR
(SEATED) AND WILLIAM PODMORE, ARE
TOLD BY MRS HUDSON (VIOLET BESSON), THAT
THEY HAVE A VISITOR IN *THE THREE GARRIDEBS*.

ANOTHER MONITOR SHOT FROM
THE THREE GARRIDEBS – HOLMES IS
TALKING TO NATHAN GARRIDEB
(JAMES SPOTTSWOOD).

Times carried a report on this very first television dramatization of Sherlock Holmes and I should like to quote from it.

'Sherlock Holmes sleuthed around the television cameras at Radio City during the past week,' the paper reported in its issue of November 28, 'and stalked across the ultra-short wave lengths in the most ambitious experiment in teleshowmanship so far attempted in the air over New York. The shadow reincarnation of Conan Doyle's master detective served to introduce the first full-length presentation of the Radio City television showmen. In six performances for members of The American Radio Relay League, the ingenious welding of film with studio production offered an interesting glimpse into the future of a new form of dramatic art.'

While the *New York Times* thought that the television version of *The Three Garridebs* offered 'no serious challenge to the contemporary stage or screen' it believed that considering television's present state of development, 'The presentation revealed how a skilful television producer may make use of the best of two mediums, how viewers may witness the realism of flesh and blood acting allied with the more spectacular scenic effects achieved by the screen.'

The newspaper then went on to give its readers a fascinating description of this pioneer production. 'The Holmes play opened with a film of the London skyline,' it reported, 'and then shifted to the "live" studio where Louis Heron, as Holmes, was seen looking out of his Baker Street window. The major portion of the Doyle tale was confined to two studio sets, one representing the detective's apartment, and the second the home of Nathan Garrideb, London ornithologist. The action shifted between these two scenes, although a film was used, and with considerable success, to tie-up the two points. This film showed Holmes and Doctor Watson riding in a hansom cab through the streets of London to the home of Garrideb in search of a new clue. Their dismissal of the cab, their entrance into the building and their inspection of the name-plate on Garrideb's door, all tended to link the action.'

Although the newspaper thought that because of the limitations of the set lighting, the figures and objects in the rooms were 'somewhat vague and shadowy', it was still possible to recognize objects such as microscopes and other items in the apartment occupied by Sherlock Holmes. The restrictive space also created problems for the camera which 'was not sufficient to show simultaneously the detective as he observed Killer Evans' manipulation of the secret passageway concealed in a bookcase – a treatment which would have heightened the scene's dramatic effect.'

The *New York Times* was, though, full of praise for the first television Sherlock Holmes and his partner. 'Louis Hector, in traditional cape, peaked cap, and double-breasted suit, played Holmes in the approved manner and at all times gave the impression that a manhunt was in progress,' it said. 'His determined manner throughout gave convincing evidence of the ultimate outcome – that the detective would surely "get his man". His demeanour was in marked contrast to the mild-mannered Doctor Watson, as acted by William Podmore. Both the actors have had considerable training in broadcast drama and proved equally at home before the television cameras.'

The Three Garridebs was no mean TV debut for Sherlock Holmes considering the facilities then available, and I have fortunately been able to secure a few very rare photographs of the production actually taken from a television receiver at the time.

BASIL RATHBONE, WHO PLAYED THE GREAT DETECTIVE ON
RADIO, TELEVISION AND IN FILMS FROM THE 1940's. HAS FOR YEARS BEEN
CONSIDERED THE ARCHETYPAL SHERLOCK HOLMES.

Interestingly, fifty years on, it is still possible to see similarities between that pioneer show and present-day techniques!

It was not until after World War II – when television at last became nation-wide on both sides of the Atlantic – that Holmes again reappeared on the small screen. In the first of these productions, he was no more than a name in the background; in the second, something of a figure of fun; and thirdly so inauspicious as to almost rule out any possibility of a return! All these productions were made in America.

The first of this trio, *Tea Time in Baker Street*, was a specially written one-act play aired over Station WWJ in Detroit, Michigan, on the evening of March 12, 1948. The creator was Russell McLaughlin, who worked on the *Detroit News*, and had been the founder of the Amateur Mendicant Society, the local branch of The Baker Street Irregulars.* The reason for the play, he said, was to mark the 94th birthday of Sherlock Holmes.

Because of copyright restrictions, McLauchlin conveniently had Holmes and Watson absent from home on an evening in 1890, and left the solving of a tricky crime to Mrs Hudson and her tea-time guest, a redoubtable Cockney lady named Mrs Wiggins. These ladies, he said, 'had developed, probably by contagion, something of the enterprise and deductive skill of the great detective himself.' Although no cast list survives of this Sherlockian exercise in Women's Liberation, it is known that all the actors were members of the Detroit Society who, by all accounts, acquitted themselves entertainingly on the screen!

In an amusing finale to the broadcast, an announcer told the audience, 'All the characters in *Tea Time in Baker Street* are real persons and any resemblance to any fictitious characters is purely coincidental. WWJ-TV regrets that it was unable to place Mr Holmes himself before you this evening, but he is much occupied at present with his bee-farm on the Sussex Downs, beside being rather crippled with rheumatism.'

There was no such reluctance to bring on Holmes on April 5, 1949 when NBC's Texaco Star Theatre, which featured Milton Berle, ran an hour-long production, *Sherlock Holmes in the Mystery of the Sen Sen Murder*. The famous comedian Berle appeared as Holmes in a farcical story which co-starred Victor Moore as Doctor Watson and the British singer, Gracie Fields, as a Mrs Vanderpool! A guest appearance was also made by a man destined to become inextricably linked with the legend of Holmes on Television – Basil Rathbone, who played Rathbone of Scotland Yard. (Rathbone, incidentally, made another appearance on the Texaco Star Theatre in September 1953 when he appeared as Holmes in full Sherlockian costume, in a murder-mystery-comedy sketch and also promoted the stage show, *Sherlock Holmes*, in which he was then appearing.)

The third US production aired over 'Story Theatre' by ZIV Television in 1949 was actually based on a genuine story, *The Adventure of the Speckled Band* and featured Alan Napier and Melville Cooper as Holmes and Watson. Although Napier was a dignified English character actor who specialized in playing noble lords or butlers and had a string of film successes behind him (including *Loyalties* made with Basil Rathbone in 1932, *Random Harvest* in 1942 and *Forever Amber* in 1947), he was hopelessly miscast as the great detective and the production directed

---

*The name given to enthusiasts of the Sherlockian canon who join together for study and discussion of the adventures.

by Sobey Martin has the unfortunate distinction of being the first televised Holmes story to be universally panned by the critics. It certainly wasn't helped by the fact that script writer Walter Doniger had to compress all the complexities of the story into just twenty-five minutes! Alan Napier has, though, been much in evidence on television again recently in the *Batman* series, playing Adam West's punctilious man-servant!

The year 1951 saw the setting up of the first projected series of Sherlock Holmes films for television in England. This pioneer idea was conceived by Vandyke Pictures, who were planning to make six, hour-long adaptations of the adventures starring John Longden, a character actor and former leading man in pictures like *The Ringer*, 1931, *French Leave*, 1937, and *Bonnie Prince Charlie*, 1948, as Sherlock Holmes, and Campbell Singer, familiar on the screen playing commissionaires, sergeant-majors or policemen, as Watson. Director Richard M. Grey was assigned to the task, and the pilot film based on *The Man with the Twisted Lip* was completed. However, TV bosses were not impressed, and the film went out on general cinema release instead. Like the projected series, it was never heard of again.

Perhaps this ill-fated idea may have given the BBC food for thought – for that same year they also planned and made their own series – the first venture of its kind, modest though it proved. The series was screened from October 20 to December 1 and featured six hour-long stories adapted from the Conan Doyle originals. Starring were Alan Wheatley as Holmes and Raymond Francis (later to become famous as a crime fighter, Detective Chief Superintendent Lockhart in Independent Television's *No Hiding Place*) as Doctor Watson.

Curiously, this series was preceded by a single story, *The Mazarin Stone*, screened on July 29, 1951 with Andrew Osborn in the leading role supported by Philip King as the good Doctor. Though initially believed to be a pilot show for the coming series, the BBC were evidently unhappy with the result and opted for a complete re-vamp with new stars, a new producer, Ian Atkin, and adaptations by Miss C. A. Lejeune, the distinguished film critic of *The Observer* newspaper.

Alan Wheatley, a suave character actor forever identified in the British public's mind for his part as the Sheriff of Nottingham in the TV version of *Robin Hood*, gave a dignified and enjoyable performance as Holmes despite horrendous problems making the show. As it was transmitted live he had to overcome unexpected noises from scene shifters at critical moments as well as wrestling with an almost impossible script.

Years later, Alan Wheatley recalled, 'I must say I found it the most difficult thing to speak I've ever done in the whole of my career. Unfortunately Miss Lejeune also did some things that are just not possible – technical things like not allowing enough time for changes. You see television was live in those days, and in one particular scene she finished up with a sentence from me, and opened the next scene also with a sentence from me, *in heavy disguise*, with no time at all for a change!

'For some time no-one could think of a way of altering this. In the end, the only

THE FIRST TELEVISED SERIAL OF
SHERLOCK HOLMES' ADVENTURES WAS
MADE BY THE BBC IN 1951 AND STARRED
ALAN WHEATLEY IN THE TITLE ROLE.

thing to do was for me to play the previous scene out of camera while I was making-up in the corner of the set. That was a nightmare – but it created quite a lot of comment because people wondered how on earth it was done. It was certainly a successful series, though, and got an enormous amount of publicity.'

The Times in its issue of October 23 had these words to say for the series, which began with the dramatic story of *The Empty House*. 'Sherlock Holmes was a great believer in the latest scientific methods, and there is therefore something appropriate in his long service to the cinema and the further lease of life he is now to have in television,' the paper commented. 'The story of *The Empty House* is not, perhaps, one of the best adventures, but it has been chosen, no doubt, for its omnibus character: complete in itself, it nevertheless serves to remind the forgetful and inform the ignoramus that behind each single episode in the adventures of the eminent Victorian detective is a long history of romance, danger, and well-nigh incredible achievement.'

Of the actor playing the part, the newspaper added, 'The performance was done in a proper spirit of seriousness. Mr Alan Wheatley, though rather younger and fuller in the face than the Holmes of his opponents' nightmares, yet catches the essential character. He is a figure, not merely of wonder or of fun, but of romantic possibility.'

Only two years passed before the 'romantic possibilities' of Sherlock Holmes encouraged CBS in America to bring him back to the television screen in their *Suspense* series. This time, though, they decided on using a wholly new adventure written by Conan Doyle's son, Adrian, and the leading crime novelist, John Dickson Carr, adapted for television by Michael Dyne.

As Holmes, they plumped for Basil Rathbone, already a veteran of the part having played it for years on the stage, over 200 times on radio and in no less than fourteen films made by Twentieth Century Fox and Universal Pictures during the years of World War II. Rathbone's dark, aquiline features – 'that dark, knife-blade face and snapping mouth' as Graham Greene once described the actor – made him ideal casting for the role from the outset, and he was by this time widely considered to be the archetypal Holmes. The disappointment as such for devoted admirers of the Sherlockian canon, was that after the initial two pictures made by Twentieth Century Fox which remained faithful to the original stories, Universal, who took over the rights, immediately up-dated the adventures and had Holmes combating a variety of villains from Nazi saboteurs to giant spiders!

To play Doctor Watson, an ideal foil had been found in Nigel Bruce, the British stage-trained actor who made a speciality of playing usually rather pompous gentlemen. His interpretation of Watson as a somewhat comic, bumbling figure was to influence several generations of actors who followed in his footsteps.

It is true to say that by the late Forties Rathbone felt himself hopelessly typecast as Sherlock Holmes.

Indeed, in January 1947 in the *Leader Magazine*, he confessed to writer, Tom Pocock, 'During the last seven years I have merged myself so much with Holmes that I have at last reached saturation point. People think I *am* Holmes!

'When Conan Doyle invented Holmes, he created a Frankenstein,' Rathbone went on. 'It got him, and now it's killing me. You see I've been Holmes for seven years in fourteen films and hundreds of broadcasts. Everybody has forgotten Basil Rathbone.

RATHBONE WITH NIGEL BRUCE WHOSE INTERPRETATION OF
WATSON AS AN OLD BUFFER STEREOTYPED THE ROLE
FOR MANY YEARS. IN THIS CURIOUS STILL FROM *PEARL OF
DEATH* (1944) A MEMBER OF THE FILM CREW CAN BE
SEEN REFLECTED IN THE MIRROR!

'It began in 1939 with *The Hound of the Baskervilles* which, I still think, is one of the *great* adventure stories. Then I made *The Adventures of Sherlock Holmes*, a hodge-podge of the short stories. They caught on, and I waded into a series of up-to-date films – complete with FBI men, bombers and Nazi spies – but all *based* on Conan Doyle. Some people thought this was sacrilege but, after all, the originals were a bit *too* well-known.'

And Rathbone added, 'Just as Sherlock Holmes took control of Conan Doyle so the same thing happened to me. To my public each film was "just another movie", but to me it was another stage in my life as Sherlock Holmes. And, whereas I was only human, Holmes was infallible. I became obsessed. Then, I thought, how did Conan Doyle rid himself of Holmes? Over a waterfall. Well, I've done the same thing. I've given him up.'

After making the twelve films for Universal, he refused a contract for a new series and tried without success to move his career in other directions. By 1953 he had wearily sensed the futility of this, and decided on a comeback in the role that had made him famous. The specially written story by the young Doyle and John Dickson Carr was called *The Adventure of the Black Baronet*, and its screening was predictably greeted by the American press as 'the return of the daddy of all super sleuths'. The major difference was that Rathbone was not reunited with Nigel Bruce, but with Martyn Green, a singer by profession and best known for his interpretations of Gilbert and Sullivan operettas! Interestingly, several of the minor parts in the drama were played by members of the New York branch of The Baker Street Irregulars.

Before the screening of the half hour show on May 26, Basil Rathbone again talked candidly about the effect Holmes had had on his life to Gordon Allison of the *New York Herald-Tribune*.

'I originally got the idea that I did not want to be Holmes and nothing but Holmes, because there might come a day when I wasn't wanted and then there would be nothing else for me to do,' he said. 'And so I quit the films and came to New York and went into *The Heiress* and *JB* and that sort of thing to establish myself. But I find it's impossible to escape Holmes.'

Why, Gordon Allison asked him, did he think there was this continual interest in the Great Detective? 'I think what's happening now is a psychological train of events – and it will happen again and again through the years,' Rathbone replied with prophetic insight, and went on to explain why he thought so. 'Well, it's not so much the mystery stories. Too much stress has been put on the stories, some of which are not too good. Matter of fact, Doyle despised them and despised Holmes, too. He considered the stories pot-boilers, even though they never brought him anything but huge success.

'In any case I think what makes Holmes live is his character. He's a strange, remote, reclusive man. He's hard to get into. How many friends does he have? One – Doctor Watson. Yet millions find him fascinating. He cares only for two things – Baker Street and crime. He's bored when he's not on a case. He reads, reads, reads. Why? A catholicity of tastes? No. Only to store up knowledge to help him in investigations.

'Who is he? If you met him at a dinner party – and you never would because he never has gone to parties – what would you say to him? I know if I went to a party and knew he'd be there I'd say to my hostess, "For heaven's sake don't put me next to Holmes!" I wouldn't know what to say to him. He knows too much. That man has extra senses.

'His extreme sensitivity is what makes him so guarded, why he keeps within himself. It's hard for him to come down to our level. That's his fascination.'

After seven years playing Holmes, Rathbone's insight into the character is both fascinating and unnerving. His views also uncannily parallel those of the latest exponent of the role, Jeremy Brett, as we shall see later . . .

Rathbone intimated in the interview that if *The Adventure of the Black Baronet* was successful, a fully-fledged series based on six other stories that Adrian Conan Doyle had written with John Dickson Carr was very much on the cards. The public and press reaction, however, doomed any such idea.

'Something was amiss,' the *New York Times'* critic, Jack Gould, wrote on May 31. 'Holmes and Watson who have proved durable characters did not seem too happy in the cathode glare. On the printed page, Mr Doyle and Mr Carr have kept faith with Baker Street, but the television adaptation by Michael Dyne appeared to have come more by way of Hollywood and Vine. The deer-stalker, pipe and comfortable tweeds were all present and accounted for, but the intellectual brilliance and personality of Sherlock was largely mislaid for the half-hour.'

Mr Gould offered a reason for the failure. 'The difficulty is that Mr Holmes happens to be a gentleman with somewhat more depth than Martin Kane, and is not too susceptible to a happy life in television's script dehydrator. In compressing *The Adventures of the Black Baronet* into a thirty-minute period, most of the traditional characterisation was left out and only the remnants of the straight narrative were seen.

'Sir Arthur, after all, was a good many years ahead of television in the matter of devising a durable format,' Mr Gould went on, 'and it's a little late to begin tinkering with his handiwork. And where he differed from the average writer of a video detective show was in making Sherlock and Doctor Watson first and foremost eminently absorbing people and then given them exciting chores to perform. Sherlock is bound to seem a little awkward if he must hurry up for the middle commercial.'

While conceding that the play had the 'usual intriguing Doyle twist', he thought Holmes and Watson 'indulged in only the most platitudinous sort of dialogue' and the great detective 'almost stumbled on the solution by accident – which, of course, would be utter nonsense'.

Mr Gould saved his strongest criticism for Basil Rathbone – and his verdict is all the more startling when one remembers the experience which the actor brought to the role.

'Mr Rathbone,' said the critic, 'did not seem too happy with a part with which he never really could come to grips.' And he added, 'Mr Green had very little to do, but even so did not seem to represent sufficient contrast to Mr Holmes. The Nigel Bruce interpretation on the radio had much more body. Doctor Watson is basically a superb foil, but on Monday evening he was only a straight man.'

The public reaction was similarly indifferent, and the idea of a Rathbone-Green series was dropped. But Basil Rathbone's words about the durability of Holmes were not long in being proven once again.

Rathbone, incidentally, had one more shot at playing Holmes that same year in a Broadway play written by his wife, Ouida, called simply *Sherlock Holmes*. Despite a spectacular scene with Professor Moriarty falling into the Reichenbach Falls from the balcony of a Swiss villa, the production was panned even more

RONALD HOWARD
AS HOLMES, ONE
OF THE STARS
OF THE FIRST
MAJOR AMERICAN
TELEVISION SERIES
OF SHERLOCK
HOLMES STORIES
MADE IN 1954.

unmercifully than the TV show, and lasted for just three days! Martyn Green, likewise was to be involved with Sherlock Holmes again in February 1955 when he played 'Mr Hargrove, a bee-keeper' in an hour-long spoof of the adventures called *The Sting of Death* starring Boris Karloff and Hermione Gingold, produced by ABC-TV.

The next man to bring Holmes to the television screen was another American, a dynamic young producer, Sheldon Reynolds, the 31-year-old writer-director-producer of the highly successful series, *Foreign Intrigue*, which dealt with European and international affairs. He had been an admirer of the Conan Doyle books since childhood, and during his visits from America to Europe conceived the idea of making *The New Adventures of Sherlock Holmes* using some of the actual locations where the stories took place.

What he did not want to do, however, was repeat the mistakes of some of the earlier adaptations. And nor did he want to perpetuate the image of Sherlock Holmes that Basil Rathbone had established in the public mind. He found the answer to his predicament in one of the Conan Doyle stories.

'It was when I was reading *A Study in Scarlet*,' he said later. 'I was suddenly struck by the difference between the character in the book and that of the stage and screen. Here, Holmes was a young man in his 30's, human, gifted, of a philosophic and scholastic bent, but subject to fateful mistakes which stemmed from overeagerness and lack of experience.

'In early stories like that one, Conan Doyle had not yet grown tired of his character, who later became a literary monster for him. And, as literature, the earlier stories are far better. But practically every stage and screen presentation of the detective is based on the later stories.'

With this idea firmly fixed in his mind, Sheldon Reynolds began to research all the Holmesian adventures and also made contact with the Conan Doyle family. He also determined to produce a series of programmes that would please the Holmesian enthusiasts. He would base a number of the stories on the original adventures, while the remainder would stay faithful to the originals but would be new cases written by men with a sympathy for the spirit of Holmes. The team he chose was Lou Morheim, Harold Jack Bloom, Henry Sandoz, Charles Early and himself.

To film the series he decided to take advantage of some new studios that had just been built at Epinay-sur-Seine, about five miles east of Paris. For location work he would hop across the Channel and use the streets of London. It all made much better sense than trying to commute from America.

Next Sheldon Reynolds needed an actor to fill the role of Holmes as he saw him. He found the man he was seeking in the slender, blond, 36-year-old Ronald Howard, the son of the late matinée idol, Leslie Howard. The younger Howard, who had been born in London but raised in America, had appeared in both films and stage plays on either side of the Atlantic. He was immediately attracted to the idea of playing Holmes and fully shared Reynold's vision of the great detective.

In December 1954 as he neared the end of filming the 39 episodes which were to make up the series of half-hour plays, Ronald Howard said that his interpretation of the part as compared to that of his predecessors was 'as different as chalk and cheese'.

'Of course it will be up to the viewer to decide who is the chalk and who is the cheese,' he said. 'I mean no disrespect to some excellent actors; I simply wish to point out that Holmes, in my portrayal, and in the text from which I work, is vastly different from the others.

'In my interpretation Holmes is not an infallible, eagle-eyed, out-of-the-ordinary personality, but an exceptionally sincere young man trying to get ahead in his profession. Where Basil Rathbone's Holmes was nervous and highly-strung, mine has a more ascetic quality, is deliberate, very definitely unbohemian, and is underplayed for reality.'

Asked if he modelled his acting style on his famous father's, Ronald Howard was very emphatic. 'Not in the least,' he said. 'However, I make no conscious effort to be different from my father. I act naturally, within my own limits, and try to bring out my personality. I honestly don't believe that my father would have considered himself suitable for Sherlock Holmes, but he might well have approved it for me!'

For Doctor Watson, Sheldon Reynolds sought a similarly distinctive actor, and cast Howard Marion Crawford, the veteran English stage, screen and radio actor, and grandson of another of the Victorian literary giants, Francis Marion Crawford. Despite all his acting accomplishments, this was to be Crawford's television debut – and he accepted the part with alacrity. It was a role he had long wanted to play, he said, and he was delighted with the chance to give the good Doctor a new image. 'I had never thought of Watson as the perennial brainless bungler who provided burlesque relief in the earlier portrayals,' Crawford said. 'He is a normal man, solid on his feet, a medical student who gives valuable advice. He is also very sincere and honest and has a keen sense of humour. In other words, he is a perfect foil to Holmes' youthful buoyancy.'

To complement the new interpretations of the Holmes and Watson roles, Reynolds contacted Michael Weight, who had built the Sherlock Holmes exhibit for the Festival of Britain, and commissioned him to build a replica of Holmes' Baker Street flat. To augment this set, Weight sought out reproductions of genuine Holmesian period furnishings including Holmes' dark lantern, coal scuttle cigar container, low-powered microscope and velvet chair.

In building Baker Street on the Epinay-sur-Seine lot, complete with its gas lights and hansom cabs, Michael Weight and his team unexpectedly received the cooperation of the Paris authorities who provided thousands of cobblestones for the street!

Another first in the history of Sherlock Holmes on the small screen was the appointment of a woman in a senior position on this production – as associate producer. She was a chic, blonde Parisienne, Mme Nicole Milinaire, who had been a lover of the Sherlock Holmes stories since she had read French translations as a teenager in her father's library.

In a delightful interview with Don Ross of *The New York Herald-Tribune* in March 1955, Mme Milinaire said she considered herself as thoroughly steeped in the Holmes tradition as any Englishman.

'I fell in love with 'Olmes when I was leetle,' she smiled mischievously. 'In France 'e is as widely read and a beeg hero. As beeg an 'ero as Jeanne d'Arc! Why, if there is a wise guy at a party, you will often 'ear someone say, "Oh, stop trying to be Sherlock 'Olmes!"'

Asked what an associate producer did, Mme Milinaire responded sharply to the popular idea that it was 'romantic, leisurely, beeg desk, flowers and tea in the afternoon.'

HOWARD MARION CRAWFORD AS WATSON.

'I actually work twelve hours a day,' she said. 'I talk over ideas with the writers and edit their scripts so that they fit into the budget limitations, cast the shows, see that the thousand and one necessary details get attended to – for example, making proper arrangements with the London authorities for shooting street scenes – and scrutinize the film rushes to see that everything has turned out all right.'

She assured Don Ross that the series was not a cheap one to produce – 'millions are involved in the period furniture we use,' she said (though she did not say whether she meant francs or dollars) – and she believed that out of all the stories 'we have only five stinkaires'. She declined to identify which they were, but there were strong suggestions that Holmes becoming involved with Red Indians while solving a tomahawk murder in the Wild West, might stretch credulity a little far!

In the final analysis, the series proved a hit when screening began over WRCA TV on October 18, 1954. *This Week* magazine urged viewers, 'You won't want to miss this 4-star video event,' while members of the Baker Street Irregulars showed their appreciation of Sheldon Reynolds' adaptation of their much-loved stories. 'They capture the full flavour of the times, and portray faithfully the characteristics and the mood which are, to us, the essence of these tales. We felt ourselves – and what could be more than this? – back in Baker Street again.'

There was praise, too, for the leading actors from the 'Bible' of the entertainment business, *Variety*. In a review on October 20, the journal called the show 'a winner that avoids the customary clichés that seem inevitable in any treatment of the Conan Doyle stories'.

Variety continued, 'Ronald Howard makes an excellent Holmes. He's got the fine features one expects in the man, plus a commanding voice. And, bless us, he doesn't overplay. H. Marion Crawford is something new in Doctor Watson, a commonplace type and by no means a buffoon. Archie Duncan is also good as the blustering Inspector Lestrade.'

Though some of the 39 stories were clearly better than others, *The New Adventures of Sherlock Holmes* enjoyed a successful airing throughout America, and in the years since has been re-run from time to time. The production was clearly an important one in the story of Holmes on TV.

Sheldon Reynolds had shown that there were special qualities inherent in Holmes that could lead to a whole range of interpretations. That the detective was an enduring figure who presented a fresh challenge to each new generation of programme makers. And with the technology of television developing every year, the gates were now wide-open . . .

It was the BBC who once again picked up the challenge in the Spring of 1964 when they decided to make a new version of *The Speckled Band* as a pilot version for a proposed Holmes series. Giles Cooper, who had recently successfully adapted Georges Simenon's Maigret for television, was commissioned to write the script, and after much deliberation the character actor, Douglas Wilmer, who had appeared in a number of screen spectaculars including *El Cid* in 1961 and *Cleopatra*

DOUGLAS WILMER, THE STAR OF THE
12-PART BBC TV SERIES,
SHERLOCK HOLMES, MADE IN 1965.

61

in 1962, was cast as Holmes. Another of the country's fine all-round actors, Nigel Stock, was offered the part of Doctor Watson.

The story was heralded with considerable publicity, including a special feature in the *Radio Times* of May 14 which declared, 'Bestriding the crime-fiction world like a colossus, the saturnine sleuth created by Sir Arthur Conan Doyle is no longer simply a character but has developed into a cult. And understandably so. For apart from his lofty place in the history of the genre, Holmes still remains one of the liveliest of all fictional investigators.'

The hour-long story was screened on May 18 as part of a series called *Detective*, and enthusiastically-enough received to be repeated on September 25. The powers-that-be at the BBC decided this was encouraging enough to justify a 12-story series the following year, and put the project in the hands of experienced producer David Goddard, with a budget of £60,000.

Douglas Wilmer, a life-long fan of the Conan Doyle stories, was well aware of the difficulties of the part he was taking on. But he was encouraged by his extensive knowledge of Holmes and by repeated remarks that he bore an uncanny physical resemblance to the original Sidney Paget illustrations of the great detective in *The Strand* magazine.

Talking about his role when the first story, *The Illustrious Client*, was screened on February 20, 1965, Wilmer said, 'Holmes was a genius, of course – that's the main thing – though an erratic one. I'd say he was the classic example of a manic depressive – a man in the mould of Van Gogh, swinging violently from one extreme to another. He was a savage genius, too.

'He had a veneer of conventional manners, but always, underneath, was this essential savagery. It wasn't merely a question of being shockingly rude when he was impatient with fools, it was a question of being literally ruthless in his determination to get to the truth.'

Wilmer continued, 'He had a brain like an acetylene lamp. It burned through the facts and he didn't care a damn whom he scarred or hurt in the process. Even if he broke a woman's heart, it was irrelevant.

'Do you remember when he pretended to be a plumber and got engaged to a housemaid? It was all in the job, and if the housemaid went through hell – that was her misfortune.

'He was astringently unsentimental. Well, I ask you! A man who could experiment in a laboratory, beating corpses to find out if the flesh bruised after death – even today, in this reputedly unsentimental age, such a man might shock even the most hard-boiled of the Mods or Rockers!

'And yet – given the particular nature of his genius – there was nothing shocking about his behaviour. It was the acetylene lamp at work again. And anyway he didn't give a hoot what people thought about him.'

It was quite evident from such words, that Douglas Wilmer had taken considerable time and trouble to get underneath the skin of the man he was playing. In another interview with the columnist, Beverley Nichols, he confessed: 'As a hard-working professional I can assure you that playing Sherlock Holmes demanded much more concentration than you'd ever believe possible. While we were making the series I was starved. Holmes stopped me going to concerts, he kept me out of art galleries, he prevented me from riding in Richmond Park; from seeing enough of my wife . . . all the things I love. There just wasn't time, with Sherlock Holmes around.'

These words, which we shall again hear being uncannily echoed by Jeremy Brett, are a clear indication of just how much dedication Wilmer put into his role. Beverley Nichols was clearly impressed.

'As Wilmer spoke,' he wrote, 'I realized that here was an actor who had penetrated as deeply as any psychoanalyst into the character he was portraying – he had walked with Holmes, dined with him, eaten and drunk and smoked and laughed and pondered with him, till Holmes, quite literally, took charge of his life.

'As a "hard-working professional" myself, I happen to respect professionalism,' Nichols added, 'and in the foregoing comments you have an example of professionalism at its ruthless best. Not that Wilmer's is merely a question of "tricks of the trade" (though it abounds in them), but it is an example of that infinite capacity for taking pains. Probably this professionalism was also what enabled Wilmer to keep his feet on the ground. For though he was saturated by Holmes, he was not "possessed" by him.'

The producer of the series, David Goddard, was also at pains to stress that great care had been taken with the original stories. 'I believe Conan Doyle to be one of the greatest short-story writers,' he said in an interview in *Radio Times*. 'I insisted that we kept strictly to the stories, simply because you cannot improve them. In particular, I was trying to convey the unique sense of horror which conterpoints the straight detection in most of the stories.'

The *Radio Times* heralded the series as the first 'full-dress, nation-wide television series in this country', and though it did not forget to mention the earlier Alan Wheatley stories, did describe them a little unkindly as 'a limited series'.

Such minor points aside, the new series proved a deserved success and achieved audience figures in excess of 11 million people for each story. There were some critics who thought Wilmer's interpretation of Holmes was perhaps not quite sympathetic enough, though his acting was excellent. Nigel Stock as Watson was universally praised.

The Times, in a lengthy review of 'this welcome revival' in its issue of February 27, said: 'In resuscitating this indisputable old master of detection, the BBC is being very venturesome. Sherlock Holmes is by now both a period character and a legend, and for both reasons not at all easy to adapt to our current conceptions of crime and retribution . . . He has certain characteristics which do not come within our conventional notion of a detective. He relaxed, for example, by playing the violin; worse still, he used to give himself shots of cocaine with a hypodermic syringe. Now here's a how-de-do. Dare any contemporary practitioner in the whole whodunit field promote a private eye who not only fiddles but dopes as well? Not even Raymond Chandler would have chanced his arm to this extent!'

Turning to the actors, *The Times* confirmed some of the misgivings about Douglas Wilmer. 'Holmes is played by Mr Douglas Wilmer who apparently bears an uncanny resemblance to the original Sydney Paget illustrations. But that doesn't matter one way or the other. What does matter, to me at any rate, is that, although Mr Wilmer is a skilful actor, he is not the man for this particular job. He impersonates the character but does not penetrate him. Sherlock Holmes was a far broodier, more meditative fellow than the figure we see . . . The producer was, though, fantastically wise (or fortunate) in his casting of Doctor Watson (never such a fool as he looks), played with immense perception by Nigel Stock.'

Although *The Times* critic thought the first story was 'by no means vintage Holmes' he was left meditating on the quality and authority of Conan Doyle as a pioneer of crime and detection. 'To me he still seems matchless: inventive, stylish and sardonic, and in a class which no contemporary screenwriters seem to achieve.'

In the aspect of fidelity, David Goddard's production certainly scored high, and within less than four years the BBC had decided to launch another Holmes series. This was to give us a peerless Holmes in the shape of the versatile Peter Cushing, who set a standard that has remained unrivalled on TV until that of Jeremy Brett. The series also brought back Nigel Stock to further enhance *his* reputation as an outstanding Doctor Watson.

Peter Cushing, one of the best-known and loved of English film actors, seemed in hindsight like an ideal man to play Holmes for years before the opportunity actually arose. With his gaunt features, piercing eyes and evident ease playing period roles, it was no surprise that he should have been one of the major stars in the horror movies of the Fifties and Sixties which made Hammer Films famous around the world.

He was, in fact, well into his stride making the various Frankenstein and Dracula pictures which made him a household name, when Hammer offered him the chance in 1958 to play Holmes in their planned version of *The Hound of the Baskervilles*. The company made no bones about the fact that they were anxious to stress the horror elements in the story, but it was a part that appealed to Peter – for reasons he was quick to explain.

'Many people had said to me before that I ought to play Holmes because I looked rather like him,' he said not long after shooting had begun at Frensham Ponds, Surrey, which, for some curious reason, was being used as a stand-in for Dartmoor. 'I had always considered it a jolly good part to play, and I was thrilled to be asked. It is also such a marvellous opportunity when you have got so much detail from the author on which to base your character.'

Cushing said he was the proud owner of a complete set of original *The Strand* magazines in which the Holmes adventures had appeared, as well as a whole range of books about the great detective. He went to great pains to get both the mannerisms and appearance of the character right before going before the cameras.

He had, in fact, a special fondness for Holmes which went back to his childhood, which he also explained. 'An uncle of mine was an absolute devotee of the adventures, and I always remember him telling me about a friend of his who had been accused of molesting a lady in a train.

'My uncle said the man proved the lady was telling a lie rather as Sherlock Holmes would have done. He called the guard and repeated what the lady had accused him of doing. "But it is absolutely impossible," the man insisted, "for look at my cigar – it has only about half an inch of ash on it. There was not enough time for me to have committed what she alleges!"'

Cushing said that this story had made him think that Sherlock Holmes must be a wonderful person – and he had promptly devoured all the books, thereafter becoming a confirmed fan of the great detective.

The Hammer film was to prove another first for Holmes on the screen – the first picture about him to be made in colour. Casting Watson, however, apparently proved something of a problem, with various studio officials favouring different actors. In the end, the part went to André Morell, an experienced film and theatre actor who had served for six years in the Royal Welsh Fusiliers, which gave him

'HE CURLED HIMSELF UP IN HIS CHAIR' –
JEREMY BRETT BRINGS A SIDNEY PAGET
ILLUSTRATION TO LIFE.

A DREAM STARTS TO BECOME REALITY.
JEREMY BRETT ON THE CASTLEFIELD LOT IN 1982
AS THE BUILDING OF BAKER STREET BEGINS.

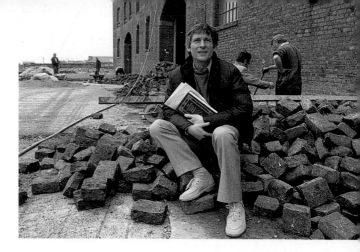

A REMARKABLE WIDE-ANGLE
VIEW OF THE COMPLETED
BAKER STREET.

221B TAKING SHAPE OUT OF A MAZE OF STEEL, WOOD, PLASTER AND PAINT.

THE VIEWS OF SALFORD AT THE END OF BAKER STREET ARE DISGUISED BY FOLIAGE.

THE INTERIOR OF 221B – AUTHENTIC IN EVERY DETAIL.

JEREMY BRETT
FILMING HIS
MAKE-UP TEST
IN MAY 1983.

JEREMY BRETT
AND DAVID
BURKE TAKE
SOME LESSONS
IN PIPE
SMOKING
BEFORE
FILMING
BEGINS.

JEREMY BRETT
AND DAVID
BURKE AS
HOLMES AND
WATSON POSE
AT THE FRONT
DOOR OF 221B
WITH MRS
HUDSON
(ROSALIE
WILLIAMS).

the valuable experience needed to play the former military man turned medical practitioner.

Directing the picture was Hammer's leading director, Terence Fisher, and playing the persecuted Sir Henry Baskerville was Christopher Lee, who ultimately became as famous as Peter Cushing for his roles in the Frankenstein and Dracula films. Curiously, Lee had for a time been seriously considered as a possible Holmes in *The Hound of the Baskervilles* – and though he did not get the part he was subsequently re-united with Terence Fisher to play the detective in a film aimed at the cinema but actually only ever shown on television. Lee also played Sherlock's brother, Mycroft, in the film of *The Private Life of Sherlock Holmes* (1970), thereby achieving a unique Holmesian double! We shall return to this later.

The attention to detail which Cushing gave his role was rewarded by favourable reviews and particular praise from the members of the Sherlock Holmes Society who voted his interpretation second only to that of Eille Norwood. The *Daily Mirror* echoed the comments of virtually all the national newspaper reviewers when it said, 'Peter Cushing is a splendid Holmes. The film, while being "Very elementary, Watson," has atmosphere and thrills.' When the picture crossed the Atlantic to open in America, *Newsweek* went even further, calling Cushing 'a living, breathing, Holmes . . . the best yet'.

Unhappily, the film was not the runaway success at the Box Office that Hammer had hoped. Or at least, so they said, and announced that plans for further Holmes films had been scrapped. According to other sources, the Conan Doyle estate were not happy with the production and declined to grant Hammer the rights to more stories.

Be that as it may, in 1968 when the BBC decided to mount another revival of the Holmes adventures, they had no hesitation in selecting Peter Cushing as their star – and pairing him with Nigel Stock who, of course, had made such an impact as Douglas Wilmer's co-star.

It is possible that part of the reason for picking Cushing for what was seen as the most ambitious and costly version to date, was because the BBC were intending to accentuate the elements of terror and violence in the stories – elements he was practised at handling. The Corporation admitted as much in an early press release on the project:

'What is new in this series is the basic approach,' the handout proclaimed, 'a daring realization of the lurking horror and callous savagery of Victorian crime, especially sexual crime. Here is the re-creation of the Victorian half-world of brutal males and the furtive innocents they dominate; of evil-hearted servants scheming and embracing below stairs; of murder, mayhem and the macabre as the hansom cab once again sets out with Doctor Watson and his debonair, eccentric and uncannily observant friend – Mr Sherlock Holmes.'

The series, under producer William Sterling, consisted of sixteen fifty-minute programmes, including a new two-part version of *The Hound of the Baskervilles* which was actually filmed on Dartmoor for the first time! Initial plans to have major stars such as Peter Ustinov, George Sanders and Orson Welles appearing as the major villains had to be dropped on economic grounds, and there were also to be cut-backs in the filming time for each of the stories. Nonetheless, Peter Cushing approached his second 're-incarnation' as Holmes with infectious enthusiasm.

He was also in the mood to blow away some myths about Sherlock while filming took place. Talking to journalist Russell Twisk, later the editor of *The Listener*, he

A PORTRAIT OF PETER CUSHING AS SHERLOCK HOLMES.

ANDRÉ MORELL WHO PLAYED CUSHING'S FAITHFUL DOCTOR WATSON.

PETER CUSHING, ONE OF THE MOST ACCLAIMED ACTORS TO
PLAY SHERLOCK HOLMES BOTH IN FILMS AND ON TV, IN A SCENE FROM
THE HOUND OF THE BASKERVILLES MADE IN 1959.

said, 'What are the first things that spring to mind about Sherlock Holmes? The way he keeps saying, "Elementary, my dear Watson," and the number of times he puffs that meerschaum pipe. But they are both untrue!

'Holmes often says the word, "Elementary" in Conan Doyle's sixty-odd stories – and he often says, "My dear Watson". But never the two together. He may say "Precisely" or "Exactly, my dear Watson" but never "Elementary".

'The meerschaum pipe – now that was really started by the actor William Gillette who played the part of Holmes on Broadway. The real pipes are described in the stories and Holmes' favourite was a dirty old black clay pipe that "ponged" the study out! He also had a long cherrywood for tranquillity,' Cushing said.

And the deer-stalker? Why was Cushing wearing a trilby in the series and not the traditional head-gear, Russell Twisk asked.

'Very perceptive of you!' exclaimed Cushing. 'But you see we have based the costumes on the original drawings by Sydney Paget. For the original serialization of *The Hound of the Baskervilles*, Sir Arthur Conan Doyle wrote only of a cloth cap – and Paget took that to mean a trilby. The deer-stalker was added later. We have also exploded the myth about Holmes' Inverness cape – it was actually a long overcoat with a hood.'

Cushing had obviously once again prepared meticulously for his part. 'I re-read all the stories in detail,' he told another journalist. 'There are just so many facets of Holmes that you have to be careful that Doyle has not contradicted himself. For example in his attitude to the country. On one occasion Holmes hates the country because he says nothing ever happens there, and then he absolutely contradicts himself and says that far worse things happen in the country than the town!'

Despite the accolades that greeted the finished series, and the stature awarded to Cushing's Holmes, he confessed later to not being entirely happy with the result.

'We had been promised ten days to do each of those sixteen episodes,' he said. 'Now that's long enough so long as you have got the scripts beforehand – because I never like to begin filming anything unless I know it backwards and then I can change things as I go along.

'Now, we got the scripts alright, but for each of the sixteen episodes there were filmed inserts and the BBC had not made allowances for the English weather. So by the time we got half way through the filming, the series was already being shown, so we had to catch up and in the end we were doing the stories in three days.

'Whenever I see some of those stories,' he added, 'they upset me terribly, because it wasn't Peter Cushing doing his best as Sherlock Holmes – it was Peter Cushing looking relieved that he had remembered what to say and said it!'

This typically-modest assessment by Peter Cushing does not really do justice to his performance – albeit that he had to work under such trying conditions. And certainly the press and public were highly impressed by the series when it came to a close just before Christmas, 1968. Cushing had established a new standard for Holmes on television that was to remain for many years the most outstanding performance. Indeed, only a few years ago he was forced to admit, 'I've played Baron Frankenstein and Professor Van Helsing many, many times, but I'm still far better known to the public as Sherlock Holmes!'

Peter has, though, never been in any doubt that Holmes will continue to outlive other heroes – even James Bond. 'In ten years time,' he said that same December after completing his role, 'we will have more fantastic gadgets than Bond ever dreamed of, and then who'll want to know him? But Holmes' brain power and gift of logical deductions leap the years: it is timeless.'

As I mentioned earlier, Cushing's co-star in the filmed version of *The Hound of the Baskervilles*, Christopher Lee, was the next man to bring Holmes to the screen – although his film, *Sherlock Holmes and the Deadly Necklace*, has only been shown to date on television. It is a picture that both Lee and the director, Terence Fisher, believe fell far short of its potential. It was a joint West German/Italian/British and French co-production, and with a screenplay by the experienced Curt Siodmak based on *The Valley of Fear* plus the fine British character actor, Thorley Walters, playing Watson, the omens *should* have been good.

But, as Christopher Lee was later to explain before the film was shown on American television in 1968, things just went from bad to worse. 'We should never have made it in Germany with German actors, although we had a British art director and a British director. It was not, in fact, taken from any specific story, although it was supposed to be based on *The Valley of Fear*. It was a hodge-podge of stories put together by the German producers which ruined it.

'My portrayal of Holmes is though, I think, one of the best things I've ever done because I tried to play him really as he was written – as a very intolerant, argumentative, difficult man – and I looked extraordinarily like him with the make-up. In fact, everyone who's seen it has said I was as like Holmes as any actor they've ever seen – both in appearance and interpretation.

'But the picture really wasn't well done. It was a badly edited hodge-podge of nonsense,' he added.

After its TV screening, Lee's verdict was also shared by Anthony Howlett of the *Sherlock Holmes Journal*. 'The title alone is sufficient comment on the film. This is the Teutonic Holmes, perpetrated in Berlin and dubbed into American. I have read the synopsis – ouch!' And Marjorie Bilbow of *TV Today* put the final nail in the coffin when she wrote, 'As a story woven around an unknown detective it would have been forgivable, but classic characters demand more accurate handling than this!'

Despite the reception of this film on both sides of the Atlantic, it was evident that foreign film-makers were aware of the potential of Holmes on the screen, and in 1972 a Czechoslovakian television company made *Touha Sherlocka Holmes* – which translates as *The Longing of Sherlock Holmes*.

According to information I have received the forty-minute colour production was screened on March 3, 1972. It was based on an original screenplay by its director, Stêpán Skalsky, and was filmed at the Barrandov Studios in Prague with location shooting also in the city as well as at Liberec and Hrádek u Nechanic. Playing Holmes was one Radovan Lukavsky with Václav Voska as Doctor Watson.

The ingenious storyline introduced Sir Arthur Conan Doyle (played by Josef Parocka) who explained that one of Holmes' greatest desires had been to escape from crime-solving for once in his life and play the part of a criminal. Freed by his creator to test his wits and ingenuity against the law rather than in defence of it, Holmes all but succeeds until the redoubtable Watson prevents him committing the perfect crime.

That same year saw yet another version of *The Hound of the Baskervilles* made specially for US television by Universal and starring one of the screen's great

CHRISTOPHER LEE, WHO ACHIEVED THE UNIQUE DOUBLE OF PLAYING BOTH SHERLOCK HOLMES AND HIS BROTHER, MYCROFT, ON THE SCREEN, IN A SCENE FROM *SHERLOCK HOLMES AND THE DEADLY NECKLACE*, WITH THORLEY WALTERS AS DOCTOR WATSON, MADE IN 1968.

GOLDEN ERA
present
"SHERLOCK HOLMES
AND THE
DEADLY NECKLACE" "U"
starring
CHRISTOPHER LEE · SENTA BERGER
and THORLEY WALTERS

HRISTOPHER
LEE
HIS ROLE AS
SHERLOCK
HOLMES ...

... AND LEE
AS MYCROFT
HOLMES IN
*THE PRIVATE
LIFE OF
SHERLOCK
HOLMES.*

THE CZECHOSLOVAKIAN FILM, *THE LONGING OF SHERLOCK HOLMES* (1972)
WITH RADOVAN LUKAVSKY AS HOLMES AND VACLAV VOSKA
AS DOCTOR WATSON.

romantic swashbucklers, Stewart Granger. The 90-minute production directed by Barry Crane from a script by Robert Williams was intended to be the pilot of a series – should it succeed.

If Stewart Granger at first seemed an unlikely choice for Holmes, he had in fact already appeared in films with several of his famous predecessors in the role including Arthur Wontner and Peter Cushing. For Watson, the character actor, Bernard Fox, was chosen, and the teleplay also introduced William Shatner, of *Star Trek* fame, as Stapleton.

Despite the fact that a genuine attempt had been made to create an authentic atmosphere, the use of sets from other productions (mainly horror stories!) tended to negate all this hard work, and the pilot-feature 'failed to generate much interest or suspense above and beyond what the viewer nostalgically brought to the home set', according to *Variety* in its verdict on February 16, 1972.

The publication was not altogether scathing of the new Sherlock Holmes, however. 'Granger makes an acceptable Holmes,' it said, 'albeit playing him without the arrogant intellectual edge that was Basil Rathbone's unique shtick, but the script – especially the latter half – had very limited footage of Holmes and

THE GREY-HAIRED SHERLOCK HOLMES AS PLAYED BY STEWART GRANGER IN *THE HOUND OF THE BASKERVILLES* MADE BY ABC-TV IN 1972.

an awful lot of Watson, played straight and rather uninterestingly by Fox. This, plus an exceedingly abrupt and limp demise of villain, William Shatner, lessened dramatic suspense to a trickle.'

Variety concluded, 'The Hound unspooling reminded us again that the Basil Rathbone–Nigel Bruce imagery as Holmes and Watson is both definitive and enduring.'

Though the idea of Stewart Granger as a snow-white-haired and rather heavier-than-usual Holmes appealed to many American Sherlockians who thought him the best US actor in the role since Rathbone, Universal were disappointed by the ratings the show received and duly shelved plans for any more stories.

In 1974, the BBC tried the curious experiment of a Holmesian story in which only Doctor Watson appeared! The idea immediately grabbed the attention of journalists, for early in December, the columnist 'Peterborough' of *The Daily Telegraph* told his readers, 'The BBC are evidently taking their Christmas programme economies more than seriously. The season's productions include a new detective drama by Kingsley Amis 'in which Doctor Watson tackles a case without Sherlock Holmes'.

Doctor Watson and the Darkwater Hall Mystery was, in fact, a pastiche by Amis in which Watson – who has been left in Baker Street while Holmes goes away on holiday – is summoned by a lady in distress to help protect the life of her husband. This *Singular Adventure*, as it was subtitled, was produced by Mark Shivas, starred Edward Fox as Watson, and was filmed at Stow-on-the-Wold. It proved the good Doctor every bit as competent as his friend, solving the mystery – as a reviewer put it – 'without the aid of cocaine, violin or magnifying glass!'

One viewer, though, felt compelled to protest to the *Radio Times* in January 1975. 'I am completely lost for words to describe the utter banality of this quite nonsensical piece of writing,' said Mr H. Lefevre Pope of Harrogate. 'Since Mr Amis's Doctor Watson bore not the slightest resemblance to Conan Doyle's original character, one wonders why the author gave his central character that name at all.

'One can only assume that it was an attempt to cash-in on the universal popularity of this unique character. If the play was intended to be a parody, then it failed dismally.'

This was not a view shared by most viewers – nor the newspaper critics for, as Mr Amis himself pointed out in a spirited defence of his play, 'the reviews were excellent.'

It was not long, however, before Sherlock himself turned up on the television screen again – though in the interim a potentially exciting adaptation to be made by NBC in 1975 was widely publicized and then failed to materialize.

At a press conference in Los Angeles on June 23, William F. Storke, a Vice-President of NBC, announced that a new series of adventures featuring the great detective were to be made, starring the much acclaimed actor, Robert Shaw, fresh from his screen triumphs in *Jaws*, *The Sting* and the James Bond movie, *From Russia With Love*.

The one-hour mystery drama was to be produced by Joseph Cates who told the assembled newspapermen that he had obtained the rights to three Sherlock Holmes stories from the Conan Doyle estate, and the adaptation of these by Terence Feely would be taped in England in the winter under the direction of Alan

Bridges for showing the following spring.

Sadly, the project was swallowed up in the mists of a Holmesian winter and never heard of again. However, a few months later on June 16, 1976 in the suitably titled, *The Return of Sherlock Holmes*, the great detective was back – albeit in a somewhat different guise – in yet another production from Universal studios.

The script, subtitled *Alias Sherlock Holmes: A 90-Minute Pilot for a 1-Hour Series*, was a loose take-off of *The Red-Headed League* written by Ronald Kibbee and Dean Hargrove (who was also the director) and starred undoubtedly the most unlikely actor ever to have tackled the part of Holmes – Larry Hagman, famous world-wide as 'J. R. Ewing' of the *Dallas* TV series! His Doctor Watson was also a revelation – a *woman* psychiatric social worker played by Jenny O'Hara! What *would* Conan Doyle have thought of this latest 'first'?

According to *TV Guide*'s précis of the play, 'Sherman Holmes (Hagman) is a bumbling Los Angeles cop who comes to think he's really Sherlock. With Doctor Watson, his female psychiatrist, he sets out to solve the puzzling murder of an embezzler'.

Once again, this pilot failed to generate a series, although the *Devon County Chronicle* said that 'Hagman makes the figure of Sherlock Holmes, melodramatically outwitting an off-stage Moriarty in today's Los Angeles, more entertaining and sympathetic than silly or incongruous. And Jenny O'Hara plays 'Doc' Watson with a sort of Shirley MacLaine dazed innocence.'

The same year also saw another perhaps equally unlikely actor playing Holmes – Leonard Nimoy of *Star Trek* fame (following in William Shatner's footsteps perhaps?) in a fifteen-minute short, *The Interior Motive* written by Richard L. Smith and directed by George Rasmussen for Kentucky Educational Television. With Burt Blackwell as Doctor Watson, this Holmes received a globe of the world and a note asking him to discover the contents of its interior without disturbing the surface.

The next major production came in 1976 and was made by Twentieth Century Fox Television for NBC. *Sherlock Holmes in New York* may well have risen from the ashes of the Robert Shaw project, but it certainly transported Holmes across the Atlantic with one of Britain's major stars, Roger Moore, of James Bond fame, taking on the role of Sherlock.

The script, by Alvin Sapinsky, had Holmes and Watson travelling to New York in the year 1901 to come to the aid of Irene Adler – 'the' woman in Sherlock's life – and also to combat the latest evil machinations of Professor Moriarty who is trying to create an economic crisis which could lead to war. Cast in the various leading roles were the debonair Patrick Macnee (of *The Avengers* fame) as Watson, beautiful Charlotte Rampling as Irene Adler, and John Huston the famous director and writer playing Moriarty. (This was surely a remarkable twist of fate if it had been, in fact, his father who had played the very first screen Sherlock Holmes in films 75 years earlier!) Among the guest stars were Gig Young, Jackie Coogan and Geoffrey Moore – Roger Moore's nine-year-old son – playing Irene Adler's illegitimate child, Scott.

The role of Holmes was not one that particularly attracted Roger Moore when he was first offered the part, as he was honest enough to admit. 'But I was urged to read the script and I found it funny and original so I changed my mind,' said Roger during the making of the two-hour long picture. 'Holmes seems to come alive in this story. I have a love affair with a beautiful actress who has a young son named

73

Scott and we learn as a result of this that Holmes' middle name is Scott. And, of course, there is Moriarty threatening to steal all the gold in the world!

'But what I like most about playing Holmes is that there is more dialogue than I ever had in 120 *Saint* episodes and two *Bond* films. The script is a bit campy, but I play it straight. And, most important, I do my own interpretation and don't copy any previous actors who have played the role.'

As the son of a London policeman, Roger Moore has always been interested in law and order, and indeed has only ever played 'good guys' in films. And despite the fact that he is one of the few actors not to have read all the adventures of Sherlock Holmes before he played the part, his admiration for the character is considerable.

'It would be difficult to think of a figure who has had a greater following for generations than Sherlock Holmes,' he also said during filming. 'In fact, he's one of the most vibrant characters in literature and I'm delighted to have had the chance to play him. Still, he *is* rather eccentric. I mean, he plays the violin in the middle of the night, lives among rows of books, and has a disguise for any situation. All this is great fun except for one thing – the disguises take forever to put on and take off. I know they work better in fiction than reality!'

Equally interesting, the versatile and debonair Patrick Macnee revealed while filming his part as Watson that he, too, had a crime fighter in his past. For he is a descendant of Robin Hood! 'On my mother's side, I am a member of the Hastings family, the Earls of Huntington,' he said. 'They go back to the 12th century and they insist that Robin Hood is one of their very own!' With this ancestry, he said, playing Watson as a man with both flair and ingenuity when tackling criminals was something that came *quite* naturally to him!

For all the time, money, effort and star names that went into it, *Sherlock Holmes in America* did not live up to expectations. The *Los Angeles Times* was full of praise for the lavish sets and costumes, but the production 'missed the mark by the length of several hansom cabs (with horses).' The *New York Times* agreed, and added, 'Roger Moore was a much-too-handsome Holmes, with all the dynamic verve of an Arrow collar model,' while Patrick Macnee 'had little to do except for two rather stilted Watsonian outbursts'.

The paper concluded, 'The plot was stretched as thin as a fat lady's panty-hose and the dialogue bounced from Brooklynese to turn-of-the-century East Lynn'. Bang went any chance of a new series!

As if prompted by the American parodies, both the BBC and ITV Channels produced spoofs of Sherlock Holmes in 1977.

In September, ITV unveiled *The Strange Case of the End of Civilisation as We Know It*, a 60-minute comedy which starred two of Britain's most inventive funny men, John Cleese of *Monty Python's Flying Circus*, playing Holmes, and Arthur Lowe, of *Dad's Army*, as Watson.

For Cleese, it was a second attempt at bringing an amusing Holmes to the small screen. In January 1973 he had appeared in the BBC Comedy Playhouse series in a story called *Elementary, My Dear Watson* written by N. F. Simpson and co-starring Willie Rushton as Watson. Although an authorized spoof, it was not a success, and provisional plans that it might be the forerunner of a series were dropped.

The script for *The Strange Case* was by Joe McGrath, who also directed the show, and it took Holmes and Watson in the company of the Commissioner of Police

TWO PARODIES OF THE HOLMESIAN ADVENTURES:
JOHN CLEESE AND ARTHUR LOWE IN
THE STRANGE CASE OF THE END OF CIVILISATION;
AND (OVERLEAF) THE POPULAR DUO OF
PETER COOK AND DUDLEY MOORE IN A SEND-UP OF
THE HOUND OF THE BASKERVILLES,
BOTH MADE IN 1978.

(played by ex-*Z-Cars* star, Stratford Johns) on a madcap pursuit of Professor Moriarty in a London bus.

During filming scenes in this bus in the spring of 1977, John Cleese explained how he had arrived at his Holmes' particular relationship with Doctor Watson.

'The key to any parody like this is to find the right relationship,' he said. 'The trouble is the pair have been played a hundred times or more and what Arthur Lowe and the director and I agreed was that in this modern version, Holmes would think he is efficient when he is evidently not, and Watson was worse, occasionally realizing how dim he was.

'We have scaled everything down from the great height that Holmes was originally. All of his deductions now are blindingly obvious: only Watson could possibly say how astute they are. The point about this type of comedy is that however mad it is there must be some kind of inner logic which the audience will accept.'

Cleese also added, 'I always wanted Arthur Lowe to play the part of Watson: our styles are totally different. I like to rush on and get the audience to laugh in case I lose them. Arthur is prepared to take the most tremendous risks by timing a line very precisely and then waiting for the laugh.'

Unfortunately for both men, the laughs did not come from the public or the reviewers. The *Daily Mail* found it 'a palpable disappointment' although 'Cleese had flashes of excellence – and from a lesser performer the show's shortfall might have been less apparent.'*

There was not a much better fate awaiting the BBC's parody of *The Hound of the Baskervilles* which was transmitted on November 24, 1977. It featured the marvellous comic partnership of Peter Cook and Dudley Moore as Holmes and Watson, but again their mixture of satire, slapstick comedy and even some high drama was not a complete success.

Dudley Moore who, of course, later left Britain and found super-stardom in America, was to confess that he thought Sherlock Holmes was 'impossible to parody successfully'. As far as his version of the Baskerville story was concerned, he felt the Irish wolfhound, Sean, had stolen the show – though he was pleased with his short cameo sequence as Sherlock Holmes' mother!

Christmas 1977 saw a very different interpretation of the Holmesian adventures, with a striking new Sherlock in the form of the Shakespearean actor, Christopher Plummer, and the return to the small screen of Thorley Walters, playing Doctor Watson for a second time.

The new production was the handiwork of HTV who assigned producer

---

*On October 5, 1980, *The Sunday People* carried a report from Italy that Arthur Lowe had been 'pencilled in' to play Watson for a second time, but in a more traditional manner, opposite the old screen heart-throb, Edmund Purdom, in a series of 26 new adventures of Sherlock Holmes. Reporting from Rome, John Deighton said that after a self-imposed exile of 23 years away from Britain, Purdom, who made his name in *The Student Prince* was preparing to return to the country to play Holmes in the series. 'At 54 I'm the perfect age to play him,' Purdom said. 'I'll bring a new kind of physical dimension to the part. There'll be none of the Basil Rathbones – his style has been lampooned. But there will still be one flaw in my interpretation whatever I do – Holmes will still come out looking a bit square. His modern equivalent would be an electronics expert using human beings like pieces in a jig-saw puzzle.' Despite Edmund Purdom's evident optimism over the project, nothing further was ever heard about the Purdom-Lowe adventures.

William Deneen and director John Davies to film the exciting racing story of *Silver Blaze*. Ambitious location shooting took place at Chepstow race-course and on the Severn Valley Railway line, recently re-opened by volunteer enthusiasts. (This same line was also used in the feature film, *The Seven Per Cent Solution* (1975) which starred Nicol Williamson as Holmes.)

Christopher Plummer, a Canadian by birth, proved yet another actor with the traditional hawk-like features associated with Holmes. (He was not, as a matter of interest, the first Canadian to have played Sherlock – that distinction belongs to Raymond Massey who appeared in Herbert Wilcox's film production of *The Speckled Band* made in 1931). Brought to international attention through his starring role in *The Sound of Music* in 1965, he was not only a long-time enthusiast of the adventures, but had a family connection with Holmes-on-screen. His cousin was Nigel Bruce!

This link gave Plummer a special delight in playing a Holmes story, but he did not let family loyalties cloud his view of his cousin's work. Speaking during location shooting in London, he said: 'Many of us were brought up on Basil Rathbone as Holmes and Nigel Bruce as Watson. The films were extremely entertaining, but I think Nigel Bruce made Watson appear a little stupid.'

An immediately noticeable feature of Christopher Plummer's Holmes was the sickly pallor of his make-up. This had been done deliberately, he explained, to underline the detective's use of drugs – a feature of the great man he believed was often cautiously side-stepped by film-makers. 'Holmes was always taking cocaine,' he said. 'And since the subject of drugs is so topical, I decided to stress this part of the detective's life by having the pallid colouring associated with drug addiction.

'Not all Holmes' admirers want to admit to the fact that he was hooked. They prefer to dismiss his habit as being little more than a taste in exotic tobacco. But, of course, Doctor Watson made no bones about it and you may remember that in *The Sign of Four* he discovered his friend applying a hypodermic needle to his scarred left forearm. "Which is it today?" Watson asks. "Morphine or cocaine?" To which Holmes replies, "It is cocaine . . . care to try it?"

'Drugs undoubtedly helped Holmes relax,' Christopher Plummer added, 'but I feel sure that if he was a real person and alive today he would be working to crack the drugs ring – even though he was a victim himself.'

Thorley Walters was also pleased at the chance of playing Watson again, and felt his television appearance to be a decided improvement on the earlier role playing opposite Christopher Lee. 'This Watson is more intelligent if at times a bit like a rather overgrown schoolboy,' he explained. 'He is amiable, obliging, co-operative, enthusiastic and full of integrity – and to cope with Holmes and his hypodermic a man would need to be all these things!'

The two actors' enthusiasm for their parts produced a stylish and well received production. Elizabeth Cowley, writing in the *Daily Mail*, said, 'The under-exposed Christopher Plummer has always wanted to play Sherlock Holmes, and indeed, his austere, aquiline face is a natural. Accompanying Holmes, as ever, is the adoring Doctor Watson – admirably cast here with Thorley Walters. They compared splendidly with that classic movie pairing of Basil Rathbone and Nigel Bruce . . . *Silver Blaze* was a real weekend winner!'

Interestingly, Christopher Plummer returned to play Holmes again the following year in the cinema film, *Murder by Decree* (1978), in which James Mason appeared as a rather melancholic Doctor Watson. The film, scripted by John Hopkins and directed by Bob Clark, was quite outside the Holmesian canon with the great detective being called in to solve the Jack the Ripper murders!

There was also another 'return' to the Holmes stories shortly afterwards when Sheldon Reynolds, who had masterminded the 39 Ronald Howard adventures in 1954, decided to make a second series about the great detective.

Reynolds' new series, *Sherlock Holmes and Doctor Watson*, was scaled down to 24 half-hour episodes, and not surprisingly when the first details were released in 1980, it was believed this was merely going to be a re-screening of the earlier success. In fact, Reynolds had set up a co-production deal with Polish television, and once again turned to an Englishman to play Holmes.

The producer's choice was TV actor Geoffrey Whitehead, a man not unlike Ronald Howard in appearance, who had previously scored something of a success on English TV as the tough and ambitious policeman, Detective Sergeant Miller in *Z-Cars*. As Watson, Reynolds cast Donald Pickering, previously seen in the film, *Zulu Dawn*, while from *The Avengers* he took Patrick Newell to play Inspector Lestrade. The part of Mrs Hudson was played by Kay Walsh.

Other actors including Richard Green, Derek Bond, Catherine Schell and Stacy Dorning were also taken to Poland for guest appearances – which provided journalist Jack Bell with an intriguing story in January 1980. 'What have a host of TV stars been doing flying in and out of Poland?' he asked. 'Elementary, my dear readers! They've been taking part in a new 24-part Sherlock Holmes series that ITV seems certain to screen in the Spring. Poland was chosen because costs there are low. But the whole production, dubbed "Sherlock Holmski" has been carried out in a cloak-and-dagger atmosphere that would have pleased the immortal sleuth.'

Bell said that no one had been keen to talk to him about the series and added, 'Perhaps the silence has something to do with the treatment Holmes is receiving. I am told that all but one of the yarns is original, and there is a feeling that Holmes purists might be upset by them.'

Only Donald Pickering has subsequently spoken about the series which ITV did not, in fact, screen.

'The schedule for filming was very hectic,' he said, 'and there were the odd dangerous moments. I remember once that the shafts of a hansom cab snapped when we were in hot pursuit of a suspect. That was *very* hairy!'

Talking about his role as Watson, Pickering added, 'Although there are moments when Watson is pretty dim, I didn't play him as a fool – the usual way to project him. I did use plenty of disguises, though – more than Holmes, in fact!'

In the light of his previous success, it is curious that Sheldon Reynolds gave such little publicity to his new series. All the more so when one learns that the best-selling novelist and writer, Anthony Burgess, was involved as a consultant, and some of the writers commissioned were leading television names like Tudor Gates and Harold Jack Bloom.

Despite the mysteries that surround this production – and despite claims that all the stories were new while, in fact, several of the episodes were clearly identical to adventures that had appeared in the earlier Ronald Howard series – it was shown on American television in certain states in 1982 and received generally favourable reviews. Peter Farrell, in *The Oregonian* of February 4, for instance, complained about the general lack of information, but nonetheless added, 'In any event, the English actors, Geoffrey Whitehead and Donald Pickering, are excellent!

'This version has Holmes as a slim, sensitive-looking young man and Watson as middle-aged and robust,' he continued. 'Each half-hour is a complete story, and this Holmes could easily be habit-forming.'

Farrell was also very intrigued by the interpretation of the first meeting of Holmes and Watson as given in the first episode, *A Motive For Murder* as against the description in *A Study in Scarlet*.

'It has Holmes and Watson meeting when Watson comes to share the flat Holmes has just rented. The Housekeeper informs the Doctor on his arrival that Mr Holmes is a fine gentleman, but of rather strange habits. His most recent oddity is that he visited the morgue to hit a corpse with a stick. Watson is intrigued.'

Aren't we all! And, teasingly, Peter Farrell closes his review. 'Yes, I *do* know why Holmes was beating a corpse with a stick. But I'm not telling!'

The whole of America was treated to the next Holmesian adventure on TV – and this proved to be a new televised version of that original 1899 play which Sir Arthur Conan Doyle himself wrote with the actor, William Gillette, incorporating elements from *A Scandal in Bohemia*, *The Boscombe Valley Mystery* and *The Final Problem*.

Sherlock Holmes was staged before a live audience at the Williamstown Theatre Festival in Massachusetts and subsequently aired no less than seven times by its makers, Home Box Office TV. Playing Holmes was Frank Langella, who had previously played the role on stage back in 1977, with Richard Woods as Doctor Watson.

Variety carried an interesting review which gave some insight into the filming of the production. 'Taped by a battery of video cameras, this technique, at first distracting, soon became credible, and the work plays out with ease,' said the paper. 'The intricate plot moved smoothly through the handsome sets designed by John Kasaeda, working up tension and high humour. Using radio mikes concealed in David Murin's costumes, the actors sounded as though they were indeed speaking from the stage, and they gave Gillette's meller a sure presentation, once more showing just how theatrical a figure Sherlock Holmes really is.'

Variety found that the participation of the audience was not an annoyance, 'it's no laugh track distraction,' and added, 'director Gary Halvorson opts for style and flair, with every indication that the re-mounting of Gillette's play abounds in authenticity. More, it's great fun, and the HBO production shows how much theatre can be a part of TV – and, as a TV event, it might serve to interest home audiences in visiting local theatres.'

There was similar praise for the actors in the national press. John J. O'Connor of the *New York Times* of November 19, 1981, wrote: 'Mr Langella is noticeably

FRANK LANGELLA AS THE GREAT DETECTIVE IN THE STAGE PRODUCTION OF *SHERLOCK HOLMES* WHICH WAS FILMED BY HOME BOX OFFICE IN 1981.

restrained as Holmes, focusing on the more disturbing, brooding aspects of his character . . . though he does take some chances. His accent is more mid-Atlantic than British, and his low-keyed approach threatens to disappear from the stage entirely in the first act.

'But gradually he succeeds in making Holmes a fascinating character, even a bit of a romantic who is drawn to a relationship even while declaring that he is incapable of love and is only playing a game.'

Lee Winfrey of the *Arizona Republic* was even more complimentary. 'Frank Langella is a superb Sherlock. With his flashing eyes and his whippet body, he is immediately convincing as the immortal tenant of London's 221B Baker Street.

'Richard Woods is the chubby embodiment of Holmes' faithful sidekick Doctor John H. Watson, while George Morfogen provides an interesting and winning characterisation of Holmes' most famous foe, Professor James Moriarty, the evil mastermind whom Holmes calls, "the Napoleon of crime".'

Lee Winfrey was also greatly impressed by the scene in which Moriarty climbs the steps that leads to Holmes' apartment and there confronts the great detective. 'The antagonists sit in silence for some moments,' Winfrey writes. 'Finally, Moriarty says, "All that I have to say has already crossed your mind". Never one-upped, Holmes replies, "Then my answer has already crossed yours". This first-rate new depiction of the master detective is full of such pleasures!'

There were similar pleasures in store for British television viewers a year later when one of the most extrovert and larger-than-life English character actors, Tom Baker, was lined up for the BBC's third version of *The Hound of the Baskervilles*. The production in fact provided a re-union for Tom and the producer, Barry Letts – but a re-union fraught with possible problems as the two had previously worked together on the long-running series, *Doctor Who*, where Barry had also been producer and Tom the star for seven years. Even the script editor, Terrance Dicks, was a former Doctor Who man.

'It *is* rather brave casting,' Tom admitted before location shooting on Dartmoor began, 'considering it's only eight months since I left *Doctor Who*. But Doctor Who and Sherlock Holmes are both parts that I always wanted to play. And it is a challenge to swop the Doctor's K-9 mechanical dog for a Hell Hound!'

The news that Baker was also swopping his Doctor's ankle-length scarf and floppy hat for Holmes' deer-stalker and pipe, generated considerable pre-publicity for the four-part serial. An angle picked up by some writers was the fact that Tom Baker had previously appeared dressed as Sherlock Holmes in 1977 in an episode of *Doctor Who* called 'The Talons of Weng-Chiang'.

Tom, though, was rather more interested in talking about his research into Holmes for the part. 'The picture of him as the great detective has been governed by the Sidney Paget illustrations in *The Strand* magazine,' he said. 'In fact, Paget simply used his brother as the model and since then all the Holmes have been based on that – a gaunt, stooped and thin person.

'I'm rather different in appearance – but I still play the part absolutely straight.

TOM BAKER, WHO CO-STARRED WITH TERENCE RIGBY IN THE FOUR-PART SERIALISATION OF *THE HOUND OF THE BASKERVILLES* MADE BY THE BBC IN 1982.

The public don't seem to approve of spoofs on Holmes. They have never worked,' he added.

Tom also revealed that he had read and re-read the Holmes stories. 'I've got rather fond of the character,' he said. 'Despite the fact that he doesn't like women and always refers to them with a jibe or a sneer. He's a bit like Professor Higgins – in other words, a prize pig, really! Not like me – I admire women. I adore them!

'The really sad thing for me is that I won't be able to go on playing Holmes – for the works have now gone out of copyright and everyone seems to be getting in on the Conan Doyle bandwagon,' he added.

Baker did, though, make an enjoyable and extrovert Holmes, ably assisted by Terence Rigby as Doctor Watson. Rigby, a 21-year veteran of television, was familiar to British viewers playing characters on the side of law and order, and had appeared as the stolid PC Snow for seven years in the popular series, *Softly, Softly*.

The opinions of viewers about the serial were divided, however, as the correspondence columns of the *Radio Times* in November 1982 revealed.

A Mr James Rusbridger writing from St Austell in Cornwall said, 'I thought the production of *The Hound of the Baskervilles* was very disappointing. The interiors were stagy and very poorly lit, the acting was wooden, with Terence Rigby totally miscast, and the location scenes failing to capture any feeling of a moor, particularly as there was a wild track of crows cawing in the middle of the night. Even the final scenes when the hound appears were spoilt by what looked like a processing fault on the film which prevented one from seeing what was happening. What went wrong?'

Barry Letts replied tersely to this, 'Nothing. Mr Rusbridger is entitled to his opinion. I don't happen to share it.'

On the other hand, Mrs Pat Hicks of Ashford in Middlesex was full of praise. 'Having just watched the final episode of *The Hound of the Baskervilles*,' she wrote, 'I feel I have to write and congratulate the BBC on a very good interpretation of the story. The scenery and costumes appeared very authentic and the cast was outstanding, especially Tom Baker and Terence Rigby. It really was compulsive viewing and I sincerely hope that Sherlock Holmes and Doctor Watson will solve some more mysteries in the near future.'

Curiously, both actors *did* have hopes of appearing in Sherlock Holmes adventures – but neither came to fruition.

While filming his part, Terence Rigby revealed, 'After I have finished this serial I'm playing Inspector Lestrade in a new Holmes series to be shown in a year or so. It's not really a demotion,' he added. 'The part is smaller, but I'm always there at the end. And it suits me, because I haven't so many lines to learn!'

For his part, Tom Baker confessed at the end of the serial that he now had a burning ambition to play . . . Professor Moriarty. 'I'd just *love* that part,' he told Joe Steeples of the *Daily Mail*. 'It's a great ambition of mine: to play Holmes – *and* Moriarty. It's a double that's never been done before.'

In fact, he hoped he might have got the part in the ambitious $20 million, 13-part made-for-TV series of Sherlock Holmes cases which was announced that same year of 1982 by American film-maker, Sy Weintraub.

This proposed series of 90-minute films was to be made in England over a three-year period, Weintraub announced to the press, and he was being joined in the venture by English producer, Otto Plaschkes. The English classical actor, Ian Richardson, had been signed to play Holmes.

When filming of the first story, *The Sign of Four*, began in September, Otto Plaschkes told journalists at a news conference, 'The stories are so good that we want to do them properly, not send them up. The old Basil Rathbone versions, with locations on the back lots of Universal Pictures, seem silly and bizarre and stupid when you see them now. We're trying to use the very latest techniques to preserve the original atmosphere, but at the same time give the stories, a new frisson.'

In between location shooting, the new Holmes also talked about his feelings for the role in an interview with Michael Billington of the *New York Times*. Ian Richardson, who is a veteran of the Royal Shakespeare Company, was quite obviously calling on all his training as a classical actor to establish the character of his Sherlock Holmes, and at the same time was very conscious of the influence of the man he had most seen playing the part – Basil Rathbone.

'Rathbone *was* marvellous,' Richardson admitted. 'He had the face, the height, the nose and a jawline that I will never have. But the crucial thing he missed was that Holmes had a definite and quirky sense of humour. It's the sort of humour that you might feel slightly uncomfortable with if you encountered it at a dinner party.

'It's usually expressed in dry little quips. When, in *The Hound of the Baskervilles*, Holmes and Watson are following Sir Henry Baskerville and Doctor Mortimer down a street, Watson asks if he should run after them. "Not for the world, Watson," says Holmes. "I am perfectly satisfied with your company if you will tolerate mine." I missed that kind of cool irony in Rathbone's interpretation.'

Ian also explained that he had approached the business of playing the part with the same painstaking attention to detail as the great detective himself. 'Being an actor is like being a detective with a magpie sense of theft,' he said. 'And, rather like Holmes, I only really come alive when I've something to do. So when I committed myself to the role in February, I sat down to re-read the entire works and, with my wife, compile a dossier on Holmes. We made notes on each of the stories and on any clues to Holmes' character. We also got a copy of the Army and Navy Stores catalogue for 1900, which has illustrations of the cigar cases, the travelling spirit flasks, the binoculars, the magnifying glasses, the pipes, the violins of the period. We made photostats of these and pasted them up alongside the notes in a volume that now runs to 150 pages.'

Unlike the performance of his predecessor, Christopher Plummer, Richardson decided to play down Holmes' use of drugs. He felt this presented a major problem as far as his interpretation of the role was concerned.

'The trouble is that at the beginning of every story, he's low, depressed, drugged out of his mind. Now you can't start a film with the leading character so laid back you think he's out of his mind with boredom. So what I've done instead is to concentrate on the sort of intensity of excitement that you can see in the eyes.

'On the screen you can show that progressing just as on the stage you would show an upright walk changing to a coiled spring. I let the lids of my eyes come down so that they look hooded and when the germ of a case becomes a reality, the eyes open and we're off. The game's afoot.'

There were, however, problems over getting this particular game afoot. David Healy, who played Watson in the first film of the series, *The Sign of Four*, could not continue thereafter because of contractual obligations to the National Theatre, and his part had to be taken over in *The Hound of the Baskervilles* by Donald

Churchill. And, at the time of writing, these are the only two stories of the projected series that have been completed. As it is possible they may be screened in Britain by ITV, this should offer viewers the chance of judging for themselves what has been described as an impressive performance of Holmes by Ian Richardson.

It is a curious twist of fate that the Granada production of Sherlock Holmes should also have become involved in a change of Watsons. And for the record, I must mention that it was originally Granada's intention during the pre-planning of their series in 1982 to begin with a two-hour adaptation of *The Sign of Four*. But, as producer Michael Cox explained, 'When the Ian Richardson version of the story went into production, we decided to abandon that idea and concentrate on the short stories only.'

Interestingly, in October 1982, Granada began screening a new family drama series, *Young Sherlock*, which detailed one of Holmes' earliest adventures as a 17-year-old schoolboy! The eight-part story, *The Mystery of the Manor House*, starring Guy Henry, was devised and written by Gerald Frow as an insight into how Sherlock began his interest in crime detection.*

According to Frow, the account of the young detective's adventures had been left on dictaphone cylinders to be listened to by Doctor Watson only after the death of his companion. Says Holmes in introducing the series, 'Since our last meeting all those years ago, I have assiduously devoted my retirement to recording details of certain events that took place during my youth; adventures that took place some years before you and I met, and of which I have hitherto apprised no-one.'

Guy Henry as the young Holmes had been picked for the role after a nation-wide search by producer Pieter Rogers for a young actor who matched the general conception of what the great detective *might* have looked like as a teenager. The son of an actor, Guy was spotted at RADA, and certainly his physical appearance was striking. And although 22 years old, he made a very convincing 17-year-old in what was his television debut!

One unique moment from the filming of *Young Sherlock* was when Guy was called on to impersonate Holmes' arch-enemy Moriarty! He took on the guise for a scene when the villainous professor was scheduled to arrive at a lonely manor house astride a black stallion.

Guy explains: 'The thing was that the extra who had been hired for the job took one look at the horse's flaring nostrils and said, "I'm not riding *him*!" I said I didn't mind because I've always been used to riding horses and, anyway, by the time I did the shot disguised and seen from a distance, the stallion was as quiet as a lamb!'

And that explains just how once on television Holmes and Moriarty were one and the same person!

* Subsequent to this, the American film director Steven Spielberg has produced a cinema version of the great detective's early years, *Young Sherlock Holmes* (1986), with Nicholas Rowe as Holmes and Alan Cox as Watson investigating a mysterious Inca sect with a vast pyramid hidden beneath London.

GUY HENRY,
THE STAR OF GRANADA'S
YOUNG SHERLOCK
(1982).

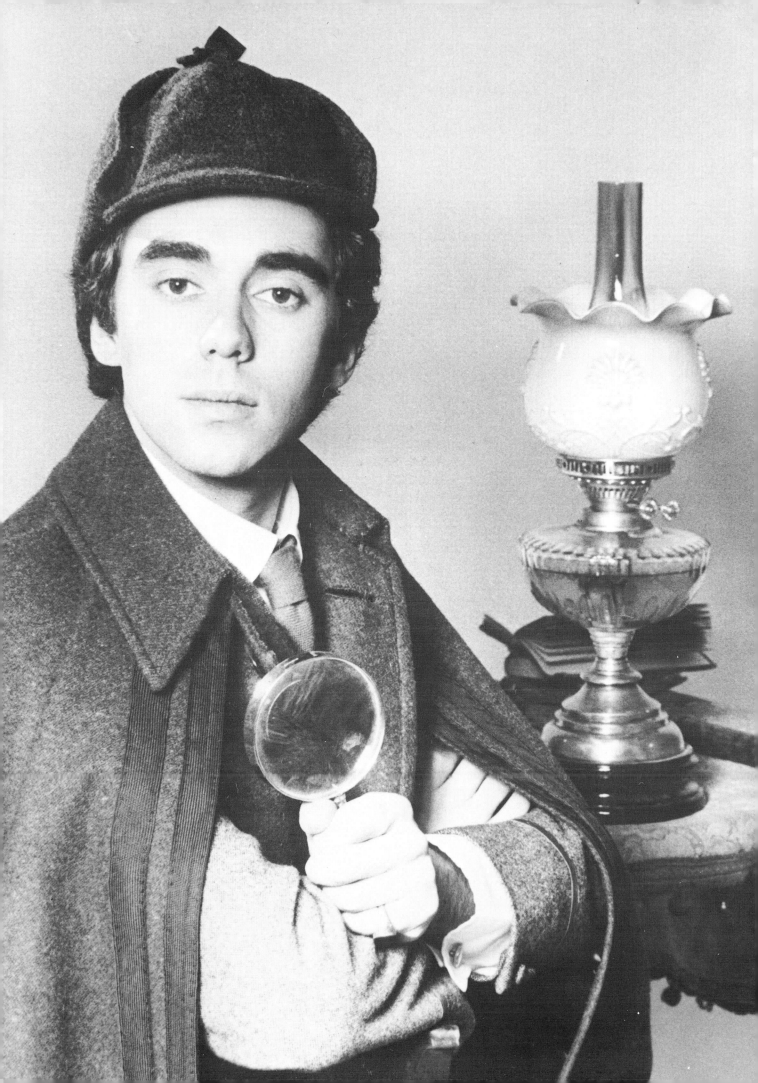

ON THE SET OF THE 1982 RUSSIAN VERSION OF
SHERLOCK HOLMES AND DOCTOR WATSON, WITH PRODUCER
IVOR MASLENNIKOV (CENTRE); VITALY SOLOMIN AS WATSON,
AND VASSILY LIVANOV AS HOLMES.

Early in 1983, readers of British and American newspapers were somewhat startled to learn that one of the most outstanding television successes of recent years on Russian television had been . . . Sherlock Holmes! And not pirated films from the West, but original 80-minute teleplays filmed in Russia and starring leading Soviet actors.

Of course, Holmes has long been a favourite all over the world and there have been innumerable films made about him in countries like France, Spain, Italy and even South America. Behind the Iron Curtain, too, it was known that the super sleuth was very popular (*viz.* the Czechoslovakian and Polish involvements in films mentioned earlier) and that in Russia unauthorized editions of the works of Sir Arthur Conan Doyle had been selling by the hundreds of thousands for much of this century – depriving the family of huge royalties. But this was the first knowledge anyone had of Holmes on Russian TV.

'Soviet citizens cannot bear to part with beloved Sherlock Holmes' ran a headline in the leading Soviet newspaper, *Izvestia*, on February 10, 1983. And the paper reported that as a result of public demand, two more telefilms about Holmes were to be made as follow-ups to the three recently shown so successfully over Soviet TV.

'In response to public appeals,' the story said, 'Lenfilms producer Ivor Maslennikov is planning to film *Trouble In Bohemia* and *The Sign of Four* with Vassily Livanov and Vitaly Solomin continuing as the master detective and his assistant.

'These new stories will be partly filmed at Stone Island, the old quarter of Riga on the Baltic Coast which resembles London. This time, though, they will feature replicas of 19th Century Thames river boats which are being built specially by members of the Neva Rowing & Sailing Club, who are also devoted admirers of Sherlock Holmes.'

This aspect of Holmes on television was also a surprise to me and I have fortunately been able to fill in the details with the aid of a correspondent in Moscow.

It seems that 'Serlock Golmes' – as Holmes is mispronounced in Russia – has become so popular that a permanent Baker Street set has been built in the heart of Leningrad. For location shooting, the producers use either the nearby Steppes as English moorland, or the famous Winter Palace, once the home of the Czars, to serve as country mansions. The success of the first three stories, *A Study in Scarlet*, *The Speckled Band* and, inevitably, *The Hound of the Baskervilles* encouraged Ivor Maslennikov to go further afield to the Baltic coast.

Maslennikov says that the appeal of the stories to Russians is a combination of a passionate interest in Victorian England, the fact that they are extremely good adventures, and Sherlock Holmes himself. 'Anyone who goes to him feels secure,' the producer explains. 'He is reliable. Whereas the police are out to punish someone, Holmes wants to help the victims. He is a personification of gentlemanly behaviour. Audiences are always in need of someone with those qualities.'

Lenfilms have spent a great deal of money and care faithfully recreating Holmes' rooms in Baker Street, as well as dressing the characters in thoroughly authentic clothes. The stories have also remained faithful to the originals – there are no political undertones – and the leading actors have been selected for their resemblance to the traditional ideas of Holmes and Watson as depicted by Sidney Paget.

Vassily Livanov who plays Holmes is aged 47, and the son of the late Boris Livanov, the famous Moscow Arts Theatre actor, once described as the Russian Olivier and a long-time friend of our own Sir John Gielgud. He is disarmingly frank about his own abilities and his part in the TV success.

'My grandfather was a good actor,' he says, 'and my father was a great one. I am just an actor. I first discovered Sherlock Holmes when I was a young boy. I was so impressed that I wrote a fan letter to Conan Doyle who I thought was still alive. I never imagined, though, that I'd grow up and play Holmes on television one day!'

Livanov says that he has never been very impressed by Hollywood's attempts to portray Holmes. 'I've seen a lot of the films,' he says, 'but it seems to me that the actors are not playing the part but playing *with* it, as if they were trying to make fun of the detective. I just try to play him as the perfect English gentleman.'

The part of Watson is played by Vitaly Solomin, an actor who prior to this role specialized in Soviet hero roles. Now with reddish moustache, starched collar and tweed suit, he has been described in *Izvestia* as being 'as English as a beefeater'.

He told a Russian journalist, 'Doctor Watson is usually shown as a bumbling old man, but we have stuck much closer to Conan Doyle's books. Here he is much younger and much more vigorous.'

Solomin has, though, been rather scathing of some of Conan Doyle's 'inventions'. 'Some of the things he wrote were nonsense,' he says. 'We had all sorts of snags when we tried to stick to the text too literally.

'For instance, take the story of *The Hound of the Baskervilles* which calls for a dog covered with fluorescent paint. We couldn't find anyone to loan us a dog because they said the paint would kill it!'

Undoubtedly the success of this series has surprised people *in* Russia as much as outside the country. For years the most popular movies have been those dealing with modern technology and the latest gadgets. And then along comes the detective from Victorian London and – as *Izvestia* so neatly put it – 'arrests the entire Soviet people!'

It seems somehow very appropriate that the actor to make the last appearance as Sherlock Holmes on television before Jeremy Brett's triumph in the part should be the man whose reputation he has surpassed – Peter Cushing.

Over the years that I have known Peter – including working with him on a joint book entitled *Tales of a Monster Hunter* which was published in 1977 – I know that he has always considered playing Sherlock Holmes as one of his favourite roles. It was not, therefore, a very hard decision for him to decide to return to the part for a third time when Channel 4 planned to make their entry into the Holmes-on-TV stakes with a completely new 90-minute adventure for showing at Christmas 1984. His only reservation was that he might be too old for the part.

'The trouble is that I'm 70,' he said in October of the previous year, 'far too old to play Holmes as he appears in the stories written by Sir Arthur Conan Doyle. People are now more used to seeing me on TV in films I made over 20 years ago for Hammer, and they don't realize how I've aged since then. When they see this rather elderly gentleman pedalling around on his bicycle, they think I'm Peter Cushing's father! So you can see why I just don't know if people will accept me as an older Holmes.'

But Peter need not have worried, because the whole idea behind N. J. Crisp's story *The Masks of Death* was that Holmes *was* much older and living quietly in retirement in Sussex tending to his bees. 'The adventure is actually set in 1913 just before the outbreak of World War I, so that Holmes is past 60, not that far from my own age,' he explained when filming began. 'Holmes is on a brief visit to his old apartments in Baker Street when he gets a visit from the Home Secretary who begs him to undertake one more vital mission. He learns that the Germans have invented a deadly secret weapon, and he has to get to the bottom of the mystery.

'I think that the writer, Norman Crisp, has done a very good job of keeping within the bounds of Conan Doyle,' he added.

Apart from the pleasure of playing Holmes again, Peter was delighted to be re-united with some old friends from nearly 50 years in show business. Another veteran actor, Sir John Mills, was Watson; Anton Diffring who played in many Hammer Horror films featured as an evil German diplomat; and Ray Milland, the durable Hollywood old-timer, made a rare appearance in what was his eightieth year, as the Home Secretary. On the other side of the cameras were Kevin Francis, son of Peter's many-time producer, Freddie Francis, and now a producer himself; as well as Roy Ward Baker, another Hammer alumnus.

Sir John Mills was equally delighted to be playing Watson, a role he had coveted for many of his 76 years as an actor. 'Like millions of others I read the books as a child and saw Basil Rathbone and Nigel Bruce in the parts in the cinema forty years ago,' he said. 'Nigel Bruce always played Watson as a rather splendid halfwit, almost an imbecile, which isn't the character at all. Watson was an Army man and a doctor.

'He wasn't in any way a buffoon,' Sir John added, 'and one of the delights about this new production is that it takes pains not to portray him as an idiot.' In fact, Sir John's portrayal of Watson as a dapper, correct, traditional sort of man earned praise from the critics, as did the entire production.

Peter Ackroyd, writing in *The Times* of December 24, 1984, for instance, said, 'After all the attempts at parody, and no less frequent inflictions of sexual innuendo or psychoanalysis, Holmes has emerged unscathed – the reason being that he has so vigorous and emblematic a character that he can be neither diluted nor obscured. He has even survived the transition to television, which is more than can be said for most real people. And as Peter Cushing proved last night, age cannot wither him: he was a Prospero rather than a Hamlet in this production, but none the worse for that.

'Once again, the Holmes adventure becomes an opportunity for the exploration of characters and settings on a *grand guignol* scale, last night's plot having to do with a German plan to leak poison gas into the homes of Londoners. And once again it can become the vehicle for that peculiarly English combination of genuine horror and spirited comedy. This is a difficult tone to catch without self-parody, but N. J. Crisp's script managed to perform the trick, apparently to the satisfaction of everyone concerned: this was altogether an excellent production.'

Steve Grant in *The Observer* was almost as enthusiastic. '*The Masks of Death* is a jolly confection,' he wrote, 'which not only pays homage to the gaslight, the tinkling clock, the leather-backed armchair, the hansom cab and the corridorless train, but joys in the cottonwool embrace of familiar faces . . .

'The production was a kind of "Dad's Army" Conan Doyle with Mills and Cushing, though well past their Victorian peaks, still capable of pushing German would-be assassins from the doors of moving trains, climbing onto roofs and in Cushing's case donning various disguises.

'Cushing, whose gaunt, bird-like features are now positively frail and cadaverous, still brings great dignity and subtlety to the role of Holmes. He says there's even talk of a series – "although they'd better hurry up or I'll have to do it from my wheelchair!"'

It is, in fact, unlikely that there ever will be a Cushing and Mills serial. And by this time, also, a definitive new Holmes had been hailed in Britain and was on the verge of being launched to even greater acclaim in America.

This new man's name was Jeremy Brett and the story of his success takes us not to London as you might expect, but to the grey Northern city of Manchester, famous mainly for its weather and football teams. It also introduces us to an enthusiastic, dedicated and hard-working group of television people who might easily be called 'The Castlefield Irregulars'. The story of their remarkable achievement is what now follows . . .

A CHRONOLOGY ❧OF❧ HOLMES ON TV

THE THREE GARRIDEBS (1937)
NBC Television, New York
Adapted by Thomas H. Hutchinson
Produced by Robert Palmer
Cast: Sherlock Holmes, Louis Hector;
Doctor Watson, William Podmore; John
Garrideb, Arthur Maitland; Nathan
Garrideb, James Spottswood; Mrs
Hudson, Violet Besson; Inspector
Lestrade, Eustace Wyatt

THE ADVENTURE OF THE SPECKLED BAND (1949)
Marshall-Grant-Realm Television, USA
Adapted by Walter Doniger
Produced by Sobey Martin
Cast: Sherlock Holmes, Alan Napier;
Doctor Watson, Melville Cooper

ONE OF THE MOST FAMOUS SPOOFS OF
SHERLOCK HOLMES – THE GREAT COMIC TOMMY
HANDLEY PLAYING 'PICKLOCK HOLES,
THE GREAT DEFECTIVE' WITH SYDNEY KEITH AS
'DOCTOR FLOTSAM', MADE BY THE BBC IN 1944.

THE MAN WITH THE TWISTED LIP (1951)
Vandyke Pictures, GB
Adapted by William Johnson
Produced & Directed by Richard M.
Grey
Cast: Sherlock Holmes, John Longdon;
Doctor Watson, Campbell Singer;
Neville St Clair, Hector Ross

THE MAZARIN STONE (1951)
BBC Television
Adapted by Alan Harmer
Produced by Duncan Richardson
Cast: Sherlock Holmes, Andrew
Osborn; Doctor Watson, Philip King

SHERLOCK HOLMES (1951)
BBC Television
Six-part series adapted by C. A. Lejeune
Produced by Ian Atkin
Cast: Sherlock Holmes, Alan Wheatley; Doctor Watson, Raymond Francis; Inspector Lestrade, Bill Owen
Episodes: *The Empty House* (October 20); *A Scandal in Bohemia* (October 27); *The Dying Detective* (November 3); *The Reigate Squires* (November 17); *The Red-Headed League* (November 24); *The Second Stain* (December 1)

THE BLACK BARONET (1953)
CBS Television, New York
Adapted by Michael Dyne from a story by Adrian Conan Doyle and John Dickson Carr
Produced by Himan Brown
Cast: Sherlock Holmes, Basil Rathbone; Doctor Watson, Martyn Green; members of the New York Branch of the Baker Street Irregulars

SHERLOCK HOLMES (1954)
Series of 39 films by Guild Films
Adapted by Sheldon Reynolds, Harold J. Bloom, Lou Morheim, Henry Sandoz, Charles M. Early, George and Gertrude Fass
Produced by Sheldon Reynolds
Cast: Sherlock Holmes, Ronald Howard; Doctor Watson, Howard Marion Crawford; Inspector Lestrade, Archie Duncan
Episodes: *The Case of the Cunningham Heritage*; *Lady Beryl*; *The Winthrop Legend*; *The Mother Hubbard Case*; *The Pennsylvania Gun*; *The Red-Headed League*; *The Belligerent Ghost*; *The Thistle Killer*; *The Shoeless Engineer*; *The Shy Ballerina*; *The Deadly Prophecy*; *The Split Ticket*; *Harry Crocker*; *The Reluctant Carpenter*; *The Texas Cowgirl*; *The Laughing Mummy*; *The Diamond Tooth*; *Blind Man's Buff*; *The Greystone Inscription*; *The French Interpreter*;

The Vanished Detective; *The Careless Suffragette*; *The Baker Street Nursemaids*; *The Tyrant's Daughter*; *The Imposter Mystery*; *The Christmas Pudding*; *The Jolly Hangman*; *The Impromptu Performance*; *The Singing Violin*; *The Violent Suitor*; *The Night Train Riddle*; *The Perfect Husband*; *The Unlucky Gambler*; *The Exhumed Client*; *The Neurotic Detective*; *The Baker Street Bachelors*; *The Eiffel Tower*; *The Haunted Gainsborough* and *A Case of Royal Murder*

THE SPECKLED BAND (1964)
BBC Television
Pilot programme adapted by Giles Cooper
Produced by David Goddard
Cast: Sherlock Holmes, Douglas Wilmer; Doctor Watson, Nigel Stock

SHERLOCK HOLMES (1965)
BBC Television
Series of 12 stories adapted by Giles Cooper, Vincent Tilsey, Anthony Read, Clifford Witting, Jan Read and Nicholas Palmer
Produced by David Goddard
Cast: Sherlock Holmes, Douglas Wilmer; Doctor Watson, Nigel Stock; Inspector Lestrade, Peter Madden; Mrs Hudson, Mary Holder; Mycroft Holmes, Derek Francis
Episodes: *The Illustrious Client* (February 20); *The Devil's Foot* (February 27); *The Copper Beeches* (March 6); *The Red-Headed League* (March 13); *The Abbey Grange* (March 20); *The Six Napoleons* (March 27); *The Man With The Twisted Lip* (April 3); *The Beryl Coronet* (April 10); *The Bruce-Partington Plans* (April 17); *Charles Augustus Milverton* (April 24); *The Retired Colourman* (May 1) and *Lady Frances Carfax* (May 8)

THE CASES OF SHERLOCK HOLMES (1968)

BBC Television
Series of 16 stories adapted by Jennifer Stuart, Hugh Leonard, Michael and Mollie Hardwick, Bruce Stewart, John Gould, Harry Moore, Alexander Baron, Richard Harris and Stanley Miller
Produced by William Sterling
Cast: Sherlock Holmes, Peter Cushing; Doctor Watson, Nigel Stock; Inspector Lestrade, William Lucas; Mrs Hudson, Grace Arnold; Mycroft Holmes, Ronald Adam
Episodes: *The Second Stain* (September 9); *A Study in Scarlet* (September 16); *The Dancing Men* (September 23); *The Hound of the Baskervilles* (2 episodes: September 30, October 7); *The Boscombe Valley Mystery* (October 14); *The Greek Interpreter* (October 21); *The Naval Treaty* (October 28); *Thor Bridge* (November 4); *The Musgrave Ritual* (November 11); *Black Peter* (November 18); *Wisteria Lodge* (November 25); *Shoscombe Old Place* (December 2); *The Solitary Cyclist* (December 9); *The Sign of Four* (December 16) and *The Blue Carbuncle* (December 23)

SHERLOCK HOLMES AND THE DEADLY NECKLACE (1968)

Constantin Film Verlag
Adapted by Curt Siodmak
Produced by Artur Brauner
Cast: Sherlock Holmes, Christopher Lee; Doctor Watson, Thorley Walters; Ellen Blackburn, Senta Berger; Professor Moriarty, Hans Sohnker; Mrs Hudson, Edith Shultze-Westrum

THE LONGING OF SHERLOCK HOLMES (1972)

Czech Films AD, Prague
Adapted by Stepan Skalsky and Ilja Hurnik
Produced & Directed by Stepan Skalsky
Cast: Sherlock Holmes, Radovan Lukavsky; Doctor Watson, Vaclav Voska; Sir Arthur Conan Doyle, Josef Parocka

THE HOUND OF THE BASKERVILLES (1972)

ABC-TV
Adapted by Robert E. Thompson
Produced by Stanley Kallis
Cast: Sherlock Holmes, Stewart Granger; Doctor Watson, Bernard Fox; Stapleton, William Shatner; Inspector Lestrade, Alan Caillou; Laura, Sally Ann Howes

DOCTOR WATSON AND THE DARKWATER HALL MYSTERY (1974)

BBC TV
Adapted by Kingsley Amis
Produced by Mark Shivas
Cast: Doctor Watson, Edward Fox; Mrs Hudson, Marguerite Young; Emily, Elaine Taylor; Sir Harry, Christopher Cazenove

THE INTERIOR MOTIVE (1975)

Kentucky Educational TV
Adapted by Richard L. Smith
Produced and Directed by George Rasmussen
Cast: Sherlock Holmes, Leonard Nimoy; Doctor Watson, Burt Blackwell

THE RETURN OF THE WORLD'S GREATEST DETECTIVE (1976)

NBC-TV
Adapted by Ronald Kibbee and Dean Hargrove
Produced by Ronald Kibbee and Dean Hargrove
Cast: Sherlock Holmes, Larry Hagman; Doctor Watson, Jenny O'Hara

THE FAMOUS BBC RADIO PARTNERSHIP OF
HOLMES AND WATSON: CARLTON HOBBS AS SHERLOCK
AND NORMAN SHELLEY AS THE GOOD DOCTOR,
PHOTOGRAPHED IN THE SHERLOCK HOLMES HOTEL
IN LONDON IN 1958.

SHERLOCK HOLMES IN NEW YORK (1976)

NBC-TV
Adapted by Alvin Sapinsky
Produced by John Cutts
Cast: Sherlock Holmes, Roger Moore;
Doctor Watson, Patrick Macnee;
Professor Moriarty, John Huston; Irene
Adler, Charlotte Rampling

SILVER BLAZE (1977)

HTV
Adapted by Julian Bond
Produced by William Deneen
Cast: Sherlock Holmes, Christopher
Plummer; Doctor Watson, Thorley
Walters; Colonel Ross, Basil Henson;
Inspector Gregory, Gary Watson

SHERLOCK HOLMES AND DOCTOR WATSON (1980)

Filmways
Series of 24 stories adapted by Sheldon Reynolds, Tudor Gates, Andrea Reynolds, George and Gertrude Pass, Joe Morhaim, Robin Bishop, Harold Jack Bloom and George Fowler
Produced by Sheldon Reynolds
Cast: Sherlock Holmes, Geoffrey Whitehead; Doctor Watson, Donald Pickering; Inspector Lestrade, Patrick Newell; Mrs Hudson, Kay Walsh
Episodes: *Baker Street Nursemaids*; *Blind Man's Buff*; *The Case of the Body in the Case*; *The Close-Knit Family*; *The Case of the Deadly Prophecy*; *The Case of the Deadly Tower*; *The Final Curtain*; *Four Minus Four is One*; *The Case of Harry Crocker*; *The Case of Harry Rigby*; *A Case of High Security*; *The Case of the Luckless Gambler*; *The Case of MacGruder's Millions*; *Motive for Murder*; *Murder on Midsummer's Eve*; *The Case of the Other Ghost*; *The Case of the Perfect Crimes*; *The Case of the Purloined Letter*; *The Case of the Shrunken Heads*; *The Case of the Sitting Target*; *The Case of Smith and Smythe*; *The Case of the Speckled Band*; *The Case of the Three Uncles* and *The Case of the Travelling Killer*

SHERLOCK HOLMES (1981)

Home Box Office TV
Adapted by William Gillette
Produced by Peter H. Hunt
Cast: Sherlock Holmes, Frank Langella; Doctor Watson, Richard Woods; Professor Moriarty, George Morfogen; Alice Faulkner, Laurie Kennedy

THE HOUND OF THE BASKERVILLES (1982)

BBC TV
Four-part serial adapted by Alexander Baron
Produced by Barry Letts
Cast: Sherlock Holmes, Tom Baker; Doctor Watson, Terence Rigby; Sir Henry Baskerville, Nicholas Wodeson; Stapleton, Christopher Ravenscroft; Inspector Lestrade, Hubert Rees

SHERLOCK HOLMES AND DOCTOR WATSON (1982)

Lenfilms, Russia
Five-part series adapted by Boris Steepinov
Produced by Ivor Maslennikov
Cast: Sherlock Holmes, Vassily Livanov; Doctor Watson, Vitaly Solomin
Episodes: *A Study in Scarlet*; *The Speckled Band*; *The Hound of the Baskervilles*; *Scandal in Bohemia* and *The Sign of Four*

SHERLOCK HOLMES (1983)

Mapleton Films
Projected 13-part series adapted by Sy Weintraub of which two have so far been completed
Produced by Otto Plaschkes
Cast: Sherlock Holmes, Ian Richardson; Doctor Watson, David Healy (in *The Sign of Four*) and Donald Churchill (in *The Hound of the Baskervilles*); Major John Sholto, Thorley Walters; Inspector Layton, Terence Rigby; Mary Morstan, Cherie Lunghi; Doctor Mortimer, Denholm Elliott; Sir Henry Baskerville, Martin Shaw; Inspector Lestrade, Ronald Lacey; Geoffrey Lyons, Brian Blessed; Mrs Barrymore, Eleanor Bron.

THE MASKS OF DEATH (1984)

Tyburn Production
Story by N. J. Crisp
Produced by Kevin Francis & Norman Priggen
Cast: Sherlock Holmes, Peter Cushing; Doctor Watson, John Mills; Irene Adler, Ann Baxter; Home Secretary, Ray Milland; Graf Udo Von Felseck, Anton Diffring; Alec MacDonald, Gordon Jackson; Miss Derwent, Susan Penhaligon; Mrs Hudson, Jenny Laird

MICHAEL COX,
PRODUCER OF THE GRANADA SERIES.

THE ADVENTURE OF THE CASTLEFIELD ❧TRIUMPH❧

The Making of the Granada Series

It was a case – as Sherlock Holmes himself might have said – of a number of special circumstances combined with the significant roles played by several people, that led to the Castlefield Triumph.

As elaborate as one of the great detective's adventures, the story of the making of Granada's television series about Sherlock Holmes is one of remarkable ingenuity, painstaking hard work and the good fortune which blesses those who dare to be bold. For bringing Sherlock Holmes – beyond question one of the most striking figures of modern literature – to the screen yet again after one hundred years of intense public familiarity presented no mean task.

It was a challenge, indeed, of which the faithful Watson had already indicated he had something of the measure when he philosophized in *The Valley of Fear*: 'Mediocrity knows nothing higher than itself; but talent instantly recognizes genius.'

I do not count myself as a Watson, but as the duly appointed Chronicler of this fascinating story, there is no better place to begin than at the beginning . . .

Granada Television's modern complex of office blocks, studios and technical facilities at Castlefield,* a few miles from the centre of Manchester, are light years

---

*Castlefield is one of the most historic areas of Manchester with a history that goes back 2000 years. Features of the area are a reconstructed Roman fort and the world's first railway station, Liverpool Road, rubbing shoulders with The Manchester Museum of Science and Technology and The Air and Space Museum. Granada have developed their section of Castlefield into an international TV production centre which now shows every sign of becoming a tourist attraction – with Baker Street and the neighbouring Coronation Street sets as prime features.

away from the gaslit, fog-shrouded London of Sherlock Holmes. Yet here the story of the making of the series begins, five floors up in the office of the quietly-spoken, friendly and energetic Michael Cox, initially the executive producer of the drama, and latterly freelance producer of the *Casebook* series. For his was the dream, his the vision, and his the gamble that brought Holmes alive in this latest of many television adaptations. Not his alone, though, as Michael is quick to explain when the talk turns to the series of which he is hugely and justifiably proud.

Beyond the large picture window of his office lies the most immediately visible sign of his achievement – the 60 yard stretch of Baker Street, specially created at a cost of £250,000 with immense attention to authenticity and fine detail, and which formed the backdrop to the whole series. It is believed to be the largest TV set ever built. This stunning facade – for such it is – is bounded on one side by an old Victorian Bonded Warehouse which Granada have restored and modernized for use as a location base, production centre and offices – and on the other side by . . . Coronation Street.

Though at first glance there is something strangely incongruous about the set of Granada's famous Northern soap opera standing terraced house by low slate roof alongside the towering grandeur of Baker Street's three-storey houses and genteel shops, it is also curiously *right*. For here, a few yards apart, lie two of the most famous streets in the world.

The singular appropriateness of this close proximity is not lost on Michael Cox, for in fact they both represent important factors in his career. For in his early years with Granada after he joined them in the early sixties, he was for a time producer on *Coronation Street*. And, equally interestingly, before becoming executive producer of drama serials in 1974, he also had a foretaste of Holmesian days when he was producer of *Victorian Scandals*.

It was in 1980, however, that he was made head of drama series, and not long afterwards began to consider realizing a long-held ambition. An ambition he was determined to fulfil not by proxy, but by returning to the role of producer. Michael's ambition was to make a thoroughly authentic and wholly faithful adaptation of the best cases of Sherlock Holmes. And, as he explains, this fascination with the Master of Detectives was something he could trace back to his childhood.

'My personal interest in Sherlock Holmes began in an almost text book way,' he says. 'My father was a fan and he had an actual collection of the bound volumes of *The Strand* magazine containing the original stories. I was introduced to them as a schoolboy, loved them, and in an enduring way I have loved them ever since.

'It was as an adult that I realized that they are wonderfully crafted pieces of popular fiction – and I can read them now both for the enjoyment of the stories themselves and also with an admiration for Conan Doyle and how he made what were sometimes not the greatest plots in the world *work* because of his characterization and eye for eccentric detail.'

For thirty-odd years Michael harboured this delight in the Holmes stories until fate presented him with the chance to bring them to the small screen. 'It was a date that provided the opportunity – the year 1980,' he explains candidly. 'Because Conan Doyle had died in 1930, I understood that the next year would mark the end of the 50 year copyright period in his works. Therefore the Sherlock Holmes stories which had previously been unavailable to Granada TV – or anyone else except those who owned the copyright at the time – became available because they entered the public domain.

'So I put up the idea of a series to Granada Television, pointing out that the stories had never been done as a television series, in colour, at a really grand level. I said we should set out to do the best Sherlock Holmes series *ever*. Brave, bold words!'

Michael smiles at the remembrance of those times. 'Fortunately, Sir Denis Forman [then Chairman of Granada] shared my enthusiasm, and between him and David Plowright [then Managing Director] we plotted to do just that.'

Michael keeps among his souvenirs of the series, a copy of the brief but nevertheless explicit memo from Sir Denis which gave him the go-ahead. It reads: 'The more I think of it, the more my enthusiasm grows for Sherlock Holmes – but it does mean that if we really roll up our sleeves on Sherlock, other period works will have to be discarded, because his period is more "period" than any other period I know. He cannot live alongside Cribb, Dickens or anything like that. One or the other.' From such little inter-office acorns do the trees of mighty series grow!

Michael knew that he had committed himself to a daunting objective – just how daunting he was to find out. 'So in the early Eighties we set about discovering how it could be done, what it would cost, and whether there was – as I believed – an overseas market. Which, of course, was rather important to us, because to make the series in an expensive way it would be a great deal easier if there was some certainty of sales elsewhere in the world. And, very fortunately, one of the public broadcasting stations in America, WGBH in Boston, and their underwriters, Mobil, responded to the idea with similar enthusiasm, and so we started to get it together!'

Michael recalls that it was in 1981 that the series really became a possibility, but there were to be two more years of hard work before actual filming began.

Right at the forefront of his objectives was to ensure the series returned to the image of Holmes and Watson as portrayed by Conan Doyle's text and Sidney Paget's illustrations in those fondly-remembered volumes of *The Strand* from his childhood. He was also anxious to avoid the variations in the characters which earlier actors had introduced – in particular the famous Basil Rathbone and Nigel Bruce partnership.

'In the same way that I had grown up with *The Strand* magazines, I also as a schoolboy used to watch the Rathbone and Bruce films at the cinema,' he recalls. 'Now, I am a great admirer of Basil Rathbone, and I think he was a wonderful Holmes. I am not so wholehearted about Nigel Bruce, because I think he was trapped into playing it too much for comedy.

'But my disappointment in their films – apart from *The Hound of the Baskervilles* – was that they had abandoned the original stories, and to a large extent the original atmosphere of Victorian London, and taken Holmes to places like Washington and Algiers: which I thought was a mistake. So I thought that if we could find a Holmes at least as good as Rathbone, and if we could cast Watson in a way that was more faithful to the original idea, then what I wanted to do was to be faithful to the original stories and the original atmosphere.'

Having settled his policy of returning to the basics of the stories, Michael next recruited a consultant to help him develop the scripts which would be the basis of the success – or failure – of the project. He went straight for one of the most respected names in television, John Hawkesworth, whose many contributions to the small screen included one of the best received of all independent television series, *Upstairs, Downstairs*.

'I went to John right at the beginning,' Michael remembers. 'He was, of course, not only well known here but also in America, which was an important factor in my plans. It seemed to me that with the help of someone like him who is a writer, also a producer and a great television professional, I might find the right way through quite a number of tricky problems. Decisions like which of the stories to do, whether or not to make any attempt to get the chronology of the stories right as the various commentators are always trying to do, what do you do about Watson's wife – or wives – and so on. All of these problems had to be solved, I believed, or else we would be contradicting ourselves all the way along.

'So I put all of this to John and asked if he would be interested in working with me. To my delight, he said he would love to be involved in a really good Sherlock Holmes series,' Michael says.

The first thing the two men did was to separately make a list of the stories they thought should be used in the series. 'When we compared notes we found there was a remarkable degree of unanimity between us,' Michael says. 'Then we made lists of the people we would like to dramatize them.

'Now the big bee in my bonnet is that you can't simply take the stories off the page and say, "The client comes up the stairs, sits down and tells his story and off we go". You have got to make as good a job of a television script as Conan Doyle made of a short story. So we needed some very good writers.

'Despite being an enormously busy man, John was prepared to do some of the scripts himself, and between us he brought in half a dozen other distinguished television writers like Bill Craig, Alan Plater, Jeremy Paul, Derek Marlowe, to do a couple of stories apiece.'

While John Hawkesworth worked with the writers to develop the scripts of the series, Michael threw himself into the whole variety of tasks necessary in setting up such an elaborate undertaking. He also acquired an associate producer in the person of Stuart Doughty, a man who had worked on several productions including the National Theatre Production of *The Double Dealer* as well as helping to develop new writing talents such as Trevor Hoyle, author of *Whatever Happened To The Heroes?* and Tony Dunham who wrote *Marathon*.

'John Hawkesworth gave me a wonderful start,' Michael Cox goes on, 'because by the time we were ready to begin filming that absolutely essential, precious work of scriptwriting was complete and he handed me thirteen splendid scripts to get on with.'

The scripts also enabled Michael to fulfil that objective of painting pictures on the screen that were mirror images of what he remembered from *The Strand*. 'I always had in my mind's eye Sherlock Holmes as Sidney Paget drew him,' says Michael, 'and I think one of the reasons for Basil Rathbone's success was that he looked so like a Paget illustration. I wanted to stick as close to those pictures as I could – though there was one small worry that bothered me.

'In America, when Sherlock Holmes first appeared in *Collier's* Magazine the Paget illustrations were not used, and instead he was illustrated by a different artist, Frederick Dorr Steele, who naturally enough drew a different Holmes. So the Americans have always had that vision of him, which made me wonder how they would react when we chose an actor to play the part. Nevertheless, I decided to stick with the Paget image.

"HE TORE THE MASK
FROM HIS FACE."

"A DRUNKEN-LOOKING GROOM."

105

"HOLMES
LASHED
FURIOUSLY."

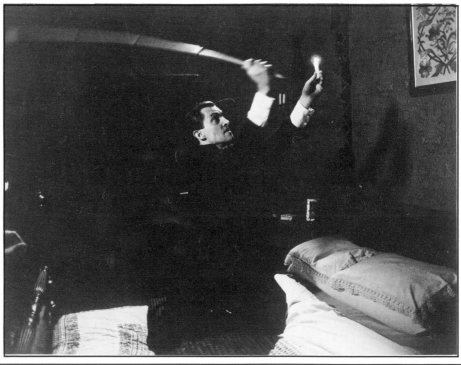

'There are also, of course, certain key scenes in the stories which Paget illustrated brilliantly – as, for example, when Holmes lashed out furiously at the snake around the bell-pull in *The Speckled Band* or the classic scene where he is talking to Watson in the railway carriage – and I wanted to hit those moments just as Paget had hit them. The same with Holmes' disguises – those occasions when he disguises himself as a groom or an old clergyman. I wanted to show it like it was!' he adds.

Just how well Michael and his team achieved this element of the stories you can judge by comparing the selection of Paget illustrations and the corresponding scenes from the television series which are included in the pages of this book.

Now the time had arrived for one of the most important decisions of all – *who* was to play Sherlock Holmes? In hindsight, the choice can be seen to be an inspired one – but how did Michael Cox face the crucial decision which could make or break his dream back in the early days of 1982?

'To begin with I made a long list of the actors who I thought more or less resembled my notion of Doyle's and Paget's Holmes,' he says frankly. 'But I knew at the end of the day I could not just pick someone for a resemblance: it had to be an actor of great classical experience. Preferably classically trained, not necessarily a familiar face, but inevitably someone who had played some of the "big" parts of his generation. In a word, it had to be someone who was good – *really* good.'

Michael pauses for a moment, looks out of his window towards Baker Street as if recalling a moment from the past, and then adds, 'From the time that Jeremy Brett's name popped out onto the list, I can honestly say there didn't seem to be a better bet – and my only worry then was, "Would he do it?"'

'Jeremy had the look for the part – physically he is a very good equivalent of the Paget Holmes. He has the right background as an actor, too, and the energy the part demanded. He also has that aristocracy, elegance and poise that Holmes possesses.'

So sure, in fact, was Michael Cox in his choice, that he did not even feel he needed to ask Jeremy Brett to make a test for the role. Instead, on February 26, 1982, he invited the former rumbustious young leading man, now one of the country's most mature stage performers, to be the latest in a long line of Sherlock Holmes.*

Michael knew he could not guarantee Jeremy Brett success. Nor could he offer anything other than many months of demanding and exhausting work in a part that had defeated numerous actors before and left its indelible – and not always happy – mark on others.

It was obviously a far from easy decision for Jeremy to make, for he sensed immediately that the role would demand considerable sacrifice as well as a big slice of his life. But even *he* did not imagine quite how much sacrifice it would entail – the facts of which I shall recount a little later.

---

*It is a curious coincidence, but Jeremy Brett's great predecessor as Holmes, Basil Rathbone, was also picked for the role by a similar instinctive feeling. It was at a dinner party in Hollywood in 1939 that George Markey, a distinguished screenwriter, suddenly said to his host, Darryl F. Zanuck, the head of Twentieth Century Fox, 'You know, someone ought to film Conan Doyle's classic, *The Adventures of Sherlock Holmes*.' The idea immediately appealed to Zanuck, but he asked who could play Holmes. To which Markey instantly replied, 'Basil Rathbone – who else?' And a few moments later, George Markey completed the cast list by proposing Nigel Bruce for Doctor Watson!

REHEARSING AN EARLY SCENE IN THE SERIES
ON THE 221B APARTMENT SET IN THE CASTLEFIELD WAREHOUSE.

Having selected such a perfectionist as Jeremy Brett for his Holmes, Michael
knew he must prepare him for the role not only with outstanding scripts – which he
had – but the most thorough background information on the familiar yet
enigmatic figure of the sleuth from Baker Street. Aided by Stuart Doughty and
Nicky Cooney, the programme's research assistant, he exhaustively combed the
56 short stories and four novels which make up the Sherlockian canon to assemble
The Baker Street File, 'a guide to the appearance and habits of Sherlock Holmes and
Doctor Watson', to quote the 77-page book's sub-title. Not only did he hope this
would be of use to Jeremy Brett, but also the other principal artists in developing
their characterizations, and the entire production team where matters of design,
props, wardrobe and make-up were concerned.

In fact, *The Baker Street File*, with its almost 1,200 entries, quickly became the
entire company's 'Bible' and thanks to Michael some extracts are included in this
book. He also explained to me how it came about.

'It is very easy when embarking on a project about Sherlock Holmes to assume
that everyone you are talking to knows as much about him as you do,' he says, 'but
we are not all Sherlock Holmes freaks. I thought sympathetically of designers,
make-up artists, costume designers, cameramen, property buyers, set-dressers –
all the people who were going to work on the series – and I thought to myself, "I

THE SPECIAL BARBER SHOP SET CREATED BY THE
DESIGN TEAM IN USE DURING A SCENE FOR *THE SOLITARY CYCLIST*.

can't expect them to know that Holmes kept his tobacco in the toe of a Persian slipper or that he kept his unanswered correspondence nailed to the mantelpiece with a dagger''.

'So I decided what we needed was a reference manual that was not as bulky as the short stories and novels, and which could be referred to quickly and easily. The sort of thing you could look up that would tell you what Holmes would wear if he went out to buy a newspaper – whether it was spats or a top hat or whatever. So, Stuart, Nicky and I divided up the stories and wrote down every fact in them we considered worth recording.'

He allows himself another smile at the memory of laboriously reading those stories, line by line, and of some of the discoveries he and his colleagues made. 'You know the sort of thing: what kind of cigarettes Holmes smoked, what he and Watson wore when they went into the country, even whether they liked cats or dogs!'

However, one of the main problems the trio encountered were the evident discrepancies to be found in Conan Doyle's texts.

'We found you just cannot take every fact in the adventures for gospel,' Michael says, 'because Conan Doyle wrote so fast and so fluently – not to mention over a span of thirty years – and not surprisingly occasionally contradicted himself. As a

AN EARLY PUBLICITY PHOTOGRAPH OF JEREMY BRETT AND DAVID BURKE AS HOLMES AND WATSON.

JEREMY BRETT, DAVID BURKE
AND PRODUCTION BUYER
DAVID ROUND (CENTRE)
RECEIVING INSTRUCTION IN
THE ART OF PIPE SMOKING
BEFORE FILMING
ON THE SERIES BEGINS.

result of this we had to supply some missing links – although there is a clear warning about this at the beginning of *The Baker Street File*.

'But we did *not* use this as an excuse to change the stories in any way,' Michael adds quickly, 'how the crimes were committed, facts about the characters, or even how Holmes reached his conclusions . . .'

Every bit as important to the series as *The Baker Street File* – even to Sherlock Holmes himself – was, of course, Doctor Watson. And here again Michael Cox found his original man in much the same way as he had done Holmes.

'David Burke was an instinctive piece of casting,' he recalls. 'He is an actor that I had worked with two or three times before, and I had always remembered his qualities – although he is not an internationally-known star, as you might describe Jeremy Brett.

'It seemed to me that if we were going to get Watson right – and I believe that he is the ordinary, middle-class man in the street – then one needed an actor who could do that without being boring.

'Now, David tells a wonderful story against himself about some friends who thought he was right for the part of Doctor Watson because he *was* boring – which is terribly insulting and dreadfully unfair because he is a very warm and witty and inventive person!

'It was just those qualities,' Michael continues, 'that made him so right for Watson, the man in the street who is us – you and I – and who is always outclassed by this superhuman figure. He was also able to bring to that ordinariness a degree of charm and intelligence and wit, as well as the flair for getting on with the ladies which Holmes, of course, said was "Your department, Watson". In the final analysis, what one needed was a pretty rounded person – and David fitted the bill perfectly.'

David Burke's completely fresh interpretation of Watson was profoundly to change the entrenched public image of Watson as a rather bumbling, comical figure – a fact we shall investigate later – and it also made his decision to leave the series at the end of the first thirteen episodes to join the Royal Shakespeare Company come as something of a shock to his many admirers. But, as in any form of entertainment business, the show must go on – and Michael Cox was faced with finding a replacement who would be acceptable to the viewing public.

'Of course, when it happened it seemed absolutely disastrous,' he admits. 'But then you think to yourself, "Well, it can't be all that disastrous because there is always someone *else* to play any part." I mean if Jeremy Brett had not agreed to play Holmes I am sure we would have found someone else who would – perhaps just as well. And I'm sure Jeremy would agree with that!

'No, the real difficulty was to find an actor who would not give the audience a huge problem by his totally different appearance. Equally, he had to be a man with a mind of his own who would bring to the series his own qualities just as David Burke had done – but at the same time be a reasonable look-alike for Watson.

'Fortunately, of course, three years have elapsed in the stories from the time of *The Final Problem* when David Burke's Watson is last seen, so the transition to the slightly older man as played by Edward Hardwicke was quite acceptable.

'I think you can argue that Holmes, because he is such a superman, doesn't perhaps change too much with the years, while Watson *does* change and you are allowed to see him age a little. That's why Edward played him as a slightly older man, a little more gravely, and I think it worked most satisfactorily in the light of the time lapse,' Michael adds.

The transition from one actor to another was, indeed, carried out with an ease that was surely the envy of that other television character much given to transmogrifications, the BBC's Doctor Who!

Michael Cox also shares the view of all enthusiasts of the Sherlock Holmes stories that Holmes without Watson is inconceivable. That the success and durability of the adventures is very much due to both men, who are inseparable.

'There are two things we had to bear in mind right from the start,' he says. 'Firstly, we had to get Holmes and Watson right individually, and, secondly, to get the relationship between them just as right. To me their relationship is one of the great friendships in English literature.

'The Holmes-Watson relationship is, in fact, only delicately sketched in the books – Conan Doyle doesn't spend a lot of time describing their lives, apart from their involvement in each particular story. But over the whole stretch you do get a pretty good idea of how these two men shared their lives in the Baker Street apartment, when they got on each other's nerves and so forth.

'And, of course, they are absolutely interdependent on each other. This is an important factor – and it is something that Jeremy Brett latched onto very early on: that without Watson, Holmes would probably have gone mad. With his all-consuming interest in crime he would have driven himself mad if he didn't have this sensible fellow by his side to keep his feet on the ground, to get him to eat, to remind him to dress properly, to wean him off his addiction to cocaine.

'Equally, without Holmes, Watson would have died of boredom. I mean, as a retired Army doctor on a small pension and with a boring practice in somewhere like Paddington he would have made a rather sad figure.

SOME QUICK ATTENTION TO MAKE-UP FOR JEREMY BRETT
WHILE FILMING ON LOCATION.

THE TRACTION ENGINE WHICH STOLE THE SCENE
FROM SHERLOCK HOLMES IN *THE NORWOOD BUILDER*.

'In fact, they are so different that they fit together enormously well – they have great patience with each other – and they make a wonderful pair,' Michael adds.

The question Michael has been most asked since he decided to produce the television series has, perhaps inevitably, been *why* are Holmes and Watson still so popular.

'It is a question that I have also frequently asked *myself*,' he replies after a moment's thought, 'and I don't think I have any better answer than anyone else. It does seem to me, though, that Holmes particularly is the sort of wonderfully strong, reliable, intelligent person that everyone would like to have in their lives.

'We have all probably got glimpses of it in a parent or an uncle or someone like that. The kind of person one could go to if you were in doubt about something, or needed to resolve a moral issue. Holmes, I think, fills that bill, although we would hate to be like him. Surely no one would *want* to be this dark, obsessive, depressive bachelor?'

Michael also does not believe the fascination with Holmes continues just because of nostalgia for the past. 'There is something deep inside people that responds to Holmes,' he continues. 'He has a genuine sense of natural justice, a sense of honour. People wish that he *did* exist. They feel somehow that society would be a safer place if he did.

'Holmes is interested in the preservation of order, of course. He's a kind of

JEREMY BRETT VISITS THE BAKER STREET SET DURING CONSTRUCTION WITH DIRECTOR, PAUL ANNETT.

114

knight errant – a throwback to the Knights of the Round Table.

'Holmes is undoubtedly a difficult person, moody, uncompromising, living erratically and even being a little frightening. Yet he is what we would like our leaders to be, someone whom you trust, will never have feet of clay, is never going to get caught out. Whatever else changed in the world, you feel he would always remain as the fixed point.'

Michael Cox's deep commitment to the original Conan Doyle stories has proved perhaps the finest tribute to Sherlock Holmes in his centenary year – restoring his image to that which his creator intended. Certainly one feels that he and his team have rescued the great sleuth from the mire of clichés, distortion and Hollywood razzmatazz that was threatening to permanently damage his reputation.

MIKE GRIMES, ONE OF THE DESIGNERS OF THE SHERLOCK HOLMES SERIES,
ON THE CASTLEFIELD LOT DURING THE CONSTRUCTION OF THE SET.
AND (OVERLEAF) THE FINISHED PRODUCT WITH THE VIEW
OF SALFORD CAREFULLY SCREENED BY TREES!

The other element of this series which was of such major importance was, of course, the design of the production. That painstaking reconstruction of a world long passed which is absolutely crucial if the stories of Sherlock Holmes are to be believed by a critical audience.

A stroll along the set of Baker Street at Castlefield immediately underlines the achievement of Michael Cox's talented design team, Mike Grimes, and his colleagues, Tim Wilding and Margaret Coombes.

All three of them worked together on the visual style of the series before dividing the considerable task between them. Perhaps the interior of Baker Street owes more to Mike Grimes, while the street itself was executed by Tim Wilding. At the

same time Margaret Coombes was setting up some of the more exotic locations such as Aldershot and India for *The Crooked Man*.

Probably all designers prefer their work to speak for them and the design of Sherlock Holmes speaks volumes for these three people. Nevertheless, Mike Grimes describes some of the problems he and his colleagues had to solve.

'The first thing we had to settle before we could do any research or even begin to think about sets and props, was the exact period in which we were going to set the production,' says Mike.

'Once we had settled on the year 1890, we then had the problem of incorporating something that was imaginary – 221B Baker Street – into a locality that actually existed,' he says. 'And this was not made any easier by the discrepancies in Conan Doyle's stories. We knew he had to be as faithful to the original as possible – that Michael Cox would not let us take too many liberties – so we settled for amalgams of fact and reasonable conjecture.'

All three members of the team brought considerable experience to their task. Mike had previously been the designer on several of Granada's most prestigious productions including *The Collection* starring Laurence Olivier, the major drama *The Good Soldier* and the highly acclaimed, *Philby, Burgess and Maclean*. Earlier he had worked with Ken Russell on *Clouds of Glory*. Tim Wilding's design credits included *A Kind of Loving* and *A Pattern of Life*, while Margaret Coombes had worked on series such as *The Mallens* and *Brideshead Revisited*. Prior to joining her two colleagues, she had worked on Granada's seven-episode series for children, *Young Sherlock*.

The first part of the team's task was a thorough investigation into the London of 1890. This involved the study of street maps, the utilization of contemporary photographs and illustrations, and the use of old street directories and catalogues from stores such as Harrods.

'This gave us the feel of the city at that time,' says Mike. 'Then we had to translate it into specific designs for Baker Street which at that time was evidently a mixture of three-storey houses and shops. The shops we made an amalgam of the kinds of establishments which were in business then – a post office, a furniture shop, a fruit shop, a wine merchant's, a tailor's, a bookshop, a jeweller's, a barber's, an estate agent and even an undertaker.

'As to the street itself, our original plan was that it should appear to go on into infinity. But because of the nature of the buildings outside the Granada lot, and the view of Salford beyond, this proved impossible. It was a big disappointment when we found that out.'

Mike pauses, and a smile creeps across his face. 'We found the answer to our problem by moving up Regent's Park from its normal location to the end of the street!'

Next came the somewhat smaller problem of locating 221B. 'The fact is everyone seems to have their own ideas about where precisely Conan Doyle intended the apartments to be,' Mike says. 'We plumped for the left-hand side looking south just a few doors up from a T-junction with York Street.'

Once it came to drawing the actual houses and shops, however, the team stuck religiously to the architectural principles of the 1890s. The buildings themselves were to be grey-green in the contemporary London Brick style, while the street itself would be tarmacadamed.

'This caused quite a long argument,' Mike recalls. 'Everyone seemed convinced that Baker Street was cobbled – I suppose people have just had this image in their minds for so long of cobbled streets that they assume it must be true. But when we did our research we found that Baker Street in 1890 *was* tarmacadamed.'

The design team were given a rather bleak open space alongside the Victorian Bonded Warehouse which Granada had recently renovated, on which to create Baker Street. In normal circumstances, sets such as this are constructed of scaffolding on which the various sections of scenery are fixed. But because of the height of the three storey buildings – not to mention the unpredictability of the Manchester weather which Mike and the team knew the set would have to withstand for a couple of years, if not longer – they opted to use steel.

'We did our homework and found that not only would a steel frame be tougher but it would also be cheaper,' says Mike. 'In the end we had over 200 sections bolted onto the steel frame to give us the Baker Street facade.

'We also decided to spend the larger part of our budget on what we call street level detail. In other words we wanted the front doors and the shop windows and what was in them to stand up to the closest scrutiny. Once we got up above twelve feet we were into cardboard country!'

One of their big worries were the tall chimney pots which were a feature of Victorian houses at this time. Perched over thirty feet above street level, they looked dangerously vulnerable to high winds. Fortunately, though, these fears proved groundless, and the soundness of the entire structure enabled it to weather a number of heavy storms.

The building of Baker Street was achieved in a remarkable five months. 'We went from the first rough scribbles to a finished set between January to May 1982,' Mike remembers, allowing himself a little smile of satisfaction at the thought.

In the meantime, work was also going on inside the Bonded Warehouse, building Holmes' apartments. This was Mike's particular preserve, and here again he was as faithful as possible to the original concept – while still adding some ingenious touches of his own.

'We not only took a lot of care to make the place look authentic, but also to fill it with genuine props wherever possible. We went all over the place to find the right period furniture and furnishings,' Mike says. 'Some of the people who sold us antiques were so excited at the thought of them being used on television that they asked for the first option to buy them back after we had finished. I suppose anything to do with Sherlock Holmes goes up in value as a result!'

To create the right colour wallpaper for the apartments, Mike used brown wrapping paper rather than wallpaper! He was, though, catholic in his taste when it came to selecting the pictures and drawings to go on the walls.

'The one real liberty we took was the picture that hangs over the fireplace,' he says. 'It's the usual practice to stick a mirror there, but this is actually rather distracting for the actors, and if you are not very careful it will show the film crew and technicians.

'So what I did was introduce a picture of a huge Swiss waterfall which looks forward to the fight at the Reichenbach. I thought this would be a nice touch and also give Holmes something to contemplate when thinking about what *might* have happened there. Jeremy Brett thought it was a great joke!'

Mike also came up with the idea of a barber shop set. 'I thought it would eventually become boring if Holmes and Watson were only *ever* seen discussing cases in their rooms. They might have met in a coffee shop, of course, but I believed a barber's shop offered more potential in terms of mirrors that could be used for interesting and unusual camera shots.'

Mike took a lot of care with Holmes' chemistry corner, and here as everywhere else on the set the props were deliberately made to look worn and used.

'We wanted to play everything down, to give it the feel of the period,' Mike adds. 'We even had newspapers printed up from the 1890s though they were mostly never seen in anything other than long-shot.'

Just how successful Mike, Tim and Margaret had been in creating a totally authentic Baker Street was dramatically demonstrated on the very first day of filming. Mike still grins at the memory.

'They were working in the studio when suddenly all the fire alarms went off. Apparently the heat from the lights had triggered off the heat sensors. These alarms are also linked to the local fire station – and before we could get a message to the brigade that it was a false alarm, a couple of engines screeched up outside the Granada complex.

'Now it's not the easiest place in the world to get into, and the only way they could finally gain access was directly onto the Baker Street lot. I shall never forget the look of total bewilderment on those firemen's faces. They just couldn't *believe* what they were seeing!'

Those Manchester firemen might have been even more surprised if they had turned up to find some of the authentic working Victorian transport vehicles which were hired for use in the series. Apart from the inevitable horse-drawn cabs, the team also brought in carriages, milk-carts and even a splendid traction engine which quite stole one scene from Sherlock Holmes!

Interestingly, Mike told me that nearly all the 'coachmen' seen in the series were girls! 'The reason for this is that they come with the vehicles when we hire them and they are the only ones who can handle the horses. We have to disguise them, of course, and stick on moustaches, but no-one seems to have complained. The only time we had to drop one of the girls was when she tried to play a hussar!'

Mike encountered several problems when searching for suitable places for location shooting. 'The trouble all stemmed once again from the inconsistencies in Conan Doyle's stories and the fact that he sometimes invented things that were quite impossible to duplicate. Let me give you the two best examples.

'In *The Musgrave Ritual*, for instance, he uses the shadow cast by a tree as a clue to the mystery. Now we looked everywhere to find a suitable house which had such a tree in its grounds, but without any luck whatsoever. So in the end, I decided to put a weathercock shaped like a tree on the roof which cast the shadow.

'And *The Speckled Band* was even more impossible. I mean the business with the snake is nonsense. A snake just will not go up and down a rope. And whoever heard of there being a ventilator between two *inside* rooms? I sometimes think Sherlock Holmes is the worst detective in the world!' he smiles ruefully.

Whatever problems Mike Grimes and his team encountered, they nonetheless overcame them to give the whole series the authentic atmosphere and look which are such a distinctive feature of the production. The Baker Street set alone is a construction to delight and impress any visitor, while in the apartments only the tell-tale evidence of the camera prevents the same visitor from believing he has stepped back one hundred years in time.

When filming of the second series, *The Return of Sherlock Holmes*, began in the autumn of 1985, pressure of other duties made Michael Cox decide to hand over the reins of producer to June Wyndham Davies, while he retained the position of executive producer.

June, a charming and purposeful lady, has also been a life-long fan of the adventures of the great detective, having read the Conan Doyle books when she was young and subsequently having seen many of the movie versions.

While filming *The Second Stain* in Manchester and on location at Baddesley Clinton in December 1985, she told me that some years earlier she had been so impressed by the story of *The Hound of the Baskervilles* that she had written a musical version of the adventure which she hoped to see performed one day. (She did, in fact, later produce the *Hound* for the Granada series.)

JUNE WYNDHAM DAVIES,
PRODUCER OF
*THE RETURN OF
SHERLOCK
HOLMES*
WITH
JEREMY BRETT
AND
EDWARD HARDWICKE.

June is, in fact, an experienced series-maker, having come to Sherlock Holmes after being producer on another of Granada's Victorian drama serials, *Cribb* about the adventures of a crime fighter named Sergeant Cribb, played by Alan Dobie.

'It was a great challenge to be asked to take over the series when it was already established and enormously popular, and give it added impetus,' she says. 'I think the pairing of Jeremy Brett and Edward Hardwicke is superb, and they have continued to evolve the characters in every story.

'I am also full of admiration for Jeremy Brett – he is such a caring actor and gives tremendous encouragement to all those around him. Sherlock Holmes has never had a better interpreter in my opinion!'

Today, looking back on the Castlefield Triumph, Michael Cox believes it owes much to being a team effort.

'Everyone from the scriptwriters, actors and directors, to the production team, the designers, costumers and make-up people, not forgetting the cameramen, technicians and grips – even the secretaries – all have made their contribution,' he says. 'But if anyone deserves special praise, it has to be Jeremy Brett for being like a father figure to the whole company. He created a real family feeling in which everyone wanted to do well. The success is very much theirs.'

And to which one might just add the comment of Holmes himself, 'A singular set of people, Watson!'

HOLMES THE BOOK-LOVER – JEREMY BRETT AND DAVID BURKE
IN A SCENE FROM *THE RED-HEADED LEAGUE*.

THE BAKER STREET ❦FILE❦

A Selection of 200 Entries from the Guide to the Appearance and Habits of Sherlock Holmes and Doctor Watson

COMPILED BY MICHAEL COX, STUART DOUGHTY AND NICKY COONEY

KEY TO THE FILE

After each entry a 4-letter reference identifies which story the item comes from. The abbreviations used are:

ABBE *The Abbey Grange*
BERY *The Beryl Coronet*
BLAC *Black Peter*
BLAN *The Blanched Soldier*
BLUE *The Blue Carbuncle*
BOSC *The Boscombe Valley Mystery*
BRUC *The Bruce-Partington Plans*
CARD *The Cardboard Box*
CHAS *Charles Augustus Milverton*
COPP *The Copper Beeches*
CREE *The Creeping Man*
CROO *The Crooked Man*
DANC *The Dancing Men*
DEVI *The Devil's Foot*
DYIN *The Dying Detective*
EMPT *The Empty House*
ENGR *The Engineer's Thumb*
FINA *The Final Problem*
FIVE *The Five Orange Pips*
GLOR *The Gloria Scott*
GOLD *The Golden Pince-Nez*

GREE *The Greek Interpreter*
HOUN *The Hound of the Baskervilles*
IDEN *A Case of Identity*
ILLU *The Illustrious Client*
LADY *The Disappearance of Lady Frances Carfax*
LAST *His Last Bow*
LION *The Lion's Mane*
MAZA *The Mazarin Stone*
MISS *The Missing Three-Quarter*
MUSG *The Musgrave Ritual*
NAVA *The Naval Treaty*
NOBL *The Noble Bachelor*
NORW *The Norwood Builder*
PREF Preface to *His Last Bow*
PRIO *The Priory School*

REDC *The Red Circle*
REDH *The Red-Headed League*
REIG *The Reigate Squires*
RESI *The Resident Patient*
RETI *The Retired Colourman*
SCAN *A Scandal in Bohemia*
SECO *The Second Stain*
SHOS *Shoscombe Old Place*
SIGN *The Sign of Four*
SILV *Silver Blaze*
SIXN *The Six Napoleons*
SOLI *The Solitary Cyclist*
SPEC *The Speckled Band*
STOC *The Stockbroker's Clerk*
STUD *A Study in Scarlet*
SUSS *The Sussex Vampire*
THOR *The Problem of Thor Bridge*
3GAB *The Three Gables*
3GAR *The Three Garridebs*
3STU *The Three Students*
TWIS *The Man with the Twisted Lip*
VALL *The Valley of Fear*
VEIL *The Veiled Lodger*
WIST *Wisteria Lodge*
YELL *The Yellow Face*

I SHERLOCK HOLMES

Clothes and Dress

1 In the morning (about 8.30am) Holmes lounged about in his purple dressing gown reading the agony column of *The Times* (ENGR)

2 Had amazing power in disguises (SCAN)

3 Wore a tweed suit (SCAN)

4 Has long grey travelling cloak and close-fitting cloth cap (BOSC)

5 This is of enormous importance, said Holmes making a note on his shirt cuff (NAVA)

6 He affected a certain quiet primness of dress (MUSC)

7 The wax bust had 'an old dressing gown of Holmes' draped over it' (EMPT)

Eating and Drinking

8 Watson, you have never yet recognised my merits as a housekeeper (SIGN)

9 Had toast and coffee for breakfast (SCAN)

10 Drinks whisky and soda (REDH)

11 Breakfast at 9.30am (BLAC)

12 Holmes dined at 7pm (BLUE)

13 His diet was usually of the sparest (YELL)

14 Sometimes ate out: 'We can stop at Marcini's for a little dinner on the way' (HOUN)

Smoking

15 Blew great cloud of cigarette smoke when triumphant (SCAN)

16 Has pipe rack. Has oily, old black clay pipe (IDEN)

17 Had an old brier pipe and smoked shag. Could smoke a whole ounce in the course of one night (TWIS)

18 His long cherrywood pipe replaced his clay when he was in disputatious rather than meditative mood (COPP)

19 Smoked cigars, which were kept in a box. He blew smoke rings

20 His before-breakfast pipe consisted of all the plugs and dottles left from his smokes of the day before, all carefully dried and collected in the corner of the mantelpiece (ENGR)

21 Smoking – 'kills the appetite' (GOLD)

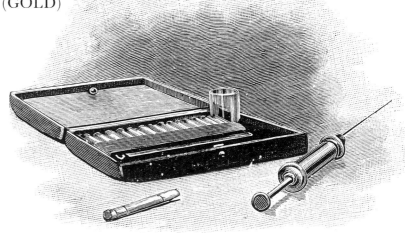

Drugs

22 Used cocaine regularly: alternated between the drowsiness of the drug and the fierce energy of his own nature (SCAN)

23 Injects himself with cocaine – and has 'other little weaknesses'. Does not smoke opium (TWIS)

24 He injected into his left arm (Holmes was right-handed therefore) (SIGN)

25 He injected himself three times a day for many months. Sometimes he took morphine, usually a seven per cent solution of cocaine (SIGN)

Chemistry/Music/Special Skills

26 Has thoughts of writing a monograph of the typewriter and its relation to crime (IDEN)

27 His hobby to have an exact knowledge of London (REDH)

28 An enthusiastic musician: a very capable performer, and a composer of no ordinary merit (REDH)

29 He busied himself all the evening in an abstruse chemical analysis which involved much heating of retorts and distilling of vapours (SIGN)

30 You would have made an actor and a rare one (SIGN)

31 He spoke on a quick succession of subjects – on miracle plays, on medieval pottery, on Stradivarius violins, on the Buddhism of Ceylon, and on the warships of the future (SIGN)

32 Catalepsy is a very easy complaint to imitate. I have done it myself (RESI)

33 Few men were capable of greater muscular effort. He was one of the finest boxers of his weight (YELL)

34 Burglary has always been an alternative profession, had I cared to adopt it, and I have little doubt that I should have come to the front (RETI)

35 I'm a bit of a single-stick expert . . . (ILLU)

Limits of Knowledge

36 There is no branch of detective science which is so important and so neglected as the art of tracing footsteps. Happily, I have laid great stress upon it and much practice has made it second nature to me (STUD)

37 Knowledge of graphology (STUD)

38 I am fairly familiar with all forms of secret writing, and am myself the author of a trifling monograph upon the subject in which I analyse 160 separate ciphers (DANC)

39 I propose to devote my declining years to the composition of a textbook, which shall focus the whole art of detection into one volume (ABBE)

40 It would be difficult to name any articles which afford a finer field for inference than a pair of glasses (GOLD)

41 Sherlock Holmes was pursuing some laborious researches into early English charters (3STU)

42 I have some knowledge of baritsu, or the Japanese system of wrestling, which has more than once been very useful to me (EMPT)

43 Football does not come within my horizon (MISS)

44 I knew the opening of safes was a particular hobby with him (CHAS)

45 I am familiar with 42 different impressions left by tyres (PRIO)

46 There can be no question, my dear Watson, of the value of exercise before breakfast (BLAC)

Books/Newspapers/Reading

47 His cases were reported in the press (SCAN)

48 System of docketing all press cuttings about people, places and things (SCAN)
49 Quotes Flaubert, Hafiz, Latin, Horace (REDH)
50 He reads nothing (in the papers) except the agony column and the criminal news (NOBL)
51 Would lounge on the sofa, a pile of crumpled newspapers beside him on the floor (BLUE)

EDGAR ALLAN POE –
THE 'FATHER OF THE
DETECTIVE STORY'
– WHOSE TALES
OF CRIME
HOLMES ENJOYED.

52 Read Edgar Allan Poe (RESI)
53 My Biblical knowledge is a trifle rusty (CROO)
54 Holmes' magazine article, *The Book of Life* – what an observant man might learn by his accurate and systematic examination of all that came in his way (STUD)

Personal Possessions
55 Had a notebook: he scribbled receipts on page of this and made notes in it (SCAN)
56 Holmes had and used a pair of forceps (BLUE)
57 Had a long, thin cane (SPEC)
58 Holmes scribbled a few words upon the back of one of his visiting-cards (CARD)
59 He whipped out his lens and a tape-measure and hurried about the room on his knees (SIGN)

126

60 He took out his revolver . . . and having loaded two of the chambers, he put it back into the right-hand pocket of his jacket (SIGN)
61 Holmes' handcuffs of steel, taken from a drawer (STUD)
62 He had himself picked up the loaded hunting crop, which was his favourite weapon (SIXN)
63 I'll blow this police whistle (ABBE)
64 Here, too, is my dark lantern (CHAS)

Women/Emotions
65 Irene Adler was referred to as 'the' woman – she eclipsed and predominated the whole female sex – although he felt nothing akin to love for her (SCAN)
66 All emotions – and love in particular – were abhorrent to his cold, precise mind (SCAN)
67 He had been beaten four times: three times by a man, once by a woman (FIVE)
68 He had a remarkable gentleness and courtesy in his dealings with women. He disliked and distrusted their sex, but he was always a chivalrous opponent (DYIN)
69 The motives of women are so inscrutable their most trivial action may mean volumes

Attitude to his Cases
70 Cleared up cases abandoned as hopeless by the police (SCAN)
71 Worked for the love of his art rather than for gain (SPEC)
72 Does not mind committing a felony (BLUE)
73 Days of the great cases are past. Man, or at least criminal man, has lost all enterprise and originality (COPP)
74 He is the only 'unofficial consulting detective in the world' (SIGN)
75 Despises the police force (SIGN)
76 Out of my last 53 cases, my name appeared in only 4, and the police have had all the credit in 49 (NAVA)
77 There's the scarlet thread of murder running through the colourless skein of life, and our duty is to unravel it, and isolate it, and expose every inch of it (STUD)
78 Sherlock Holmes was a past master in the art of putting a humble witness at his ease (MISS)
79 Lestrade: We're not jealous of you at Scotland Yard . . . there's not a man, from the oldest inspector to the youngest constable, who wouldn't be glad to shake you by the hand (SIXN)
80 Holmes' contempt of blackmailers: 'The worst men in London'. I had seldom heard my friend speak with such intensity of feeling (CHAS)

Attitude to Watson
81 He has no friends – with the exception of Watson. He does not encourage visitors (FIVE)
82 Refers to Watson on several occasions as 'my boy' (NAVA)
83 'You're not hurt, Watson? For God's sake, say that you are not hurt!' (3GAR)
84 I felt Holmes' hand steal into mine and give me a reassuring shake, as if to say that the situation was within his powers and that he was easy in his mind (CHAS)
85 To Watson: 'I need your company and your assistance' (PRIO)

Philosophy

86 'Always a joy' for Holmes to meet an American. Great believer in Anglo-American friendship. Talked about the unification of the two countries (NOBL)

87 Crime is common. Logic is rare (COPP)

88 The great unobservant public . . . (COPP)

89 To a great mind, nothing is little (STUD)

90 Work is the best antidote to sorrow, my dear Watson (EMPT)

91 I am very anxious that I should use the knowledge which I possess in order to ensure that justice be done (DAN)

92 I have learnt caution now, and I had rather play tricks with the laws of England than with my own conscience (ABBE)

Character and Nature

93 Had immense faculties and powers of observation (SCAN)

94 Had a Bohemian soul – but did not miss company (SCAN)

95 He was the most perfect reasoning and observing machine that the world has seen (SCAN)

96 Had a dual nature: swung from extreme langour to devouring energy (REDH)

97 Very persuasive manner (TWIS)

98 Egotism was a strong factor in his singular character (COPP)

99 Thinks Watson's retelling of his cases is too romantic and fanciful (SIGN)

100 A brain without a heart, as deficient in human sympathy as he was pre-eminent in intelligence (GREE)

101 There are in me the makings of a very fine loafer, and also of a pretty spry sort of a fellow (SIGN)

102 Sensitive to flattery on the score of his art as any girl could be of her beauty (STUD)

103 I am not a fanciful man (EMPT)

104 We were all marshalled by Sherlock Holmes (NORW)

105 Holmes stood before us with the air of a conjuror who is performing a trick (NORW)

106 Without his scrapbooks, his chemicals and his homely untidiness, he was an uncomfortable man (3STU)

107 You would not call me a marrying man, Watson? (CHAS)

108 My simple wants: a loaf of bread and a clean collar (HOUN)

Mannerisms

109 Pacing room: head sunk upon chest, hands clasped behind him (SCAN)

110 Rubbed his long, nervous hands together (SCAN)

111 Laughed – sometimes heartily and for some time; sometimes till limp and helpless (SCAN)

112 Curls up in chair with his knees drawn up to his hawk-like nose. His eyes closed and with his black clay pipe thrusting out like some strange bird (while pondering a problem) (REDH)

113 Has a keen, questioning glance (BOSC)

114 Like a dog picking up the scent (BOSC)

115 He sat with the weary, heavy-lidded expression which concealed his keen and eager nature (ENGR)

116 Leaned his chin upon his hands and stared into the fire (SPEC)

HOLMES HOT IN PURSUIT OF CRIME – A MOMENT FROM *THE SPECKLED BAND*.

AN UNUSUAL ANGLE ON JEREMY BRETT UTILISING A MIRROR IN *THE GREEK INTERPRETER.*

A FOG BLOWS DOWN BAKER STREET DURING THE MAKING OF *THE COPPER BEECHES.*

A LIGHT-HEARTED MOMENT AS HOLMES AND WATSON PEER OUT FROM THE FACADE OF BAKER STREET.

THE SHIP THAT SAILED INTO
BAKER STREET! – A REVEALING
PHOTOGRAPH FROM THE MAKING OF
A SCANDAL IN BOHEMIA.

ANOTHER REVEALING SHOT FROM *THE SPECKLED BAND*,
AND A SIMILAR SCENE FROM THE OTHER SIDE.

SHERLOCK HOLMES THE MASTER OF DISGUISE.
IT TOOK TWO HOURS FOR THIS
MAKE-UP FOR A SCENE IN
THE FINAL PROBLEM TO BE APPLIED!

ALTHOUGH IN
DISGUISE ONCE
AGAIN FOR *A
SCANDAL IN
BOHEMIA*,
HOLMES DID
NOT FOOL
THESE YOUNG
FANS.

THE
MULTI-
TALENTED
SHERLOCK
HOLMES.

MASTER
OF CHEMICAL
ANALYSIS IN
*THE SOLITARY
CYCLIST*.

SKILLED
BOXER,
ALSO IN
*THE
SOLITARY
CYCLIST*.

ACCOMPLISHED
MUSICIAN IN
*THE RESIDENT
PATIENT*.

HOLMES AND MORIARTY STRUGGLE ON
THE BRINK OF THE REICHENBACH FALLS.

JEREMY BRETT BEING MADE UP
FOR THE FIGHT SEQUENCE IN
THE FINAL PROBLEM.

117 Are you going to bed, Holmes? No, I am not tired. I never remember feeling tired through work. Though idleness exhausts me completely. (After a whole night chasing about London) (SIGN)

118 Holmes cocked his eye at me . . . like a connoisseur who had just taken his first sip of a comet vintage (SILV)

119 It is quite exciting, said Sherlock Holmes, with a yawn (STUD)

120 Again in the utter silence I heard that thin, sibilant note which spoke of intense, suppressed excitement (EMPT)

121 Moran calls Holmes, 'You clever, clever fiend!' and 'You cunning, cunning fiend!' (EMPT)

122 Sometimes he was making progress and whistled and sang at his work . . . (DANC)

123 Holmes gave an enigmatic smile (3STU)

124 I watched Holmes unrolling his case of instruments and choosing his tool with the calm and scientific accuracy of a surgeon (CHAS)

125 Never have I seen a man run as Holmes ran that night. I am reckoned fleet of foot, but he outpaced me . . . (HOUN)

Miscellaneous

126 Prefers German music to Italian or French: it is more introspective (REDH)

127 Mr Sherlock Holmes, I began; but the words had a magical effect (SIGN)

128 My ancestors were country squires . . . my grandmother was the sister of Vernet, the French painter (GREE)

129 Holmes was at college for 2 years (GLOR)

130 It was the same month that Holmes refused a knighthood for services which may perhaps some day be described (3GAR)

HORACE VERNET,
THE FRENCH PAINTER,
WHO WAS HOLMES' UNCLE.

II DOCTOR WATSON

Clothes and Dress
131 Characterized by a military neatness, proud of his appearance (BOSC)
132 Wears slippers of patent leather (STOC)
133 When returning from consultation: kept his stethoscope in his top hat. Had black mark of silver nitrate on his right fore-finger (SCAN)
134 Wore an ulster overcoat (SCAN)
135 Wears a hat in London (and everywhere presumably) (SIGN)

Eating and Drinking
136 Had toast and coffee for breakfast (SCAN)
137 Sometimes takes snuff (IDEN)
138 Has been known to drink Beaune with lunch (SIGN)
139 Drank beer (in a pub) (BLUE)

Smoking
140 You still smoke the Arcadia mixture of your bachelor days, then! (STUD)
141 Smokes cigars (BOSC)
142 Watson's cigarettes from Bradley's, Oxford Street (HOUN)

Books and Newspapers
143 Watson's scrapbook contained clippings from various newspapers – *Daily Telegraph*, *The Standard*, *The Daily News* (STUD)
144 Reads *The British Medical Journal* (STOC)
145 Tries on one occasion to read a yellow-back novel but finds it too thin and trashy for his taste – finally flings it away (BOSC)
146 'Worked back' to Richter (the German philosopher) through Carlyle (SIGN)

Personal Possessions
147 My old service revolver (Adams .450 standard issue for Army of the period) (STUD)
148 Has an old (gold?) watch inherited from his father (SIGN)
149 Has a desk in the sitting room (SIGN)
150 Has no key to 221B (has to be let in by Mrs Hudson) (BLUE)
151 The diary which I kept at the time (HOUN)

Women and Emotions
152 With your natural advantages, Watson, every lady is your helper and accomplice (RETI)
153 Notices attractive women (SIGN)
154 Now, Watson, the fair sex is your department (SECO)
155 I gave my arm to the frightened girl (SOLI)

Medical Practice
156 Did his MD at London University in 1878, then went to Netley Military Training Hospital near Southampton (STUD)
157 Comparison of human skulls 'which is my special study' (HOUN)
158 A glance at his wound told me that it had not penetrated the bone (SOLI)

159 My term of service in India had trained me to stand heat better than cold, and a thermometer of 90 degrees was no hardship (RESI)
160 He sat nursing his wounded leg. The wound did not prevent him from walking but it ached with changeable weather (SIGN)

Attitude to Holmes and Cases
161 My respect for his powers of analysis increased wondrously (STUD)
162 I have all the facts in my journal, and the public shall know them (STUD)
163 Accustomed to Holmes' success, he never dreamed of him failing (SCAN)
164 Hated Holmes taking drugs: his conscience troubled him . . . (SIGN)
165 Sometimes actively investigates cases on his own (TWIS)
166 Would not miss an interesting case for anything (SPEC)
167 Sometimes introduced cases to Holmes. He recommended people to go to Holmes rather than the police (ENGR)
168 I managed to satisfy his curiosity without telling him too much – I have not lived for years with Sherlock Holmes for nothing (HOUN)

ONE OF THE 'YELLOW-BACK' NOVELS THAT DOCTOR WATSON READ.

131

169 I have notes of many hundreds of cases to which I have never alluded (SECO)

Character and Nature
170 I object to rows because my nerves are shaken. I get up at all sorts of ungodly hours and I am extremely lazy (STUD)
171 He had a grand gift of silence – which made him invaluable as a companion (TWIS)
172 A prompt and ready traveller – after his experiences in Afghanistan. Travels light. Has few wants (BOSC)
173 My dear Watson, you were born to be a man of action. Your instinct is always to do something energetic (HOUN)
174 Holmes: 'I trust your judgement' (ABBE)
175 Watson on Holmes: 'I found myself seated beside him in the hansom, my revolver in my pocket, and the thrill of adventure in my heart.' (EMPT)

Mannerisms
176 Holmes and I burst simultaneously into an uncontrollable fit of laughter (SIGN)
177 I read the account aloud to him while he finished his breakfast (SECO)
178 I must have fainted for the first and last time in my life (EMPT)
179 I struck him on the head with the butt of my revolver (EMPT)

Miscellaneous
180 Believes war a preposterous way of settling a dispute (RESI)
181 Both Holmes and I had a weakness for the Turkish bath (ILLU)
182 He had neither kith or kin in England (STUD)
183 'By the way, Watson, you know something of racing?' – 'I ought to. I pay for it with about half my wound pension!' (SHOS)

III BAKER STREET

The Street
184 It was a blazing hot day in August. Baker Street was like an oven, and the glare of the sunlight upon the yellow brickwork of the house across the road was painful to the eye (CARD)
185 The solitary plane tree which graces the yard behind our house (THOR)
186 When it snowed the traffic of Baker Street ploughed the snow into a 'brown, crumbly band.' The grey pavements were scraped clean, however (BERY)
187 Yellow fog swirls down the street and drifts across the dun-coloured houses (SIGN)
188 The droning of the wind . . . the long grind of a wheel as it rasped against the curb (GOLD)

Inside 221B
189 We heard a loud knock, a deep voice below, and heavy steps ascending the stair (STUD)
190 There is a long row of yearbooks which fill a shelf and there are the dispatch cases filled with documents, a perfect quarry for the student (VEIL)

191 A bath at Baker Street freshened me up considerably (SIGN)
192 A spirit case and gasogene in the corner (SCAN)
193 There is a bell in the sitting room – to summon 'the maid' (!) (FIVE)
194 Holmes had a strong box (BLUE)
195 Somewhere in 221B was a bow-window (!) (BERY)
196 A joint of beef and a loaf were kept on the sideboard (Permanently?) (BERY)
197 The gas was lit and shone on the white cloth and glimmer of china and metal (COPP)
198 Watson's bedroom was on the floor above the sitting room (COPP)
199 Holmes' bedroom . . . pictures of celebrated criminals adorned every wall (DYIN)
200 Massive manuscript volumes which contain our work (GOLD)

A VIEW OF GRANADA'S BAKER STREET
LOOKING TOWARDS REGENT'S PARK.

THE
❦STATELY❦
HOLMES

A feature of all Granada's Holmesian adventures has been the use of period buildings to evoke the atmosphere of Victorian England. The combination of civic buildings, mansion houses and even ordinary suburban dwellings have provided an authentic background to the stories and reflect credit on the care with which the design team have picked the locations.

Two branch line railways have also been featured, the charming Keighley & Worth Valley Railway in Yorkshire which was specially used for the pursuit of Holmes by Moriarty in *The Final Problem*, and the famous Bluebell Railway in Uckfield, East Sussex, on which the great detective travelled in *The Greek Interpreter*.

For those who might care to seek out the 'Stately Holmes of England', here is a list of the various properties and the stories in which they were used. In addition there has also been some footage shot in the cities of London, Manchester and Liverpool and in the Welsh countryside.

HOLMES AND WATSON WITH
HELEN STONER (ROSALYN LANDOR)
IN FRONT OF ADLINGTON HALL IN
CHESHIRE DURING FILMING OF
THE SPECKLED BAND.

THE ADVENTURES OF SHERLOCK HOLMES

The Naval Treaty: Heaton Hall, Heaton Park, near Manchester; Lyme Park, South Manchester; and Pott Hall, Pott Shrigley, Macclesfield, Cheshire.

The Dancing Men: Leighton Hall, near Carnforth; Tatton Hall, Cheshire.

The Crooked Man: The Manor House, North Rode, near Macclesfield; Great Moreton, near Congleton.

The Copper Beeches: Private House near Carnforth, North Lancashire.

The Norwood Builder: Beech Mount, Bowden Road, Altrincham, Cheshire.

The Greek Interpreter: Arley Hall, South Manchester; Tatton Park, Cheshire; Capesthorne Hall, Macclesfield, Cheshire.

The Resident Patient: Leck Hall, Over Leck, near Kirby Lonsdale, Cumbria.

The Speckled Band: Adlington Hall, near Prestbury, Cheshire; Tatton Park, Arley Hall.

The Solitary Cyclist: Willington Hall, near Tarporley; Adlington Hall, Overdale, near Delamere.

A Scandal in Bohemia: South Road, Grassendale, Liverpool; 5, North Road, Grassendale; Tatton Park.

The Final Problem: Chethams College, Manchester; Tatton Hall.

The Red Headed League: Chethams College.

The Blue Carbuncle: Croxteth Hall, Croxteth, Liverpool.

THE RETURN OF SHERLOCK HOLMES

The Abbey Grange: Dunham Massey, Altrincham; Tabley House, Knutsford, Cheshire; Adlington Hall.

The Musgrave Ritual: Baddesley Clinton, Lapworth, near Warwick.

The Second Stain: Capesthorne Hall.

The Empty House: Tatton Hall.

The Man with the Twisted Lip: Uphall, Hillington, near King's Lynn.

The Priory School: Lyme Hall; Haddon Hall, Bakewell, Derbyshire; Chatsworth, Derbyshire, home of the Duke and Duchess of Devonshire.

The Six Napoleons: no specific locations.

The Devil's Foot: Caerleon Cottage, the Lizard and surrounding area of Cornwall.

Silver Blaze: Peover Hall; Knowlmere Manor, near Clitheroe; Bangor racecourse.

Wisteria Lodge: Nether Alderley Rectory; Grimsditch Hall, Warrington.

The Bruce-Partington Plans: Crosby Hall, Liverpool.

THE SIGN OF FOUR

Allerton Park, near Knaresborough; Tower of London and London Docks; Tabley Hall; Walker Art Gallery, Liverpool; Malta.

THE HOUND OF THE BASKERVILLES

Heath House, near Cheadle, Staffordshire; Mobberley Old Hall; Croxteth Hall, Liverpool; Castern Hall, near Ashbourne.

THE CASEBOOK OF SHERLOCK HOLMES
The Disappearance of Lady Frances Carfax: Underscar Hotel, near Keswick; Port of Liverpool Building; Hoghton Towers, near Preston.

The Problem of Thor Bridge: Capesthorne Hall; St George's Hall, Liverpool; Abbey Gateway, Chester.

The Boscombe Valley Mystery: Arley Hall; Mobberley Old Hall; Gawsworth Hall; Bromley Cross Quarry; Peckforten Castle, near Taporley.

The Illustrious Client: Lotherton Hall, Abberford, near Leeds; Croxteth Hall, Liverpool.

Shoscombe Old Place: Tatton Hall; Dunham Massey, near Knutsford; Peover Hall.

The Creeping Man: Hatton Grange, near Telford.

THE MASTER BLACKMAILER
Flintham Hall, near Newark; Chatsworth, Derbyshire; Lyme Hall, Cheshire; Tatton Park, Cheshire; Adlington Hall, Cheshire; Dunham Hall, Dunham Massey, Cheshire; Winstanley Hall, Wigan; Tabley House, Knutsford, Cheshire; The Queens Park Art Gallery, Manchester; St Bede's College, Manchester.

THE LAST VAMPYRE
Adlington Hall, Cheshire; Mobberley Old Hall, Knutsford, Cheshire; Delamere Forest, Cheshire; Bramall Hall, near Stockport; Pitchford Hall, Pitchford, Shrewsbury; Guys Cliffe, Warwickshire; Stanton Village, Gloucestershire.

THE ELIGIBLE BACHELOR
Croxteth Hall and Country Park, Liverpool; Bolton Town Hall; The Hulme Hippodrome; Eastnor Castle, near Ledbury, Hertfordshire; The Town Hall, Manchester; The Albert Hall, Deansgate; Harewood House, Leeds; Lyme Park, Stockport; Tatton Park, Knutsford; Capesthorn Hall, near Macclesfield.

THE MEMOIRS OF SHERLOCK HOLMES
The Three Gables: Heaton Hall, Heaton Park, Manchester; Tatton Hall, Tatton Park; Lyme Hall, Lyme Park, Disley, Cheshire; Grimsditch Hall, Whitley, near Warrington.

The Dying Detective: Dorfold Hall, Nantwich, Cheshire; Adlington Hall, Cheshire; Dunham Massey Hall, Altrincham.

The Golden Pince-Nez: Spectrum Arena, Birchwood, Warrington; Albert Hall, Peter Street, Manchester; Manchester Town Hall; Lymm Hall, Rectory Lane, Lymm, Cheshire; Nether Alderley Church, Alderley Edge, Cheshire; Adlington Hall, Cheshire.

The Red Circle: Moravian Settlement, Droylesden, Manchester; Knowsley Hall, Knowsley Park, Merseyside; HMS *Plymouth*, Birkenhead; Buxton Opera House; Croxteth Hall, Liverpool.

The Mazarin Stone: locations unconfirmed at time of going to press.

The Cardboard Box: Tatton Park, Cheshire; Manchester Town Hall; Stanley Docks, Liverpool; Sefton Park, Liverpool; Bowden, Cheshire.

A CASE
❧OF❧
IDENTITY

The
Coincidental Story of
Two Bretts

There is probably no more curious case of coincidence in all the annals of Sherlock Holmes than the facts concerning the two Bretts. (As Doctor Watson might have put it.) For history has repeated itself in a very extraordinary way sixty-five years apart.

Back in 1921, a series of silent films made in Britain by Stoll Picture Productions were released as *The Adventures of Sherlock Holmes*. Sir Arthur Conan Doyle, who saw several of these movies, was so impressed as to proclaim that 'if William Gillette was Sherlock Holmes to theatre audiences, then this new man *is* Holmes to cinemagoers'.

In 1984, of course, Granada began to show their series also called *The Adventures of Sherlock Holmes* and the leading man was at once hailed as '*the* Sherlock Holmes of television'.

The extraordinary thing is that both men were named Brett – though both had actually changed their names! What price such odds, Watson!

The series of silent pictures made in the early Twenties were, in fact, the first serious British attempt to bring Holmes to the screen. And so successful did the initial series of 15 films prove with audiences, that the star who appeared under the rather curious name Eille Norwood, went on to make a total of 47 pictures in the role. Only the sad fact that the greater majority of these films have since

JEREMY BRETT, WHO PLAYED A NUMBER OF
HANDSOME, SARDONIC MEN OF THE WORLD
DURING HIS EARLIER SCREEN CAREER, MAKES A
CHARMING HOLMES IN THIS SCENE WITH
ALISON SKILBECK IN *THE NAVAL TREATY*.

perished and just a handful remain preserved at the British Film Institute in London, prevents Norwood from enjoying greater acclaim as the first faithful portrayer of the great detective on the screen.

Norwood was born Anthony Edward Brett in York in 1861, the son of a lawyer, who understandably wanted him to go into the legal profession. As it was, though, the boy hankered after the stage right from his college days at Cambridge, and it was some years before the father agreed to his demands. As a sop to his parent, the young Brett picked a stage name for himself: Eille (after an old girl-friend) and Norwood (after the current family address).

Norwood is also, of course, the setting of one of Holmes' adventures, and it seems somehow highly appropriate that the former Anthony Brett's most memorable contribution to the cinema should be playing the famous sleuth. Before making films, however, Eille spent many years learning his stagecraft and appeared in a variety of classical and popular dramas not only in Britain but in Europe and even Australia. During these years he demonstrated a particular talent for make-up which he applied himself – once so successfully as to fool his disapproving father sitting in the audience and convinced by the interval that his son had not yet appeared – only to be told he had been on for *half* the act! He also performed as a classical violinist! Both were qualities that would serve him well when he came to play Holmes . . .

It was in 1911 that Eille Norwood graduated into films, and curiously, one of his earliest roles was in a version of Sir Arthur Conan Doyle's *Brigadier Gerard* made in 1915. In 1920 he joined the Stoll Picture Company, and made such a success in a historical adventure called *The Tavern Knight* that the following year the director, Maurice Elvey, decided to offer him the lead in his projected series of Sherlock Holmes films. Elvey has left us this account of how he cast Norwood:

'At the studio I suggested that Mr Norwood should try to make himself as much like the Great Detective in appearance as possible for the purpose of a rough test. Though the suggestion was thus sprung on him, and no special facilities were available, Mr Norwood went off to his dressing room, and within the space of a very few minutes came back to my room and astonished me. He had done very little in the way of make-up, and he had no accessories, but the transformation was remarkable – it *was* Sherlock Holmes who came in at the door!'

Before filming actually began, Norwood read all the Sherlock Holmes stories that had been published up to that time – and at once vowed to make the character as close to the original as possible. He used the Sidney Paget illustrations as his make-up guide, and was always ready to argue over changes in the script that he felt were unjustified.

He actually refused to play one scene which was described by the words, 'enter Sherlock Holmes in a white beard' protesting that Holmes would never do that. And when he and Maurice Elvey were unable to agree on another interpretation of the role, Norwood said, 'Let's film it your way first, and then mine.' So several shots were taken and the next day the two men retired to the projection room to watch the rushes. Elvey emerged a little later to confess that Norwood had been right! So convincing was Norwood in the role, that he received mountains of correspondence from cinemagoers asking him to solve their problems as well as being given advice on how to outwit Moriarty and the other criminals he encountered!

Sir Arthur Conan Doyle was also among these admirers. 'Mr Eille Norwood's wonderful impersonation of Holmes has amazed me,' he said. 'Norwood has that rare quality which can only be described as glamour, which compels you to watch an actor eagerly even when he is doing nothing. He has a quite unrivalled power of disguise.'

Conan Doyle's verdict that Norwood *was* Holmes was no mean praise from a man usually given to disparaging his great creation – and it was a view shared equally by the critics. Laurence Hale of the influential *Moving Picture News*, for example, summarized what was the general opinion when he wrote in February 1922:

'A great deal of the success of the Sherlock Holmes films is due to the remarkable impersonation of Holmes by Eille Norwood. Really, the resemblance to the figure of the imagination is uncanny. It is much more genuine than William Gillette's characterization. Norwood *is* Holmes in countenance, personality and conduct.'

There is no doubt when viewing these films that Eille Norwood *was* a perfectionist, seeking to make the most of his thin, six-foot frame, dark features, angular profile and magnetic eyes in portraying Holmes. Though all the films were silent, he mimes with conviction, and his performance ranges from moments of quiet introspection to sudden bursts of energy and activity which are very much the trademarks of Sherlock Holmes. How seriously he took his role can be easily judged from this statement which he issued to the press before beginning work on the pictures in 1921:

'It is in no light spirit of bravado that I shoulder my responsibility, but with a very full knowledge of its many difficulties. It is so easy to play the detective in private life, over the breakfast table and in an arm-chair – and so very much the reverse to play Sherlock Holmes on the screen. But I shall set about the task with a grim determination to work in all earnestness for success.'

It is a pity, in the light of Stoll Pictures' intention to be faithful to Conan Doyle, that they cast a character-comedian actor named Hubert Willis, as Watson. Though Willis played the role with a certain bravado, the comic elements do tend to predominate, and very often he appears uncannily similar to his famous successor, Nigel Bruce.

Eille Norwood, though, dedicated himself to playing Holmes as faithfully as possible, and he adopted many of Holmes' characteristics both on and off the screen. He shaved the hair from his forehead to give himself Holmes' wide expanse of forehead, for instance, took to pipe smoking with a vengeance, and perfected his art of make-up to such a degree that even those working with him could be duped. Jeffrey Bernerd, the managing director of Stoll, remembered going onto the set one day and seeing someone he believed to be an undesirable hanging about . . .

'I saw this common-looking cab driver standing there watching while a scene was being taken,' he said. 'I promptly told the stage manager to clear him out – at which the man whined in broad cockney that he "wasn't doin' no 'arm".

'He was actually being escorted off the set when Maurice Elvey suddenly called for Mr Norwood – and the cab driver turned abruptly and walked straight into the scene!'

Norwood himself was later to comment on his disguises, 'The greatest difficulty with my disguises in the Sherlock Holmes stories is that I have to remove my make-up before the camera, revealing not Eille Norwood, but Sherlock Holmes. A disguise within a disguise, you know, and it takes a bit of doing!'

Almost as striking as Eille Norwood in this series of films was the set which Stoll

EILLE NORWOOD, AKA ANTHONY EDWARD BRETT, THE 1920'S
SILENT-MOVIE HOLMES IN THE GREAT DETECTIVE'S
CLASSIC MEDITATIVE POSE.

JEREMY BRETT STRIKES A SIMILAR
MEDITATIVE POSE FOR HIS ROLE IN
THE ADVENTURES OF SHERLOCK HOLMES.

Pictures built of the interior of 221B Baker Street. Originally, it had been Maurice Elvey's plan to actually film in Baker Street, but, as he was later to explain, 'when we started there huge crowds gathered and filming became impossible'.

Instead, the company duplicated a real Baker Street house – number 144, in fact – complete with the exterior of the street, Holmes' sitting room, bedroom and hall, all interconnected as in a real house. It was an astonishingly complex set, the like of which it is said had not been seen again until Granada's version . . .

Though, as I mentioned earlier, this series of 47 films are now virtually all lost, the memory of them should not be forgotten for they *do* represent the earliest, most faithful, screen interpretation of the original Doyle stories. And, as we shall now see, there are remarkable similarities between the career of Eille Norwood, aka Anthony Edward Brett, and Jeremy Brett, formerly Jeremy Huggins.

The latest Sherlock Holmes was born Jeremy Huggins on November 3, 1935, at Berkswell, near Coventry, the youngest of the four sons of a distinguished Army man, Lieutenant Colonel Henry William Huggins. His mother was half-Irish and a Quaker.

'It was an improbable marriage of opposites,' Jeremy says. 'My father was a particularly successful soldier by which I mean he was sufficiently cowardly to be incredibly brave. Trying to prove to himself and conquer his cowardice he earned one of the first DSO's of World War I and twice won the MC.'

Jeremy's birthsign was Scorpio with Leo in the ascendancy – which means, he says, that he's passionate but emotionally unstable, suspicious and distrustful, but loyal with tenacity and devotion once the suspicions have been lulled and the person won over. 'I recognize all these characteristics in myself,' he confesses.

Both of his parents died many years ago, but Jeremy has retained a strong sympathy for his father who lost all his friends killed in the war, and then tried hard to readjust to being a soldier in peace-time.

'I would like to have been a soldier for a while, for my father's sake, but I had rheumatic fever at 16 and never saw any kind of military service,' he says. 'When I said I wanted to be an actor, it was the end. It was a great disappointment to my father.'

He was educated at Eton and with his father's reluctant consent studied for the stage at London's Central School of Speech and Drama. 'My father wouldn't let me use the name Huggins when I decided to act, although it would have been a good balance. After all, I was Jeremy Huggins at Eton, where I was known variously as Buggins, Juggins and Muggins.'

So for his stage name he chose Brett – after the man who had made his first suit, in fact! It was a brave choice of profession for up until the age of 17 he suffered from a speech impediment.

'I was tongue-tied,' he explains. 'I couldn't make "r" and "s" sounds. I had to have my tongue cut like a crow. A doctor took a pair of scissors and clipped it. Having got the tongue free, I then had to learn how to use it.

'That really got me involved with words and I had to do a lot of vocal exercises. I still do them every morning.'

Jeremy has certainly triumphed over that impediment, for not only does he speak with great clarity, but he has a pureness of diction that gives his words a striking resonance whether he is acting or talking in private.

He wanted to be an actor from the age of eight, he says, when he enjoyed singing to records in his room or else sneaking out of school to watch plays. It was his mother who quietly encouraged him and helped him get his father to agree to him going to stage school.

Jeremy began his professional career at the Library Theatre in Manchester in 1954, where his evident ability – not to mention self-confidence – quickly landed him roles as juvenile leads. A photograph of himself in the actor's 'bible', *Spotlight*, next caught the eye of the Hollywood film director, King Vidor, and almost before he knew it, he was off to play Nicholas Rostov in *War and Peace* with Henry Fonda and Audrey Hepburn in 1955.

'I was whisked off from Manchester to Rome and lived in a fantasy world for six months,' he says. 'At the end of the film there was talk of taking me to Hollywood to groom me into a star.'

Instead, though, he returned to London to appear in Tyrone Guthrie's modern-dress production of *Troilus and Cressida* which then toured the United States and Canada, earning him both popular and critical acclaim.

He looks back on those heady days with the benefit of hindsight and is not particularly pleased with what he remembers of himself. 'I was big-headed,' he says, frankly. 'I think it may have stopped the drive a bit. I thought I was better than I really was. I was able to choose my own roles and that's a heady thing for a young man. I was always being described as "personable" and "promising", but the fact is I then had six flops in two years. I knew I was going in the wrong direction. If you think in terms of Upstairs, Downstairs, I was Upstairs and stuck with it.'

In 1964, what should have been a highlight of his career, going to Hollywood to co-star with Audrey Hepburn, Rex Harrison and Stanley Holloway in the film version of *My Fair Lady*, proved a big disappointment. He had to spend the best part of six months sitting around waiting to play his part of Freddy Eynsford-Hill – and in the meantime had to pass up a lot of other interesting offers. 'They were the most miserable six months of my life,' he remembers.

He was also married to actress Anna Massey in 1958 and though they had a son, David, the couple parted three years later.

But Jeremy was learning from his experiences, and when in 1967 he was given the chance to join the National Theatre Company by Sir Laurence Olivier, he suddenly found himself surrounded by a group of brilliant young actors such as Robert Stephens, John Stride and Ronald Pickup. His career has not looked back since.

He became particularly associated with the roles of handsome, sardonic men-of-the-world whom women found irresistible, and this led to a variety of other work in both films and on television.

Curiously, Jeremy believes that his good looks have worked *against* him at times. 'Until I was about 36 I photographed very wetly,' he says, 'there was nothing written in my face.'

This, he maintains, is also the reason why he has had to resist the temptation to put on too much make-up. 'I remember playing a sex maniac in a British film called *The Very Edge* back in 1963. I had yellow eyes and a green skin. My appearance so shocked my father that he said to me, "If you're going to do such terrible films, will you make sure they don't come to the village?"'

However, when Sean Connery announced that he was giving up the role of James Bond, the debonair Jeremy was one of those tested for the part. 'It's the sort of role you cannot afford to turn down,' he says, 'but I think if I had got it, it would have spoiled my life.'

In 1963, though, he notched up a most satisfying achievement when he was voted 'The Most Promising Actor on TV' for his performance in *The Picture of Dorian Gray*. It was to prove the first of two dark Victorian stories which led him to Sherlock Holmes.

In 1978 he was offered the lead in an American touring company's production of *Dracula*, which broke box office records in Los Angeles, San Francisco and Chicago. And then in 1981, also in the States, he had his first encounter with Sherlock Holmes in the play *The Crucifer of Blood*. He was not, though, cast as Holmes, but as Doctor Watson, playing opposite Charlton Heston as Holmes. But the honours went to him – he carried off the coveted Los Angeles Drama Critics' Choice award for his performance.

Though he obviously had no idea then of the significance that the stories of the great detective were to have in his life – he even went so far in one interview as to sarcastically describe his model for Watson as the cartoon character, Snoopy – he is today glad to have had the chance to play the good Doctor.

'It was tremendous fun,' he says, 'and it taught me a lot about how to approach Holmes when the Granada series got under way. I learned a great deal about the inter-relationship of the two men.'

One of the things that attracted Jeremy to playing Holmes was the thought of returning to Manchester where he had spent those early days in rep.

'Despite my forays into America, my career is in England,' he says. 'The whole of my origins are deeply English. I could not live anywhere else for long. I am also at an age where I feel a duty to return to the profession here what I have got from it.'

Another attraction – once he had overcome his initial misgivings about the part – was the chance of being able to create a genuinely fresh Holmes modelled on the original.

After completing the first series of stories, *The Adventures of Sherlock Holmes*, Jeremy was able to take a break – switching 221B Baker Street for West 47th Street – where he took New York by storm in the play *Aren't We All* co-starring Rex Harrison, Claudette Colbert and Lynn Redgrave. According to the *New York Times* he was 'the second tall, debonair English charmer to become the toast of Broadway – following Jeremy Irons in 1984'. It was also a role light years away from the gloomy world of Sherlock Holmes, which, said *The Times*, 'is currently bringing him fame and fortune on TV screens on both sides of the Atlantic'.

Jeremy was, though, most proud of a letter he had received from his 82-year-old grandmother. He quotes from the letter, 'Now, suddenly, this burst of stardom. It's almost frightening! Do you feel the same way?' Jeremy grins, 'What she is really saying is, "Are you staying humble?"'

Only one tragedy has marred Jeremy's life since Sherlock Holmes changed it irrevocably. His second wife, Joan Wilson Sullivan, an American television executive in Boston, died in July 1985 after a year-long battle with cancer. The couple had met ten years earlier when Jeremy was appearing in America.

'She saw me on stage and said, "That's the man for me". She organized the meeting and we married in 1976. We had a decade together – more than many. I loved her dearly, she was so beautiful and gutsy,' he said in tribute.

Jeremy was still hiding his grief as best he could when he came back to Britain in August to film *The Return of Sherlock Holmes*. 'The dust has settled and I am coming to terms with it,' he told reporters. 'The problem is that it is a disease for which there is no cure. She had been fighting the cancer for the past year.'

Part of Jeremy's reason for starring on Broadway, he said, had been so that he could be near Joan. She had actually become ill while he was filming the epic struggle between Holmes and Moriarty in Switzerland.

'Joan gave me the most enormous confidence – she loved me for being exactly the way I am,' he said. 'The last thing she said to me was, "Are you going to be all right?" Under the circumstances, that was a pretty stunning question. She was 54 and she had such wonderful things ahead of her.'

Now, of course, Jeremy has to face the future without her. He will console himself with his close circle of friends in London and enjoy the world-wide acclaim that three years of dedication to Sherlock Holmes has given him.

STOLL FILM C° L^{TD}

THE HOUND OF THE BASKERVILLES

EILLE NORWOOD'S CO-STAR AS DOCTOR WATSON WAS HUBERT WILLIS,
HERE STANDING BEHIND HOLMES' ACCUSING ARM IN A DRAMATIC
MOMENT FROM *THE HOUND OF THE BASKERVILLES*. AND OVERLEAF ...
DAVID BURKE, THE FIRST OF GRANADA'S TWO WATSONS, IN A SIMILAR
SITUATION IN *THE DANCING MEN*.

'I've always been dismissed as something of an extrovert,' he says with a wry
smile. 'But Holmes has finally given me recognition as a real actor, not just an
ageing pretty face.'

Jeremy Brett is a likeable and charming man, a dedicated professional where his
work is concerned, and an actor of rare ability uncannily proficient at sublimating
his own personality into that of the character he is playing.

It is surely only fitting, therefore, that he should have received recognition
playing such a master of impersonation as Sherlock Holmes, for I am reminded of
something that Doctor Watson once wrote about his friend which could just as
easily be applied to Jeremy Brett:

'It was not merely that Holmes changed his costume. His expression, his
manner, his very soul seemed to vary with every fresh part that he assumed.'

147

A BAKER STREET ❦DAY❦ WITH SHERLOCK HOLMES

In Conversation with the Great Detective

It is a beautiful, clear winter day. The sky is an arc of blue overhead, and the morning air is crisp with just an edge of chill to it.

The wide street of three-storey terraced buildings is already bustling with people and traffic. Along the road several horse-drawn broughams and landaus clip-clop by, passing some tradesmen's vehicles, a brewer's dray, a milk pram, a chestnut-seller and a pair of flat carts, one laden with bales of hay.

On the pavement a mixture of dark-suited, top-hatted gentlemen stride purposefully through an assortment of clerks, housemaids, nannies, costermongers, policemen and the odd ragamuffin or two. Some stop to glance into the windows of the small shops which are already busy with trade.

At the junction of the street with a side road, a young newsboy is shouting the headlines.

'Murder in Westminster,' his voice shrills out into the air. 'Man stabbed to death with Indian dagger!'

First one of the dark-suited gentlemen and then another stop to take newspapers from the boy's eager hands. Momentarily they both pause to glance at the front pages before walking on past a little bevy of women in ankle-length dresses and shawls who have stopped to gossip.

Another man, similarly dressed in black-tailed suit and shiny top hat, strides

A BIRD'S EYE VIEW OF FILMING ON BAKER STREET.

across the road and up to the front door of one of the elegant houses interspersed between the shops. He seems unaware of the morning bustle around him, lost in his own thoughts.

He reaches the black, highly-varnished front door and with a decisive move, lets himself in. The door bangs shut beneath the distinctive gold-painted numbers '221B'.

At this another voice rings out even louder than that of the newsboy.

'Cut!'

As if by magic, the world of Baker Street, London comes to a halt. Sherlock Holmes is at home and a new game is afoot.

But even though the throng of Victorian people and vehicles are soon intermingled by technicians and cameramen in the warm, casual clothes of the late twentieth century, it is still necessary for the eye-witness to remind himself that what he is watching is *not* real. That it is all an impressive illusion . . .

For the year is not 1890 and the place is not a real thoroughfare in the capital city of the British Empire, but a December day in 1985 – and I am in Manchester on Granada's superb reconstruction of Baker Street watching the filming of *The Second Stain*, one of the stories for *The Return of Sherlock Holmes*.

It is a particular pleasure to be observing this story, for it was one that Conan Doyle himself considered 'among the neatest stories I ever did' and it has been dramatized by one of the masterminds of the series, John Hawkesworth.

I am also here to spend some time with the man who has created the most highly acclaimed of all television portrayals of 'The Master of Detectives'.

The street is a facade, as I said earlier – a masterpiece of steel, wood, plaster, canvas and paint – while behind it lies the old warehouse which has been converted into one of the most modern television studios in the country. And wherein is to be found the equally impressive reconstruction of Sherlock Holmes' apartments inside 221B.

The man I meet there a few minutes later is not just an actor playing a part. Not just a very good actor playing a part very well. But Sherlock Holmes *personified*.

The look of the man, the dark, very dark eyes. The high forehead and prominent, almost aquiline nose. The strong mouth, the red lips almost a gash in the pale, white skin. And the finger raised like an exclamation mark to touch his lips before thrusting out a firm handshake.

This Holmes is a man of enormous inner strength, you feel almost at once, a man who would see through a lie or an untruth immediately. A man not to be underestimated. A man to have on your side – if the side you are on is the side of law and order.

Then the face breaks into a smile and Jeremy Brett, the 117th man to have brought his talent to the demanding business of playing a legend, greets me with a warmth that I am to learn is very much a part of his character. A character that has endeared him to all who have worked on the Sherlock Holmes series and a far wider, international television audience.

For it has taken a man with the fullest range of personal emotions to translate Holmes, the enigma, to the screen. Jeremy welcomes me into Holmes' sanctum and we begin the conversation which will go on – interrupted by various bouts of filming – throughout the day and into the evening.

The set on which we talk is an almost perfect reconstruction of Sherlock Holmes' rooms as depicted a century ago in the pages of *The Strand* magazine. It has an authentic feel about it, the atmosphere slightly dusty and tinged by the smell of gas lighting. The carpets and chairs are slightly worn (Holmes and Watson were not, after all, rich men), and the place is not over-furnished. There, too, are the familiar slipper, the bullet-mark initials on the wall, the violin and the pipes which have been firmly entrenched in the imagination of every Sherlockian since he or she first discovered the sacred canon of adventures.

The room has, in fact, become an immensely important element in Jeremy's interpretation of Holmes as he is quick to tell me. 'I love this set,' he says in the same undulating, velvety tones that have helped make his performance so memorable. 'I am happier working here at 221B than anywhere else. I find it easier to work here in the womb of our home than out on location or in a strange house. I work faster here, too.'

It is interesting to hear Jeremy call the set 'our home'. It is an example – and more will follow – of his total absorption into the part. Holmes also, of course, used to do much of the thinking which led to the resolution of his cases at 221B.

'I find myself more in tune with Holmes here,' he goes on. 'In fact, I have personalized this tiny space. I even sleep in the bedroom sometimes during my lunch break.'

He pauses for a moment and a smile crosses the wan features. 'Put me outside, and what with my slicked back hair and black clothes I look like an undertaker!'

The humour cracks the formality of our meeting and I decide to ask Jeremy to go back to the beginning of his involvement with the series which has brought him international recognition and acclaim.

'I was asked in 1982 if I would like to play Sherlock Holmes,' he says, settling in his armchair, flicking back the two dark wings of his coat and placing his agile, strikingly demonstrative fingers together in a pyramid, 'and I was really quite alarmed. I was nervous about the idea of playing such a dark character because of my own metabolism. You see I am basically a very sunny guy and I was being asked to walk in a very dark place.

'I was also concerned about making a commitment to one character for such a long time. Initially, I think it was for a year with an option for another year. I wondered if I could hold my act together for that long – and if I could stay in one piece.

'I suppose you could say I panicked,' he went on, his eyes holding mine very directly. 'I didn't want to do it. "Why me?" was another reaction. Holmes seemed to me to have been done to death and I couldn't understand why they wanted to do it again. I was sure I'd have nothing original to contribute. Basil Rathbone was the definitive-looking Holmes and Peter Cushing was marvellous and had got closest to the relationship intended between Holmes and Watson. Any number of actors would have been better for the role.'

Jeremy was, of course, familiar with the Conan Doyle stories, having read the books while at college (although only because he was being tested on them then, he says) and also seen many of the earlier film and television versions. He was also naturally concerned about the effect playing the part might have on his career – as it had done to Basil Rathbone.

'I thought it might bring my career to a grinding halt,' he said – but decided to seek the counsel of two people whose opinions he respected. Their views turned out to be diametrically opposed!

Jeremy's older brother, John, a devoted fan of Holmes and a pipe-smoker to boot, was in no doubt. 'Why would they cast you,' he said. 'You're not a pipe-smoker. Frankly, Jeremy, I don't think you're right for the part!' Jeremy says now that he recognizes his brother was being 'very possessive' of the Holmes character.

'As for the pipes, I had to be very careful because I'm left-handed. I had to learn how to pack and smoke one, or else make sure they were lit when I picked them up. But I confess I took to smoking them like a duck to water!'

The reaction of Jeremy's long-time friend, the broadcaster Alistair Cooke was quite different. 'Wonderful, wonderful,' he said as if Jeremy had already signed the contract. 'You realize who you're playing don't you? One of the three most important men of the century – Churchill, Hitler and Holmes! I can see it now!'

Jeremy allows himself a smile at the memory of that conversation. 'That really freaked me,' he says, 'because it demonstrated that Holmes' fans viewed him, not as a man of fiction, but in the same breath with men who had actually *lived*. But Alistair is a very wise old buzzard and what he did was brace me up. I had been so overawed that a side of me kept saying, "Why do it again?" That side was put to rest by Alistair.'

Before Jeremy had to commit himself to the role, however, he was contracted to appear in a role in Canada. 'It was a fortunate break,' he recalls. 'For during that year I made Doyle my bedside reading. I read all the 54 short stories twice and the four novels. I saw the way to do Doyle was to do *Doyle* – the books as they were.

'I realize now that I needed that time for complete absorption. It enabled me to do my homework in a way that doesn't normally happen for an actor. When I returned to Manchester I was thoroughly marinated in Sherlock Holmes!'

The thing these readings confirmed for him, surprisingly, was that there was not a lot he *liked* about Holmes.

'I never found him interesting or attractive,' he recalled. 'I always thought of him as a machine. I found him boring to watch and quite arrogant. He's so *right* all the time. He's certainly not the kind of a person I'd gravitate to at a party. He's chilling, in fact.

'If I saw him walking down the street I'd say, "Poor soul . . . What a tortured creature. He's not a happy man." Who *could* be happy who falls apart when he's not working or has to be drugged in order to go to sleep?'

Jeremy pressed his left finger to his lips again. His lean, aristocratic features took on the slightly far-away look that is so Holmesian. Which made his next remark all the more surprising.

'I didn't think I looked like the character Conan Doyle had in mind,' he said. 'In fact, as I understand it, he felt the Sidney Paget illustrations were too good-looking, not precisely what he envisioned. It was these early illustrations that I used as a make-up guide. With my white face and hair slicked back I looked more like Basil Rathbone than anyone else.'

Although Jeremy was never tested for the role of Holmes, he *did* play a make-up test for the cameras. The memory of this occasion again creases his face into a huge smile. 'I think the mistake I made at the beginning was to endeavour to try and make myself look so completely like Holmes that I became a parody,' he says. 'I put this white line across my forehead, another one down my nose, and gentian violet under my chin. I looked like a kind of gargoyle!

'I also walked about quickly as if I had St Vitus' dance and spoke in a very sharp way. I don't know if those original camera tests still exist but you could mistake me for a lean ghost with a high-pitched voice. I just pray they *don't*!'

JEREMY BRETT GIVING AN INTERVIEW ON THE BAKER STREET SET.

We both laugh at the thought of this film, and I cannot resist mentioning how much the more fanatical Sherlockians would love to get their hands on a pirate copy of the test. Jeremy gives a mock shudder at the thought, and then goes on: 'Anyhow, when the people at Granada looked at the film, their immediate reaction was, "Is there going to be *any* of Jeremy in this Holmes at all?" It was the clue I needed, and gradually my confusion cleared and I became more and more fascinated with the part.'

Jeremy also went on a diet and lost 15 pounds to achieve the gaunt look, and applied dye to his naturally dark brown hair to give it Holmes' coal-black appearance.

'Apart from all the problems of getting my character right, I think I was also very concerned about the enormous amounts of money that were going to be involved in the production – what with the huge Baker Street set, the interiors, the location work and, of course, not forgetting the big names who were being lined up for co-starring roles,' he said. 'I think this gives you an exaggerated sense of responsibility in case it doesn't come off.'

Jeremy's determination to seek perfection was greatly encouraged when he set his eyes on the scripts for the first 13 stories. 'They were marvellous,' he says. 'Beautifully written and in the main adapted in the most faithful way. But I did still come across the occasional liberty.'

'Adaptors have a right to do their own thing,' he went on. 'But they will sometimes miss out important words and that's when I get reminders from Conan Doyle. And I'll battle to get them back.'

155

At this, Jeremy turned round in his chair and picked up a large, ornately bound book that lay on the table beside him. It was an illustrated edition of *The Complete Adventures of Sherlock Holmes*. He opened it on his knee and flicked over the pages. I saw immediately that the pages were heavily annotated in his own handwriting.

'I have had this book beside me since we began,' he said, 'because as I mentioned I wanted to keep Doyle's stories as close to the originals as possible. Now adaptors *do* have a way of changing things, and so I needed this with me to refer to. When I found something I didn't like, I would flip open the book and say, "Isn't the original better?"'

'I became a bit of a pain in the neck at times, I guess, but it was worth it to get the stories as close to the books as possible.'

Jeremy also recalled that whenever he got stuck with a scene he would try all sorts of ways to get it right. 'I would walk about all over Manchester wrestling with the problem. Sometimes I would discuss it with others or else read the lines over and over again. But in the end I realized the best thing was to go back to the original text by Conan Doyle. So I would pick up my annotated copy, read it, and sure enough there would be the answer staring me in the face!'

Another problem that he managed to resolve was the schedule allowed for filming. 'When we first started I was getting up at 3 am to prepare. It takes a lot of effort to go deeper into a story so that it's not simply a parody. I was bouncing a scene like a trampoline.

'I'd be polishing my magnifying glass, eating breakfast and making-up, all while doing 26 pages of dialogue. I seemed to have more lines than I'd had hot dinners. By 4 pm when the director wanted fire, my fire was out!'

Jeremy decided to take the matter up with producer, Michael Cox. 'I remember Michael came onto the set and I said, "Can you have a word with the powers that be? I cannot make these stories on one week's rehearsal. To bounce the words I really should have *two* weeks."

'The result was that Michael got us two weeks for rehearsal and then we had three to three and a half weeks for actual filming. It was a tremendous upheaval in the Granada schedule, but I promised them, "I will last longer if you take care of me!"'

As if on cue, a solicitous member of the production team arrived at this moment to take Jeremy away to shoot a scene. I sat back to enjoy the feeling of being in Holmes' sanctum . . .

It seemed like only a matter of moments before Jeremy returned. He sat down in the chair and lit not a pipe, as I half-expected, but a filter-tip cigarette. He inhaled then blew the smoke out suddenly. He examined the cigarette for a moment and spoke once more.

'When I was reading the books and stories I discovered that Holmes smoked a rather dirty, broken-off clay pipe in his meditative moods and a long cherrywood in his disputatious moods. He also smoked a lot of cigarettes, an enormous amount of cheroots, not to mention cocaine, opium and all that. I did smoke the curled Meerschaum pipe in *The Final Problem*, but only as a gesture to William Gillette. Otherwise, I tried to follow the books exactly.'

After a couple more pulls at the cigarette, Jeremy's face relaxes, and my initial misgivings that maybe the scene had not gone as well as he had expected are allayed. When he speaks again, my suspicion is confirmed.

'Another thing that I have found exciting about making this Sherlock Holmes has been the people working on it with me. It is very seldom that you get an entire studio of people that have actually read the script before they come to the first shoot. That does *so* help. Some of them have even read the original stories as well,' he says.

As a thoroughly professional actor, Jeremy is very conscious of the importance of having good people around him. 'If we are the skin, the flesh that is being burned,' he says waxing lyrical for a moment, 'then there must be skilled people all around doing the mechanicals. We need brilliant artistry, great lighting, pure sound to get the maximum effect. It is also good to have new people around you from time to time, giving different kinds of performances. This helps you keep your own performance moist and stop it from becoming staid like porridge.'

I took this opportunity to bring Jeremy's thoughts back to how he had finally evolved the Holmes we now know. He squashed the rest of his cigarette out and again made a pyramid of his fingers.

'Curiously, I found one or two similarities between us,' he replied. 'I realized that he was very vulnerable which I tend to be underneath. I'm also very quick. And like me, when he's not working he tends to fall apart, but from the moment he gets a job he's on fire.

'But there was no way I could identify with his dark side – the addiction to drugs and all the rest. You realize he's an isolated, lonely man, and a difficult one to live with for an actor. Some actors have actually become suicidal playing him . . .' Jeremy's voice momentarily fades.

'Fortunately, I have a very strong Christian ethic and I jettison him as fast as I can come the end of the day. If there are too many pressures I meditate or break open a bottle of champagne.

'Still, I admit I don't like the smell of him. He's very dangerous. I believe if you're dealing with criminology, you become criminal.

'I remember when I was playing John Mortimer in *Voyage Round My Father* on the stage, I went to see the playwright who is, of course, a barrister, and he agreed with me. "What happens," he told me, "is that you begin to understand the criminal mind." I find that to be true of Holmes, although he's anti-crime as well as anti-establishment.'

For a moment we were interrupted when Jeremy's make-up girl came to check his appearance. Susan Milton is a highly talented lady and, after she had left, Jeremy was quick to praise her work for him. The interruption immediately sparked his thoughts again.

'I began to find the cracks in the man,' he went on. 'To discover there *was* flesh and blood underneath. But the most important thing of all I discovered was the relationship with Watson. He wasn't the doddering plodder following behind as is so often shown. He had the compassion to stay with Holmes, picking him up. It is one of the great friendships of literature.'

Jeremy's understanding of this relationship undoubtedly started when he played Watson in 1981 in *The Crucifer of Blood*. 'If you look at it from Watson's side, Holmes emerges as about the loneliest man in literature,' he said.

'Really, Watson is much more my kind of part than Holmes – Holmes is a big stretch. I don't like working alone. I'm not a one-man band, so when I took on Holmes I came to rely on Watson as much as I could without bending the willow.

'Holmes is a very private man, a tragic genius. But Watson has his friends and his surgery. He's not a dull man, he's an ordinary, good man of great compassion,

warmth and consideration. He's a gentleman. Everybody would like a friend like Watson.

'The relationship between them is terribly British. Holmes has a great deal of trouble saying such simple things as "Help!", "Thank you" and "I'd be lost without you". Watson sees beyond that. He's fascinated by Holmes and his intuitive leaps. And he realizes that if he stays away from Holmes for too long the man will overdose.

'Yes, there is no doubt in my mind that it is Holmes who needs Watson and not the other way round. I didn't see any of that in the earlier films, nor did I see anything of the vulnerability of Holmes. So that's why I set out right from the beginning to show the insecurity and to explore the amazing friendship between those two men.'

Jeremy's evident understanding of both sides of this partnership helped me fit another piece into the jig-saw of how he has achieved his outstanding performance as Holmes. This also seemed like a suitable moment to discuss the two men who had partnered him as Watson, David Burke and Edward Hardwicke.

Jeremy's face broke into a smile at the mention of David Burke's name. 'We made a very good odd couple,' he chuckled throatily. 'Of course it was a terrific gamble that we would be able to work together, that we would see our parts in a compatible way. But in fact there was no cause to worry because we soon found we got on so well.

'David is debonair with an attractiveness about him that proved to be unusual and appealing in a Watson. That was a real bonus and helped to break the traditional mould,' Jeremy added.

Just as Jeremy's Holmes had thrown a whole new perspective on the detective, so David Burke's Watson had shattered the old image of the bumbling and rather comic doctor. How did he feel, though, when David decided against making *The Return of Sherlock Holmes.*

'I was very sorry, naturally.' Jeremy stretched his lean frame further out from the chair and contemplated the fireplace. 'But being an actor I quite understood. And if it had to happen, that was the right time between Holmes' disappearance in *The Final Problem* and his reappearance three years later in *The Empty House.* Looking back, I think the change has been very useful.'

Jeremy closes his eyes for a moment as if selecting his next words carefully. 'The thing is,' he says after a pause, 'if you work together with the same person it becomes almost like a marriage. However fresh you try to be on a day-to-day basis it becomes a known way. So for me the change of Watsons was like a breath of fresh air, a shot of adrenalin in the arm.'

Whether Jeremy had intended the pun or not, his face remains unchanged as he continues. 'What happened was a chemical change – and it *is* a chemical change – of a new person adding a new element to the friendship. Remember that three years have passed since the two men last met, so things have happened to them both which enabled us to restart the friendship at a different angle.

'It was revitalizing for me, though not easy for Edward. But he is an immensely sensitive person and a brilliant actor so it really did not take us long to find our way into a new relationship.

'I have this feeling that *The Return of Sherlock Holmes* is better even than the first 13 stories. I can't quite tell you *why* that is – it is to do with some shift of emphasis, some confidence, some chemistry between Edward and me. But there is definitely *something*.'

Jeremy has clearly been re-charged not only by this change, but others that have taken place during the series. 'You can so easily fall into a kind of complacency if things don't change,' he went on. 'It's something to do with the human animal. So I have enjoyed new directors, new actors in guest roles, even a new lighting cameraman or technician joining the team. On a long series you become terribly aware of new faces, but if you are trying to continue being creative then you need them, for each new face brings in new ideas. All the time the format is changing ever so slightly and that is terribly important, I think.'

I found Jeremy's examination of his art a fascinating insight into the man himself, and it seemed appropriate at that moment that he should be called to play another scene. He invited me to come and watch.

The story had reached the point where Sherlock Holmes was to be confronted by Watson over the news of the stabbing in Westminster. The self-same news the paperboy had been bawling out in Baker Street.

Jeremy and Edward Hardwicke took their places on the set – Edward, a small, dapper man, every inch the 'gentleman' that Jeremy had described. I was immediately struck by his almost-Victorian politeness, and the warm smile and firm handshake as we were introduced, underlined this feeling. We agreed to meet again later.

The landing of the Baker Street apartment became a flurry of technicians and lighting men as the director, John Bruce, prepared to shoot the scene. Jeremy, though, seemed to withdraw into himself, running his lines through his mind and evidently preparing his movements. One could see him visibly becoming the dark and tense figure of Holmes. Edward was stiller, but became Watson just as inexorably.

The call for 'Quiet' echoed demandingly through the set, and then 'Action' from John Bruce.

It is Watson who speaks first, a newspaper in his hand, enquiring if the man Holmes is preparing to go out to see is a certain Eduardo Lucas.

Holmes' voice is flat, 'Yes.'

'Of Godolphin Street?' enquires Watson.

'Yes.' The voice is again flat.

'You will not see him.'

'Why not?' There is a subtle change in Holmes' voice.

When Watson replies it is evident he is savouring the news he is about to impart.

'He was murdered in his house last night!'

It is obvious immediately from the reaction of both men that Watson has astonished Holmes – a very rare thing.

'Good heavens,' the famous detective replies, 'does it say murder?'

Savouring his triumph, Watson goes on to read the newspaper's account of

SIDNEY PAGET'S ORIGINAL
1904 SKETCH OF THE SCENE
I WITNESSED BEING FILMED
FOR *THE SECOND STAIN*.

Lucas' mysterious murder, stabbed to the heart by a curved Indian dagger. Holmes takes the paper from him and reads the details for himself.

After a brief discussion with Watson as to what he makes of the news, Holmes continues, 'With the late Eduardo Lucas lies the solution to our problem,' he says thoughtfully, 'though I must admit that I have not an inkling as to what form it may take. It is a capital mistake to theorize in advance of the facts.'

He then turns to his friend. 'Do stay on guard, my good Watson, and receive any fresh visitors. I'll join you when I am able.'

A moment more, and John Bruce calls, 'Cut'. He nods his approval. The scene is in the can. Both actors relax visibly.

Jeremy discusses something briefly with John Bruce and then comes over to me. He is going to lunch, he says, and will meet me in the afternoon. It fits in perfectly with the plans I have to talk to Michael Cox . . .

It had been a fascinating experience to be eye-witness to a rare moment in the life of Sherlock Holmes. A moment when he was genuinely surprised by Watson. This, in fact, was still in my mind in the afternoon when I met Jeremy once more in the Baker Street apartments and found him grinning broadly. I couldn't help wondering if he was still smiling at the memory of the morning's experience.

'Actually, it was what happened at lunch,' he said, settling down in the chair again. 'Sometimes I go to the Granada canteen to eat. Well, today I collected a piece of chicken, a tomato and two slices of crispbread, and was standing in line to pay. There were so many people about, and it was getting so hot, that I suddenly thought, "My God, my make-up is going to burst right off my face!". So I put down the chicken, the tomato and the crispbread and came back here and had a sleep! Mind you, after the nap I did pop back and get a fish cake!'

Jeremy is, in fact, as visible off the set at the Granada studios as on it – he expects no special star treatment and is quite prepared to eat in the canteen with everyone else. At the end of the day, he is also as happy to drink with a co-star or a crew member in the bar. It is not without good reason that members of the production team maintained that he had created a 'family atmosphere' among everyone involved in making the Sherlock Holmes stories.

Jeremy's amusing story gave me the chance to ask one of the most intriguing questions about Holmes – did he think the man had any humour in him?

'Yes, I do,' he replied after a moment or so of thought. 'I was not sure to begin with because Holmes suppresses so many of the emotions in himself. But once I began to find the cracks in his armoury I realized there were moments when he laughed. I was also anxious to let a little of my own humour into the part.

'I once actually suggested a scene where I fell flat on my face and Watson had to pick me up. It would have been funny, but the director was adamant. "Can we shoot the alternative?" he said – which meant, "No!" I suppose there are certain rules about what Holmes can and cannot do, and that was one of them.'

Jeremy did, though, recall some funny moments. 'I mean when Holmes falls on his knees with a lantern and a magnifying glass and, with his backside stuck up in the air, starts inspecting the cracks between some stones – *that* is funny. On another occasion he rushes through some shrubbery sniffing his way among the rhododendrons like a golden retriever on the scent! And, of course, he often teases Watson!'

He grinned and then added, 'Although Watson tells all the stories in the first person, I think it is amusing to imagine what he *didn't* write. He obviously chose

161

very carefully to show Holmes in the best light. And that is one of the great chivalries of friendship.'

But, of course, I said, it was Sir Arthur Conan Doyle who actually *wrote* the cases. What did he think of the man who had given literature one of its most famous characters?

'I imagine Conan Doyle to have been a rather extraordinary, private sort of creature. I don't find it surprising that he should have become so absorbed in spiritualism and fairies and such like in the later part of his life. Being a man with a most logical mind and at the same time saddled with this character he could not be rid of, he must have found relief in the illogical.

'We really don't know that much about Doyle, do we?' he continues. 'He was overtaken by his own invention. One wonders what he would think if he could see how we are still wrestling with Holmes a hundred years after his creation?'

Jeremy is, in fact, a fund of little stories about what he calls 'Doyle's Dynasty' – the author himself and the members of his family. Some are much too libellous to print, but three stick in my mind.

'I love the story about Doyle meeting the American actor William Gillette when he arrived in London after his huge success as Holmes on Broadway. Gillette actually turned up after all that travelling at Victoria Station in his complete Holmes costume – cloak, pipe, deer-stalker hat and all. No wonder Doyle's first words to him were, "You *are* my Sherlock Holmes!"

'I actually met one of Doyle's nieces in Lancaster and I think she probably longed never to have been his niece at all. The shadow of Holmes seemed to have kept her fossilized in the past.'

Jeremy's voice then dropped to a conspiratorial note. Like Holmes, he loves picking up gossip. 'Have you heard the story that Conan Doyle was actually removed from this life by a member of his family?'

He waits for my reaction, which is non-committal. He goes on, all the same. 'Apparently he was spending all the family goodies on the occult and one of them got a bit concerned about the inheritance . . .'

The face breaks into a huge grin and Jeremy lights another cigarette. I decided to steer the conversation away to the afternoon's shooting. Jeremy has to film a scene playing his violin: one of the most enduring images of Holmes.

'I can't play it, in fact,' he admits, 'but I have got pretty skilful at bowing the instrument. Mind you, to give the impression that I know what I'm doing, I do listen to the music for hours beforehand so that I have the feel of it.

'I have tried to vary my performances, sometimes playing in a very still fashion, and in others with lots of movement. Recently I even swung right round with my back to the camera, but still bowing the violin. Then I threw that scene at Patrick Gowers, who is the composer on the series, and challenged him to put music to it. He's a brilliant and inventive man and so, of course, he did!'

I found it interesting to learn that the soundtrack of the violin being played is actually performed by Patrick Gowers' teenage daughter, Kathy. The reason for this choice is because Patrick thought she would most sound like a 'gifted amateur' – the status accorded to Sherlock Holmes.

That Jeremy has succeeded well in this deception is evident from the compliments he has received – and this quite rapturous comment from Miv Schaff, the television reviewer of the *Los Angeles Times*, while discussing the authenticity of the whole series.

'And at the end – here comes the nerve-wracking part – Holmes picks up his violin. Please, please, we pray, he will not play that damnably ridiculous, fluffy springtime air Basil Rathbone always played. Miracle of miracles, he does not.

'The bow goes on the strings, Holmes holds it as if he were accustomed to playing the violin and yes, a slow, sad melody, a sober one that Holmes himself might have composed and clever Brett has taken the time to learn the correct bowing so that we are convinced he is playing the violin. He stops, puts down the violin and bow – look! he does not put his fingers on the bow hairs as his unthinking, non-violinistic predecessors have done – and he sits in his armchair next to the fire, fingertips together, just as Joseph Bell, the Edinburgh surgeon professor who was the inspiration for Holmes sat, thinking Holmesian thoughts.'

The words echo what I am looking at, for Jeremy prepares to play his scene with the violin and picks up the instrument from beside him. Standing up briskly, he thrusts it under his chin, and begins to play with an invisible bow. A soundless music fills the air. The maestro is performing!

It is time for me to slip away, for the rest of the afternoon will be busy for Sherlock Holmes, and we still have a dinner date to come. I am now conscious as I leave Jeremy that all the praise has been fully justified – and earned by the most dedicated hard work.

What the cost of this long and arduous performance has been to the man *himself* I decide to keep to raise in the relaxed surroundings of our meal together . . .

The dinner proves to be an evening to remember. I share it not only with Jeremy, but Edward joins us as well. Dinner with Holmes and Watson – what more could a chronicler of their adventures ask!

We dined together at the Britannia Hotel in the centre of Manchester, a most suitable venue with its huge rooms, imposing staircases, Victorian decor and ornate crystal chandeliers.

Jeremy and I had arranged to meet in the foyer – and he spotted me before I did him. For what a change from the man I had last seen in the studios! Gone were the wan features, the slicked-back hair and the funereal clothes. Instead, a smiling face, a sweep of brown hair, stylish, casual clothes, and a multi-coloured scarf wrapped around his neck.

I could not avoid commenting on the transformation, and almost before we had been seated in a corner alcove of the restaurant, Jeremy was answering the question I had wanted to put about the effect of Holmes upon him.

'I found after a time that Holmes was threatening me,' he said. 'He became the dark side of the moon because he is moody and solitary and I am sociable and gregarious. Holmes is so still and I'm like Jiminy Cricket. I had to wash the part out of me as well as the grease out of my hair.

'It got dangerous for me about the tenth film (*The Norwood Builder*). I began to feel there was nothing in my life *but* Holmes.'

Jeremy hesitated momentarily as thoughts of those dark days obviously crossed his mind. He took a sip of white wine which had already been brought to our table. I waited for him to speak again.

'Holmes is a very difficult man to live inside,' he said finally. 'He's obsessive, and he's dazzling, and I became very weary in my psyche, my head. It was rather like being a violin wound up too tight.

'The thing was, I had become changed by the stories. I was marinaded in them. They're pre-Freud, pre-psychology, and much wilder. You realize they're much more destructive and dangerous than you could have imagined. Holmes is his own Special Branch. He's a man who flirts with crime all the time, and I always think this rubs off.'

Jeremy found that as the series gathered momentum, and these feelings grew stronger, another worry also presented itself.

'I have always believed that the best way an actor can stay sane is to leave his part behind at the end of the day. But when you are living away from home as I have done in Manchester, the hotel where you are staying can become a prison.

'You close the door and you're locked in. Now that can be alright for playing a difficult part like Sherlock Holmes because it prevents any distractions. The isolation can be wonderful for the part. *For a time*. But it is definitely *not* good for your lifestyle,' he said.

'In October of 1983 I started dreaming about Holmes, and the dreams turned into nightmares. It was as well I had another part to go to in America before coming back to do *The Return of Sherlock Holmes*. For he had worn me threadbare. I was over-Holmsed.'

Now that Jeremy has quite evidently got back his sense of equilibrium and can turn off Holmes once he leaves the studios, he looks back on those days as painful, but nevertheless having provided him with a valuable lesson. And if he now once again enjoys his taste for good food in fine restaurants and occasionally singing and dancing the night away, his tangible reward for those trials and tribulations are the ecstatic reviews which greeted the first series when it began to be screened on Tuesday, April 24, 1984.

I quoted Jeremy one of the earliest of these from the prestigious *Sunday Times*, which said he was 'indisputably the best screen Holmes I have ever seen – Jeremy Brett *is* Sherlock Holmes'. He smiled at this, took the menu that was offered to him by a hovering waiter, and said, 'That was great, of course. But I rested much easier when Michael Cox put a copy of a favourable review by the Sherlock Holmes Society of London on my dressing-table with a note calling it, "the ultimate accolade".'

I was just about to tell Jeremy that I could quote similar equally enthusiastic comments from other newspapers and Sherlockians all over the world, when the good Doctor Watson in the form of Edward Hardwicke arrived to join us. He, too, had changed into less formal clothes, but the transformation was less dramatic than Jeremy's.

After we had all ordered, the conversation slipped from one topic to another, some to do with the series, others on acting, writing and life in general. If Holmes and Watson had entertained at 221B, one would like to think that they did it with the same style as Brett and Hardwicke.

Indeed, it suddenly struck me as we were passing from the main course to the sweet, that they seemed as much Holmes and Watson *off* the screen as they were on it. I said so. Jeremy chuckled . 'Oh, maybe better off it – I think we behave a bit better!'

We talked for a bit of the long hours that are required in filming – days sometimes lasting from 7.15 am to 5.30 pm. At this, Edward chipped in, 'An actor once said to me, "I do the acting for free – I get paid for waiting."' Jeremy smiled agreement. 'Yes, the days can be long – but at the same time you are doing something you absolutely love.'

Finally, as the time neared for us to part – for both men had early starts the next day – I asked Jeremy what the future held for him after this landmark in his career. Once again he paused, took a last mouthful of wine, and then said: 'I have done many acting jobs in my life and I have enjoyed most of them and tried to do my best. But this one has radically affected me. It has turned me into something of a recluse and it has also taught me to survive the most extraordinary probabilities.

'I now know that I won't take no for an answer if I believe I am right about something – and that's quite shocking. Which means, I suppose, that I am louder than I used to be!'

He laughs that deep, velvety laugh. 'Sherlock Holmes has undoubtedly changed me – though for the better or the worse I can't quite make out. But like any good marriage I just have to get on with it!'

We all shook hands, wished each other well, and walked out of the restaurant. Jeremy and Edward, ever the professionals, taking a moment to quickly discuss a matter concerning their scenes the next day.

As we left, my eye just happened to catch sight of a name on the list of hotel personnel. It was the name of the General Manager, and as I watched my two friends disappear, I thought of how Holmes would have smiled at the extraordinary coincidence it represented.

For the name of the General Manager was Shaun *Moriarty* . . .

DAVID BURKE
WHO TRANSFORMED THE OLD
STEREOTYPED IMAGE OF DOCTOR WATSON ...

THE CHANGING ❧OF A❧ FIXED POINT

The Men Who Transformed Doctor Watson's Image

It was Sherlock Holmes, of course, who called his greatest friend 'the one fixed point in a changing age' – and it is also a fact that until the transformation of the good Doctor's image in the Granada series, Watson had been almost invariably portrayed on the screen as a rather bumbling figure, baffled by Holmes' cleverness and seemingly only around to provide a little comic relief.

But in creating Watson, this had been far from Sir Arthur Conan Doyle's intention – for didn't Holmes on several occasions speak highly of his friend's intelligence, enthusiasm, humour, and perhaps most of all, utter dependability?

In the case of *The Blanched Soldier*, for example, he paid this fulsome tribute: 'Speaking of my old friend and biographer, I would take this opportunity to remark that if I burden myself with a companion in my various little enquiries it is not done out of sentiment or caprice, but it is that Watson has some remarkable characteristics of his own to which in his modesty he has given small attention amid his exaggerated estimates of my own performances.'

After the difficult business of *The Sussex Vampire*, Holmes was also equally forthright. 'I never get your limits, Watson,' he said. 'There are unexplored possibilities about you.' While in *A Scandal in Bohemia* he said unequivocally, 'I am lost without my Boswell.'

Do *these* sound like the attributes of a simpleton?

Those familiar with the original stories are, no doubt, fully aware that Watson was Holmes' right arm, and that it was the various screen adaptors over the years who had been responsible for giving the poor medical man his unfortunate and unwarranted image. In the Granada series, however, this was righted by not one but two outstanding performances – as the newspaper reviews bear testimony.

It was David Burke, playing opposite Jeremy Brett in the first 13 *Adventures of Sherlock Holmes* who broke the mould. Then Edward Hardwicke who took over in *The Return of Sherlock Holmes* confirmed that the old image had gone – hopefully for ever! The achievement was made all the more remarkable because of the necessity of a change of actor. But, thanks to the timing of this change, and the excellence of the casting, the result proved wholly acceptable and ultimately completely satisfying.

David Burke's handsome and vigorous Watson became the slightly older and more assured Doctor of Edward Hardwicke. The three years that intervened between the Doctor of *The Final Problem* and *The Empty House* had treated him kindly in every respect except the belief – so dramatically shattered – that he had lost his friend Holmes. But age had not withered his devotion a jot.

For both David Burke and Edward Hardwicke, playing Watson proved challenging and rewarding. The opportunity to change the way the public sees a character is not often presented in such a specific way as it was in this version of the Sherlock Holmes adventures – and both men took their chances with alacrity and skill.

David Burke, a tall, debonair and friendly man, was in no doubt about the challenge which faced him when he accepted Michael Cox's invitation to play Watson. 'Because Watson is the narrator of the stories, he has little to say and very little to do because he is recording,' he says. 'So an adaptor has a difficult problem: What do you do with Watson? The easiest way for a Watson to get into the show is to be slightly funny.'

David explains further, 'For this reason, I believe, many actors in the past fell into the trap of going overboard on the comedy. Watson is not a dynamic character, so to make a mark they grabbed at the comedic elements.'

'If you make Watson too stupid, though, it begs the question why would a man of Holmes' intellect put up with him?' he adds.

For this reason David steered resolutely away from the archetypal bumbling Watson performance of Nigel Bruce which he had studied with interest, if not admiration. Through reading the stories again before linking up with Jeremy Brett to film the series, he had come to greatly respect Watson.

'He is the most ordinary man in the world,' David said. 'At the same time he is the best kind of English gentleman. I think the friendship between Holmes and Watson is one of the great male friendships – on a par with Hamlet and Horatio, or Butch Cassidy and the Sundance Kid.'

David Burke came to the role with a distinguished career to his name – though as he explains he got into acting almost by chance and by displaying a gift for comedy which is not something one might immediately associate with him.

'It was while I was at Oxford University,' he explains. 'I had a small part in a university play. Just a couple of lines, but they got a gale of laughter. I walked around in a daze afterwards, knowing that I had found what I wanted to do with my life.'

David learned his craft on the stage, working for some years in the National Theatre Company, though never actually appearing with Jeremy Brett. He also spent four years with the Royal Lyceum Company in Scotland where he played a number of major roles including Othello, Macbeth, Astrov in *Uncle Vanya* and Flamineo in *The White Devil*. In the West End, he also appeared in *War and Peace*,

Hotel in Amsterdam, Bodies and *Rocket to the Moon.*

David has a string of successful television appearances behind him, too, including several BBC Shakespearean productions, and leading roles in *The Woodlanders, Kipling* and *Crimes of Passion,* while for Granada he has done *Crown Court* and *Inheritance.*

David's first reaction on being offered the part of Watson in 1983 was a typically practical one. 'In a profession where unemployment is getting worse and worse and you are lucky to get two weeks' work, almost two years in something of quality is more than you dare hope for.'

The reaction of some of his friends to this news was, however, not quite what he had expected – as he recalls with wry amusement. 'They said, "So glad you're playing Watson – you are absolutely right!" Now that wasn't quite the confirmation I was seeking, because Watson is your average man, almost bordering on the boring! I consoled myself with the thought that as there are more people like Watson around than Holmes, they would identify with me rather than with him!'

Any reservations that David might have had about partnering Jeremy Brett were also very quickly dispelled. 'We got on well right from the start,' says David. 'Jeremy was as anxious to make Holmes as much like the original as I was Watson, so our objectives were similar and we were both able to help each other in various ways.'

David was determined not to retreat into the giggles and shows of amazement which the earlier Watsons on screen had resorted to in order to make themselves evident. 'It was a problem, though, because the dialogue – 99 per cent of it – in the stories belongs to Holmes. In one story, *The Speckled Band,* for instance, I counted the number of words Watson actually spoke. It was 43!'

The adaptations provided David with a more substantial role, however, and he was naturally delighted at the reviews his performance attracted. In Britain, for instance, the *New Statesman* enthused, 'We can surely never have seen a better, milder, more intelligent and less stereotypical Doctor Watson than the one David Burke has given us.' While the *Daily Mail* said, 'Actor David Burke has transformed the image of a bumbling Doctor Watson to a razor-sharp detective'.

It was the same in America, too. The *Detroit Free Press* commenting, 'Burke has succeeded admirably in rescuing Doctor Watson from his long purgatory as Colonel Blimp' and the *Minneapolis Star* chipped in, 'Burke's character is, like the original, a patient observer and a keen student. Impressed by Holmes, certainly, but half his loyalty comes from a need to protect his lonely, occasionally cruel and somewhat fragile friend.'

David, though, particularly remembers a comment from his co-star after they had read a laudatory review in *The Times.* 'Jeremy turned to me in half-humorous consternation and said, "You realise we shouldn't show our faces in this country for two years, because they'll murder us!" What he meant was that in England people are terrified that if they praise you you'll get terribly big-headed, so if you do succeed they cut you down to size.

'He then said, "In America they believe in celebrating success, but I've gone home after a good first night in England to a boiled egg and a glass of milk!"'

As a result of his work on the series, David – who enjoys writing himself – became very interested in Sir Arthur Conan Doyle. 'My favourite story about him concerns the time a crime took place at his home. Now although the gardener who

WATSON,
THE OLD SOLDIER,
COMES INTO
HIS OWN IN
THE CASE OF
*THE
CROOKED
MAN.*

told him this news added that the criminal had *already* been arrested in the village, the old boy insisted that he must find his magnifying glass and go and search for clues himself in the grounds! He was obviously a man full of foibles!'

After playing Doctor Watson for 18 months, David decided he did not wish to make the second series, *The Return of Sherlock Holmes*. 'We were filming virtually solidly for 18 months in Manchester and I never saw my home and family,' he explains. (His family is actress, Anna Calder-Marshall, and they have a five-year-old son, Tom.) 'I had the chance to join the Royal Shakespeare Company at Stratford-on-Avon and appear with Anna, so I took it. It was marvellous fun to work with her and I had the added bonus of playing a real bastard in Maxim Gorky's *The Philistines* – something completely different from Watson!'

David does, though, remember his time as the good doctor with great affection – and always made a point of getting home from the theatre in time to watch the screening of the serial. 'If I have played some small part in refurbishing Watson's image then I count my work well done,' he says modestly.

Of that he may be in *no* doubt!

Edward Hardwicke who was offered the chance to fill the role of Doctor Watson in *The Return of Sherlock Holmes* found himself in a challenging though not altogether unenviable position.

'You see, I had seen David Burke playing Watson and my first reaction was, "Oh, God, have I got to follow that",' Edward recalls with a smile. 'He had been absolutely marvellous and I adored the stories. But we were friends and it was very much due to him that I came into the series, so I knew I had to grab the opportunity with both hands. The choice was made easier by the chance of working with Jeremy Brett, with whom I'd been at the National Theatre Company, though we had never actually worked in the same company.'

It was his work at the National which also encouraged Edward to believe he *could* fill the shoes another man had first worn. 'In my days at the National there was a lot of taking over roles from other actors,' he recalls, 'and I had my fair share of that. I used to think it was better if I had not seen the previous performance – the same feeling I first had about Sherlock Holmes.

'On the other hand, I remember Laurence Olivier calling me over when I was about to take on a new role and asked me if I had seen the earlier actor. I said I had not – to which he immediately replied, "Well, go and see him and be sure to pinch the best bits." He then listed the bits he wanted me to pinch and reassured me by saying that he had done something similar when he was a young man. "Never be afraid of stealing!" was what he told me.'

Edward, who is a dapper, grey-haired, quietly-spoken man, has strong connections with Sherlock Holmes which made his casting all the more appropriate. He is the son of the distinguished British stage and film actor, Sir Cedric Hardwicke, who not only played Sherlock Holmes on the radio (with Finlay Currie as his Watson) but when he settled in Hollywood became a close friend of Nigel Bruce!

Edward has clear memories of his childhood in the film capital and of the screen Watson who used to come calling at his home. 'When my father arrived in Hollywood the first person to meet him was Nigel Bruce, an old friend from his London days. I was about eight or nine at the time, and I remember they were great, great friends. Nigel Bruce would come over to our house every weekend to play bridge and gossip about the colony of English actors who were living in

Hollywood,' he recalls.

'The English were as thick as thieves there at that time, playing polo and cricket. It was ludicrously over the top, really – because you couldn't have found anything as "English" as that even in the heart of the English stockbroker belt back home! I particularly remember the house that belonged to C. Aubrey Smith, the character actor who was also the captain of the cricket team. It was a black and white timbered place that I think he had had built specially. It was just like a piece of the Empire! I think all those people had worked themselves into being caricatures of what the Americans *thought* the English were like!'

Among the others of his father's friends was Basil Rathbone: and although the two men actually appeared in the war-time film called *Wing and a Prayer* – which also included Nigel Bruce in the cast – Edward has no clear memories of the famous screen Holmes.

'I had read the Sherlock Holmes stories when I was young,' he says, 'but I must confess that I did not remember them that well, and I had to re-read everything when the Granada offer came up. My image of the stories was also affected by what I remembered of the Basil Rathbone and Nigel Bruce films, and so I had to go right back to the basics before filming started,' he says.

'Jeremy was absolutely marvellous helping me into the part. He is such a talented actor, and right from the very beginning he was always thinking of new ways of developing the relationship between Holmes and Watson – pushing it into new directions. This I found immensely stimulating.'

Edward brought a wealth of experience of his own to the role of Watson, having made his acting debut at the tender age of seven at the Malvern Festival in 1939. His father believed that acting was bound to be his profession, and in his delightful autobiography – or 'Irreverent Memoirs' as he called them – *A Victorian In Orbit* (1961), Sir Cedric wrote, 'I suppose Edward was doomed to be an actor. Barry Jackson was his godfather.'

Among Sir Cedric's friends was the great writer, George Bernard Shaw, who once said, 'You are my fifth favourite actor – the other four being the Marx Brothers.' Shaw was also one of the people Sir Cedric asked to contribute to a leather-bound 'Birthday Book' in which the actor invited all the famous people he met to inscribe words of advice to Edward. Among the people who wrote messages were Henry Ford ('Learn by doing'), Walt Disney ('May your conscience be your guide'), H. G. Wells ('Consider all the advice you're getting in this book and take none of it'), and Eugene O'Neill ('May your career be as brilliant as your father's').

Edward has retained the book to this day – now himself asking the famous people he meets to inscribe it for his children – yet the words of Shaw remain the most familiar: 'Don't go on the stage, Edward. You would only be Cedric Hardwicke's son at best; and it's a precarious profession anyhow.'

Edward remembers that his father added wryly to this, 'The words of Shaw went straight to the point, as usual. They were also entirely unheeded, as they often were!'

The younger Hardwicke in fact learnt his craft the hard way after graduating from the Royal Academy of Dramatic Art, playing seasons at the Bristol Old Vic and at the Oxford and Nottingham Playhouses before joining the National Theatre Company in 1964. He appeared there with Laurence Olivier in *The Master Builder*.

As well as the stage, Edward has also appeared in several film roles – including *A Flea In Her Ear* with Rex Harrison and *Matter of Honour* with Nicol Williamson, both co-starring Rachel Roberts – and on television where he was seen in *Time for Murder* and the ITV series *Drummonds* before joining *The Return of Sherlock Holmes*.

It is no surprise to learn that Edward, like his father before him, has a great interest in the Victorian era, and is full of admiration for the way Jeremy Brett has captured an important element of Victorian stagecraft in his portrayal of Sherlock Holmes.

He explains it like this. 'In Victorian times – the same period in which Conan Doyle wrote the Holmes stories – there were no microphones in the theatres and the lighting was also very bad. This meant that actors had to do something enormous to reach the audience at the back. Nowadays, we would regard such grand gestures as strange, and we have replaced them with what I might call "naturalistic acting". In other words, in a television play it is possible for the actors to signal things in a quite natural way and the audience is so close as to catch every nuance. You can even turn the sound down and understand what is happening from the gestures.

'What Jeremy has done is to quite consciously bring that Victorian "signalling" back into what is a most difficult medium for it, television, and make it totally real. I don't know how he does it, but his performance for me is an extraordinary and magical evocation of the period in which the stories are set,' he adds.

Edward has himself brought a new dimension to Watson as an older man. He is wise in the ways of the world, deeply understanding of his friend and the pressures which drive him, yet at the same time resolute in his own convictions and opinions. It is a performance strong on understatement and wholly believable.

Despite all the praise that he has received, Edward cherishes one compliment above all others. 'It was paid to me by a make-up girl not long after I had taken over the role,' he says. 'Quite unconsciously, as she was working on my face, she called me "David". She apologized and seemed genuinely surprised when I replied, "Don't be sorry – I regard that as a great compliment". It's happened four times in all, and it convinced me I had fitted into the role of Doctor Watson with barely a seam showing. And what actor could ask more?'

What indeed – and the compliment has been well-earned.

The achievement of David Burke and Edward Hardwicke has been a major one: for Doctor John H. Watson will never seem quite the same again after their interpretations. They have, in my opinion, restored to the good man the esteem in which Sherlock Holmes himself held him and which he expressed so vividly in these words in *The Hound of the Baskervilles*:

'I am bound to say that in all the accounts which you have been so good as to give of my own small achievements you have habitually underrated your own abilities. It may be that you are not yourself luminous, but you are a conductor of light. Some people without possessing genius have a remarkable power of stimulating it.'

What higher compliment can one man pay another?

EDWARD HARDWICKE WHO
COMPLETED THE TRANSFORMATION OF
WATSON'S IMAGE IN
THE EMPTY HOUSE.

A SKETCH OF
BASIL RATHBONE AND NIGEL BRUCE
AS HOLMES AND WATSON
FROM *PUNCH*, JULY 1939.

ONE OF THE MANY *PUNCH*
CARTOONS TO FEATURE
*THE HOUND OF
THE BASKERVILLES*
(NOVEMBER 17, 1982).

THOUGHTS ON SEEING *THE HOUND OF THE BASKERVILLES* AT THE CINEMA

"GOOD HEAVENS, WATSON, I FEAR WE MAY BE TOO LATE!"

This extraordinary poem is the earliest that I know of to express dissatisfaction at the way Watson was traditionally depicted on the screen. It was written in July 1939 by E. V. Knox, the editor of *Punch*, who was an admirer of the Sherlock Holmes stories, and – as he shows – less than happy with the latest Basil Rathbone and Nigel Bruce film version of the classic Dartmoor story . . .

'The stately Holmes of England, how beautiful he stood
Long, long ago in Baker Street – and still in Hollywood
He keeps the ancient flair for clues, the firm incisive chin,
The deerstalker, the dressing-gown, the shag, the violin.

But Watson, Doctor Watson! How altered, how betrayed
The fleet of foot, the warrior once, the faster than Lestrade!
What imbecile production, what madness of the moon
Has screened my glorious Watson as well nigh a buffoon?

Is this the face that went with Holmes on half a hundred trips
Through nights of rain, by gig, by train, are these the eyes, the lips?
These goggling eyes, these stammering lips, can these reveal the mind
How strong to tread where duty led, his practice cast behind?

His not to reason why nor doubt the great detective's plan –
The butt, maybe, of repartee yet still the perfect man,
Brave as the British lion is brave, brave as the buffalo,
What do they know of England who do not Watson know?

We have not many Sherlocks to sift the right from wrong
When evil stalks amongst us and craft and crime are strong,
Let not the Watsons fail us, the men of bull-dog mould,
Where still beneath the tight frock-coat beats on the heart of gold.

Watson, who dared the Demon Hound nor asked for fame nor fee,
Thou should'st be living at this hour. England hath need of thee!'
Thus did I muse and muse aloud while wondering at the flick
Till people near me turned and said, 'Shut up, you make us sick!'

THE MYSTERY
❦ OF ❦
WATSON'S
DOG

An Old Controversy Reopened

A review of *The Copper Beeches* adventure when it was screened in August 1985 re-opened one of the most puzzling of all Holmesian puzzles – the mystery of Doctor Watson's bull-pup.

The matter was started by the *Guardian* critic, Nancy Banks-Smith in her review of August 25 entitled, 'The hounded of the Baskervilles.'

'Talking of bulldogs,' she wrote, 'I don't know if you share my growing conviction that Conan Doyle was not a dog man. A dog has only to raise its handsome head in Doyle to have its brains blown out. *The Hound of the Baskervilles* (as large as a small lioness) got five barrels in the flank from Holmes. The mastiff in *The Copper Beeches* (as large as a calf) was as affable a dog as ever wagged its tail ingratiatingly at a cameraman (straight between the ears) and what about Watson's bull pup?

'When he first met Holmes, Watson mentioned he owned a bull pup (size unspecified) because these things can be accounted a flaw in a fellow lodger. "Oh, that's all right," said Holmes, "with a merry laugh". Ha, ha, indeed. Do we ever see hair nor hide of that dog again? We do not. Undoubtedly it fell victim to Holmes' reckless target practice.'

Michael Cox was as intrigued as anyone by this reference and put pen to paper to the Editor of *The Guardian*.

'Sir,' he said, 'Nancy Banks-Smith has re-opened one of the great Sherlockian mysteries – what became of Watson's bull pup. Jack Tracy, an American Holmes scholar, states that, "To keep a bull pup, in Anglo-Indian slang, means to have fits of quick temper". But there are no bull pups in *Partridge* to support this view so

Holmes remains suspected of foul play. Can anyone clear his name?'

This plea brought two immediate replies to the newspaper. Kevin Jacklin, writing from Emsworth in Hampshire, offered these thoughts: 'I'm afraid the evidence is black for Sherlock Holmes with regard to the disappearance of Watson's bull pup. Several Holmesian scholars have tried to explain away the missing dog as a military term for a rifle or a small calibre revolver (no doubt also missing from the relevant reference work). Others have suggested that the pup is a fiction of Watson's to put Holmes on his guard (bearing in mind his weakened condition from the effects of the infamous Jezail bullet). Elsewhere there are hints that Mrs Hudson objected to a pet in her house; or even that the dog was the unfortunate victim of Watson's stumbling on the stair to 221B.

'However, it is Watson himself who gives the game away by reminding us of the fact that Holmes was bitten on the ankle by a bull terrier whilst still a student at college. I am therefore forced to the conclusion that the pup reminded Holmes of this incident and that it was either ordered away or was used as target practice for Holmes' revolver.'

Steve Duffy, of Betws-yn-Rhos in Clwyd had a still more ingenious suggestion to offer. 'If we assume,' he wrote, 'that Watson has a grown bull-terrier which, out of affection, he refers to as a bull pup, the solution to the mystery may be found in *A Study In Scarlet*. Holmes has two pills which he believes to be poisonous. Rather than utilise his "profound" knowledge of chemistry in analysing the pills, he suggests that Watson bring up "that poor little devil of a terrier . . . which the landlady wanted you to put out of its pain yesterday". One of the pills proves fatal to the dog.'

Some readers, however, may have felt the *Guardian*'s cartoonist made the most succinct comment of all on the mystery with his sketch reproduced here!

THE FALL *OF* MORIARTY

‘The most frightening TV sequence ever made’

DAILY MIRROR

SIDNEY PAGET

THE CLASSIC 1893 *STRAND* MAGAZINE ILLUSTRATION OF
THE DEATH OF SHERLOCK HOLMES – AND (OPPOSITE) THE GRANADA
RECONSTRUCTION IN 1985.

PROFESSOR
MORIARTY
AS DRAWN BY
SIDNEY PAGET –
AND
ERIC PORTER'S
SUPERB
INTERPRETATION.

The spectacular fall of Holmes and Moriarty down the Reichenbach Falls which climaxed the story of *The Final Problem* at the end of *The Adventures of Sherlock Holmes* was widely hailed as one of the most breath-taking stunts ever seen on television. Indeed, the *Daily Mirror* of September 28, 1985 warned its readers, 'Get ready to see one of the most frightening television sequences ever made when Sherlock Holmes and Professor Moriarty battle it out on the edge of the Reichenbach Falls in Switzerland.'

It was a spectacular moment in the series – and one that proved as memorable for the actors who were *nearly* involved, Jeremy Brett and Eric Porter (playing Moriarty), as it was for the two stuntmen, Alf Joint and Marc Boyle, who actually *were*!

Byron Rogers, of the *Sunday Times*, who watched from the safety of his television armchair, afterwards called it 'the best fall ever filmed, much better than Butch Cassidy and Sundance, whirling arms in the spray, capes flapping. God knows how they did it.'

These sentiments were echoed precisely by Jeremy Brett who told me later, 'The event quite unnerved me. Eric and I had to film our part of the struggle about eight feet from the edge of the falls – and that was bad enough because every time I looked down I felt quite sick.'

Before the actual stunt, a dummy figure was dropped down the Falls by the film crew as a test. The party – stuntmen included – watched as the figure smashed into the cliff, lost its head, and disappeared into the torrent.

'How those two men went over the edge I'll never know,' Jeremy added. 'You should have seen their bruises the next day!'

The story of the making of this breath-taking reconstruction of perhaps the most famous moment in Sherlock Holmes' history is, I believe, well worth the telling.

Professor James Moriarty is, of course, the genius of crime, 'the organiser of half that is evil and nearly all that is undetected in London'. Though he in fact only appears in two of the stories about Sherlock Holmes, such was the impact of the 'Napoleon of crime' that he instantly caught the public imagination and has never lost this grip. His fame, indeed, is little short of that of Holmes himself.

In Moriarty, Conan Doyle created a villain worthy to test the metal of Sherlock Holmes, and it is not really to be wondered at that the author felt him to be the one man capable of ridding him of Holmes.

Certainly this is the view of Eric Porter, one of the most famous and distinguished of British actors, and now the latest man to play Holmes' arch-enemy.

'I suspect Conan Doyle knew it would take no ordinary man to kill off Sherlock

THE TWO STUNT MEN WHO PERFORMED THE DRAMATIC PLUNGE OF HOLMES AND MORIARTY, ALF JOINT AND MARC BOYLE.

Holmes,' says Eric Porter. 'And even though he created a super-criminal to carry out what he hoped would be the execution, he had not bargained for the incredible reaction of the British public.'

The chance to play Moriarty was an opportunity that Eric Porter accepted without a second thought. 'He is such an incredibly complex figure – in his way every bit as obsessed and driven as Holmes – that even on the brief canvas of his appearance in *The Final Problem* there are still endless opportunities for an actor to pursue.

'I have always felt some of the performances of the earlier Moriartys lacked any real depth. He was just played as an unregenerate villain without any attempt to show the real motivations of ego and pride that drove him to the confrontation with Holmes to prove which of them was the better man.

'I found acting with Jeremy Brett a splendid challenge, too, for he was so deeply involved with Holmes that he understood every nerve and fibre of the man. I like to think I gave a good account of Moriarty – though like Jeremy I could hardly bear to watch the two stunt men going over the cliffs.

'In fact we had all our time cut out trying to keep our feet on the ledge where we were acting, for the spray from the falls made everything terribly slippery. I can tell you I was very relieved to finish that scene and get back on firmer ground again!' he adds.

Filming of the struggle on the rocky outcrop beside the 430 foot falls took place at the end of September 1984. When Jeremy Brett and Eric Porter had completed their part of the battle against the background of the huge wall of plunging white water, they both gratefully handed the final dramatic fall over to two of Britain's most accomplished stunt men, Alf Joint and Marc Boyle.

Alf, at 53, is the country's top 'high man' – a stunt artist who will undertake dives or falls from extreme heights – and has most recently been seen diving 161 feet into the sea off Malta for a Cadbury's Milk Tray TV commercial. Marc, who is 40, specializes in doubling for actors like Charles Bronson in his *Death Wish* films. In *The Final Problem*, Alf played Moriarty and Marc Boyle, Holmes.

It was one of the biggest – and costliest – gambles that Michael Cox took to film the scene at the actual spot where the death struggle was supposed to have taken place.

The two stuntmen arranged the fall with engineer Dave Bickers, an ex-world champion motorcross rider. Each was suspended by lengths of thin steel cable fixed to harnesses under their clothes and run from a specially built winch on a platform at the top of the falls.

Then, just far enough away from the cameras so that their features could not be

ON LOCATION IN SWITZERLAND –
A LIGHT-HEARTED MOMENT FOR JEREMY BRETT
AND DAVID BURKE WHO, APPROPRIATELY,
STAYED AT THE SHERLOCK HOLMES HOTEL!

JEREMY BRETT AND DAVID BURKE
PHOTOGRAPHED BEFORE THE REICHENBACH FALLS.

A 'WEATHERPROOFED'
ERIC PORTER AWAITS HIS CALL TO FILM.

recognized, the two men were dropped spiralling and twisting down the precipice at a little over 30 miles per hour.

'That may not sound very fast,' Alf says with self-depreciating modesty, 'but it is about the speed of a parachute descent. Mind you, if the wire had snapped, or our harnesses had slipped, or the platform had collapsed, that would have been the end for us!

'It actually took about 25 seconds to make the fall,' he continues. 'As we dropped we had to pretend to wrestle and flail our arms about. We fell about 375 feet and were then stopped by the wires just a few feet short of the water.'

Alf gave a small grin when he added, 'We did ache a bit all over afterwards – but that was soon put right by the bottle of champagne that Jeremy cracked open for us!'

Jeremy Brett and the rest of the crew understandably greeted the two men like heroes when they were back on *terra firma* once more. And Granada also acknowledged their achievement later by listing their names in the credits for *The Final Problem.*

Both men were naturally pleased to have successfully made a little piece of Holmesian history – as well as living to collect their fees of around £2,500 each.

Alf even still found enough of his good humour to admit to a journalist, Paul Donovan, in an interview that he was not altogether without fear. In fact, he said, he was terrified of spiders! 'I know people who've had black widows and bird eating spiders crawl over them,' he said, 'but it's the one thing I *couldn't* do!'

Jeremy Brett has a couple of other lasting memories from the two-month period making *The Final Problem.* 'Being made up as the priest with the long nose took over two hours,' he recalls. 'But that wasn't what bothered me. I had to be sure to rip it off correctly when we were shooting or I'd have been faced with *another* two hours to put it right!'

'We were lucky there, but it took six takes to get the fight with Moriarty on the edge of the precipice right. It was a terrible strain on my back because Eric weighs 13 stone when he's dry and 14 stone *wet!*

'I remember thinking to myself as we slithered around in the mud and grass, soaked by spray, that if we were not very careful we might actually fall over the edge and then Conan Doyle would have got his wish after all.

'There really would have been *no* return for Sherlock Holmes!'

THE SPECTACULAR STUNT FALL BY ALF JOINT AND
MARC BOYLE FOR *THE FINAL PROBLEM*.

SEBASTIAN MORAN
(PATRICK ALLEN).

IRENE ADLER
(GAYLE HUNNICUTT).

PROFESSOR MORIARTY
(ERIC PORTER).

CHARLES GRAY AS
SHERLOCK'S BROTHER,
MYCROFT HOLMES.

THE INDEFATIGABLE
INSPECTOR LESTRADE,
PLAYED BY
COLIN JEAVONS.

HOLMES WITH
HIS 'NEW' WATSON,
EDWARD HARDWICKE.

AT WORK IN 221B ON
THE EMPTY HOUSE.

HOLMES AS AN
ELDERLY BOOKSELLER
MEETS WATSON
AGAIN IN
THE EMPTY HOUSE.

THE BEAUTIFUL PATRICIA HODGE
WITH HOLMES AND WATSON IN
THE SECOND STAIN.

ANOTHER SECRET REVEALED IN
THE MUSGRAVE RITUAL –
HOW HOLMES AND WATSON
ARE *REALLY* TAKEN FOR A RIDE!

A SPECIALLY
POSED PORTRAIT OF
HOLMES AND WATSON
FOR USE IN THE
AMERICAN PROMOTION
OF THE SERIES.

AFTERWORD:
❦ I ❦

by David Burke

When Granada TV, in the shape of my old friend Michael Cox, asked me to play Doctor Watson, I was very pleased (the heart of the jobbing actor always beats a little faster at the mention of a TV series), but also a little worried. I went to my wife and told her I had reservations about playing a man who had serious claims to be the most ordinary character in English literature.

'I wouldn't know how to play him,' I said.

She turned to me with genuine puzzlement and said, 'What's your problem? It's you to a tee!'

In the succeeding days her opinion was confirmed when several of my friends shook me warmly by the hand and swore that simply no other person could play the part as well as me. Since then I have had to live with the terrible truth that I was born to play Doctor Watson. The sacks of congratulatory mail which I have received since the series was shown have merely confirmed this.

Consider the effect of this on the mind of a serious and sensitive actor (who has given his Othello twice): to be at the top of everyone's list to play Mr Pooter in *The Diary Of A Nobody*. However, I have always prided myself on being a practical, pragmatic sort of person; a realist and a stoic. So I got on with it and played the good doctor for 18 months of my life.

Of course, it was child's play: I needed to change only clothes, my mind stayed exactly where it was. Indeed, I barely needed to think. I never consciously learned my lines: I opened my mouth, and the correct words uttered themselves. I leave the reader to decide whether this is a case of arrogance or humility.

If Doctor Watson is very like me, it is also true that lots of people are very like Doctor Watson, which has much to do with his success. It is difficult to identify with Sherlock Holmes unless you are brilliant, neurotic and highly successful. It is easy to find common ground with Watson. I believe he had more in common with his creator than Holmes had, and I have a true story to support this contention.

A couple of years ago I became acquainted with an old man who had, in his youth, been Sir Arthur Conan Doyle's gardener. He told me that one day the house was burgled – nothing serious, but something had quite clearly been stolen. Before anyone could shout, 'Stop thief!', Sir Arthur was on his hands and knees with his magnifying glass, checking doors and windows, and poking about in the flower beds. Two hours later he was still hard at it, when the local constable walked up the drive and announced that he had arrested the thief – a well-known local mischief-maker! Sir Arthur had been trying very hard to be Sherlock Holmes, but ended up looking much more like Watson.

In reality, the claims made for the genius of Sherlock Holmes will not stand up to more than superficial examination. His famous reasoning is full of wild surmises and shaky logic. It is only because the all-powerful author is on his side that it leads to a successful conclusion. In any case, I am convinced that it is not the detective side of the stories or even the thriller element which makes them last. It is because they are the story of a great friendship; an odd couple who formed a highly successful partnership by complementing each other.

By a curious coincidence (or maybe it was inevitable), the remarkable thing which I gained from acting Doctor Watson was the close friendship of the man who played Sherlock Holmes. It is as well that Jeremy Brett and I did become close friends, since we were obliged to live in each other's pockets for several months. We would meet in the make-up room about 7 am, and after a day's filming, frequently bid each other a convivial good-night around midnight after an excellent meal in the Midland Hotel in Manchester.

We laughed a good deal at and with each other. My favourite story of Jeremy à la Sherlock Holmes concerns the perfectionism which they shared. We were shooting a scene one day, and Jeremy had several times stopped a take going ahead in order to make some small but significant adjustment to some detail of set or costume, ending up removing a stray hair from the coat of one of the extras who was standing in the background. At last we went ahead with the take, the director shouted 'Cut!' and Jeremy relaxed.

'Jeremy!' I said. 'You had your hat on back to front!' It was true! It was some minutes before we stopped laughing.

I can still laugh at that perfectionism, and yet, if I had to pick out one element which contributed more than any other to the success of the series, it would be that. Jeremy was determined that the series should succeed, and that it should succeed by being faithful to the original in spirit and in detail. He carried the *Complete Stories* around like a Bible. When we finished, that book was almost falling apart, so often had it been thumbed through to check a line or a detail of scenery. In this he was aided and abetted by Michael Cox and, I am happy to say, by myself.

When it was all over, we three sat down to a celebratory and valedictory lunch in Manchester. Michael said he would like to propose a toast.

'It's a favourite of mine,' he said, with a twinkle in his eye. I think he said that it was a favourite of Bulldog Drummond's also. We raised our glasses.

'Here's to us,' said Michael. 'Those like us. Damn few!'

We all laughed, but we all drank, and I know that we did feel the genuine warm glow of a worthwhile job taken up and done just about as well as it could be done.

AFTERWORD:
❦II❦

by Edward Hardwicke

I was sitting at home not so long ago viewing one of those American cop series on television. It was *Starsky and Hutch*, I recall, and as I sat watching the two young men painstakingly tracking down a criminal, I suddenly became conscious of a rather extraordinary fact.

Those two partners – and all the other crime and detection stories on television and in books that have a pair of crime investigators working together – have their basis in Sherlock Holmes and his friend, Doctor Watson.

Indeed, the longer I watched, the stronger the similarities seemed to become. For all the stories like *Starsky and Hutch* start and end as the Holmes and Watson adventures do: with a discussion about the crime concerned and a little insight into their relationship.

I would not claim for one minute that all the characters in these stories represent the same aspect as the two originals, but theirs are exactly the same kind of friendships-in-law.

Making *The Return of Sherlock Holmes* was a great joy for me, not only because of my father, Sir Cedric Hardwicke's association with the stories through playing Holmes in *The Adventure of the Speckled Band* for BBC radio in 1945, and also being a great friend of Nigel Bruce – but because of having the chance to co-star with Jeremy Brett. His is a superb Holmes, and working with him was much as I imagine it must have been with one of the great Victorian Actor Managers.

For Jeremy generates such a feeling of team spirit on the set that everyone – not only the actors, but also those working behind the cameras – want to do their best for him. The resulting shows have been a success that I am sure must have been beyond most people's dreams.

It was also a fascinating experience taking over the role of Doctor Watson from my friend, David Burke, who made such a wonderful job of changing the traditional view of Watson as a bit of an old fool. That idea certainly does not equate with a person of whom Sherlock Holmes says in *The Hound of the Baskervilles*, 'There is no man who is better worth having at your side when you are in a tight place. No one can say so more confidently than I.'

And no one can say more confidently than *I* that although Sherlock Holmes will undoubtedly return to the screen again and again in the future with fresh actors in the leading roles – for such is his timeless and enduring appeal – the effect of this particular series will not, I believe, be forgotten.

Edward Hardwicke

❧APPENDIX❧

The Plots
and Credits
for

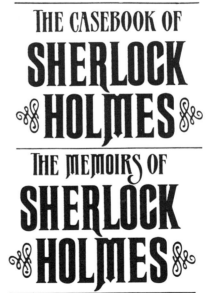

THE ADVENTURES OF SHERLOCK HOLMES

THE CASEBOOK OF SHERLOCK HOLMES

THE RETURN OF SHERLOCK HOLMES

THE MEMOIRS OF SHERLOCK HOLMES

BETSY BRANTLEY AND TENNIEL EVANS
AS THE CUBITTS IN
THE DANCING MEN.

GAYLE HUNNICUTT AS IRENE ADLER –
'THE' WOMAN – WITH WATSON AND A DISGUISED
HOLMES IN *A SCANDAL IN BOHEMIA*.

THE ADVENTURES OF SHERLOCK HOLMES

by Sir Arthur Conan Doyle
Developed for television by John Hawkesworth
Producer MICHAEL COX
Associate Producer STUART DOUGHTY
Music PATRICK GOWERS

FIRST SERIES

A SCANDAL IN BOHEMIA

Dramatized by Alexander Baron

The opening story of the series introduced the two most important women in Sherlock Holmes' life – Irene Adler 'the' woman, and Mrs Hudson, the faithful housekeeper at 221B. The American actress, Gayle Hunnicutt, played the New Jersey-born opera singer and adventuress with a 'soul of steel' who is at the centre of a scandal in Royal circles and outwits Holmes for one of the few times in his life. Playing Mrs Hudson very much in the style of the original was Rosalie Williams, who said, 'I see her as very firm, but understanding, almost a maternal presence. She has come down in the world, and is a lady with dignity'. And she added, 'In everybody's mind she is a strong character – but in fact she has no more than 20 lines in the whole saga. That is not much to build a character upon.' Nevertheless, Rosalie *did* build a memorable character, and enjoyed her work on the series as it reunited her with Jeremy Brett with whom she had worked when he was beginning his career at Manchester's Library Theatre.

Sherlock Holmes .... JEREMY BRETT
Doctor Watson ...... DAVID BURKE
Irene Adler .... GAYLE HUNNICUTT
King of Bohemia .... WOLF KAHLER
Godfrey Norton . MICHAEL CARTER
Mrs Hudson ... ROSALIE WILLIAMS
John .... MAX FAULKNER
Mrs Willard ...... TESSA WORSLEY
Clergyman .... WILL TACEY
Cabby .... TIM PEARCE

Designers .... MICHAEL GRIMES
MARGARET COOMBES
TIM WILDING
Director .... PAUL ANNETT

First shown on ITV Network on April 24, 1984 at 9 pm

BETSY BRANTLEY AS ELSIE CUBBIT AND TENNIEL EVANS AS HER HUSBAND
IN THE CASE OF *THE DANCING MEN*.

THE DANCING MEN
Dramatized by Anthony Skene

A second American lady also appeared in the next adventure, with Sherlock
Holmes and Doctor Watson called to Norfolk to solve the puzzle of some white
chalk figures drawn on a sundial. Playing Elsie Cubitt, the lady terrified by the
implications of these matchstick men, was Betsy Brantley from North Carolina,
who came to Britain to study Shakespeare and ended up in the National Theatre
and films. Betsy found an immediate affinity with her part as, like Elsie, she is 'an
American who travelled about and decided to settle in England'. During filming
she also recalled that, 'Sherlock Holmes was always my holiday reading as a
child'.

Sherlock Holmes	JEREMY BRETT	Inspector Martin	DAVID ROSS
Doctor Watson	DAVID BURKE	Walker	PAUL JAYNES
Hilton Cubitt	TENNIEL EVANS	Doctor Carthew	BERNARD ATHA
Elsie Cubitt	BETSY BRANTLEY		
Abe Slaney	EUGENE LIPINSKI		
Saunders	WENDY JANE WALKER	Designer	MICHAEL GRIMES
Mrs King	LORRAINE PETERS	Director	JOHN BRUCE

First shown on ITV Network on May 1, 1984 at 9 pm

202

THE NAVAL TREATY
Dramatized by Jeremy Paul

The dramatic case of a secret document that has gone missing while being copied causes the unfortunate clerk, Percy Phelps (David Gwillim) to call for the help of Holmes and Watson to recover it. By coincidence, David Gwillim, the son of character actor, Jack Gwillim, lived in a house similar to the one at Woking where the story is set – although location work was actually done in Cheshire! 'I was able to spend the time when I was not filming walking,' David recalled later. 'One weekend I completed 50 miles – no wonder poor Percy looked so pale!' Alison Skilbeck who played Percy's fiancée has vivid memories of filming her part in stifling Victorian clothes during the long hot summer of 1983, and she admits she had a tendency to think of the story as 'The Navy Lark'!

ALISON SKILBECK AS ANNIE HARRISON COMFORTS HER FIANCÉ, PERCY (DAVID GWILLIM) WHILE HOLMES AND WATSON LISTEN TO HIS ACCOUNT OF THE MISSING *NAVAL TREATY*.

Sherlock Holmes ..	JEREMY BRETT	Mrs Tangey	PAMELA PITCHFORD
Doctor Watson	DAVID BURKE	Tangey	JOHN MALCOLM
Percy Phelps ...	DAVID GWILLIM	Inspector Forbes	DAVID RODIGAN
Doctor Ferrier	JOHN TAYLOR	Miss Tangey	EVE MATHESON
Annie Harrison	ALISON SKILBECK	Mrs Hudson ..	ROSALIE WILLIAMS
Joseph Harrison	GARETH THOMAS		
Lord Holdhurst	RONALD RUSSELL	Designer ..	MARGARET COOMBES
Charles Gorot ..	NICHOLAS GEAKE	Director	ALAN GRINT

First shown on ITV Network on May 8, 1984 at 9 pm

THE SOLITARY CYCLIST
Dramatized by Alan Plater

The fourth story centred around the music teacher, Violet Smith, who finds whenever she cycles to and from Chiltern Grange near Farnham to give music lessons to the daughter of a widower, Mr Robert Carruthers, she is followed by a mysterious man on a bicycle. When Watson is unable to solve the puzzle, and then Carruthers proposes marriage to Miss Smith, Holmes himself thinks it is time to look into the matter. Barbara Wilshere played Violet and John Castle was Carruthers.

Sherlock Holmes ... JEREMY BRETT
Doctor Watson .... DAVID BURKE
Violet Smith   BARBARA WILSHERE
Carruthers .... JOHN CASTLE
Woodley ..... MICHAEL SIBERRY
Williamson .... ELLIS DALE
Sarah Carruthers
                SARAH AITCHISON
Landlord ... STAFFORD GORDON
Peter .... SIMON BLEACKLEY
Mrs Hudson . ROSALIE WILLIAMS
Mrs Dixon .... PENNY GOWLING

Designer ...... MICHAEL GRIMES
Director .... PAUL ANNETT

BARBARA WILSHERE AS VIOLET SMITH WHO IS FOLLOWED BY THE MYSTERIOUS FIGURE ON A BICYCLE IN *THE SOLITARY CYCLIST*.

First shown on ITV Network on May 15, 1984 at 9 pm

THE CROOKED MAN
Dramatized by Alfred Shaughnessy

Doctor Watson is asked to bring Holmes to investigate the mysterious death of Colonel James Barclay at Aldershot and the scandal that has blown up and is threatening the good name of the Royal Mallows regiment. At the heart of the mystery lies the 'Crooked Man' of the title (played by Norman Jones) and the terrible feeling of betrayal that has obsessed him for years. Lisa Daniely, who appeared as the unfortunate Colonel's wife, was actually the daughter of a war-time Army Colonel, though before the film she had never been to Aldershot! She particularly enjoyed the role of a 'put-upon' wife because, as she explained, 'I usually play ladies who are strong and sexy.'

THE STRANGE FIGURE OF
THE CROOKED MAN
PLAYED BY NORMAN JONES.

Sherlock Holmes .. JEREMY BRETT
Doctor Watson .... DAVID BURKE
Henry Wood .... NORMAN JONES
Young Henry Wood
         MICHAEL LUMSDEN
Col. James Barclay
         DENYS HAWTHORNE
Young James Barclay JAMES WILBY
Nancy Barclay ..... LISA DANIELY
Young Nancy Barclay
         CATHERINE RABETT
Major Murphy .. PAUL CHAPMAN
Miss Morrison ...... FIONA SHAW
Jane ... SHELAGH STEPHENSON
Bates .... COLIN CAMPBELL
Mrs Fenning .. MAGGIE HOLLAND

Designer .. MARGARET COOMBES
Director .... ALAN GRINT

First shown on ITV Network on May 22, 1984 at 9 pm

THE SPECKLED BAND
Dramatized by Jeremy Paul

The sixth episode introduced the overbearing Doctor Grimesby Roylott (played by Jeremy Kemp) in the gruesome story of death in a Surrey mansion. Holmes ignores Roylott's threats not to meddle in his affairs and finally confronts the 'speckled band' of the title – a deadly snake. Rosalyn Landor, who played Helen Stoner, Roylott's stepdaughter, admitted she had not read the story before filming and did not know *what* she would have to confront. 'But I was brave enough to have my photograph taken with the snake!' she said afterwards. During filming, the snake became affectionately known among the crew as 'Kevin' – 'after a director we all knew,' one of them explained with a smile.

JEREMY KEMP AS THE HOT-TEMPERED DOCTOR GRIMESBY ROYLOTT AT THE HEART OF THE MYSTERY OF *THE SPECKLED BAND*.

Sherlock Holmes ..	JEREMY BRETT	Mrs Hudson .	ROSALIE WILLIAMS
Doctor Watson	DAVID BURKE	Thorne	TIMOTHY CONDREN
Doctor Grimesby Roylott		Percy Armitage	
	JEREMY KEMP		STEPHEN MALLATRATT
Helen Stoner ...	ROSALYN LANDOR		
Julia Stoner	DENISE ARMON	Designer	MICHAEL GRIMES
Driver	JOHN GILL	Director	JOHN BRUCE

First shown on ITV Network on May 29, 1984 at 9 pm

HOLMES AND WATSON WITH PETERSON (FRANK MILLS) EXAMINE THE JEWEL KNOWN AS *THE BLUE CARBUNCLE*.

THE BLUE CARBUNCLE
Dramatized by Paul Finney

The seventh, and last, story of the first series of *Adventures* was about a mysterious gem found in China which brings murder and suicide to those who come into contact with it. When the stone is stolen from its latest owner, the Countess of Morcar, and a man is arrested who protests his innocence, Holmes is drawn into the case to solve the mystery in his own inimitable way. Playing a key witness was Frank Middlemass, with Ken Campbell, Frank Mills and Rosalind Knight, the unfortunate Countess of Morcar, as co-stars.

Sherlock Holmes .. JEREMY BRETT
Doctor Watson .... DAVID BURKE
Inspector Bradstreet BRIAN MILLER
Mrs Hudson .. ROSALIE WILLIAMS
The Countess of Morcar
    ROSALIND KNIGHT
John Horner
    DESMOND McNAMARA
James Ryder .... KEN CAMPBELL
Catherine Cusack .. ROS SIMMONS

Henry Baker FRANK MIDDLEMASS
Windigate .DON McCORKINDALE
Jennie Horner .. AMELDA BROWN
Peterson .... FRANK MILLS
Breckenridge .... ERIC ALLAN
Mrs Oakshott .... MAGGIE JONES

Designer .... TIM WILDING
Director .... DAVID CARSON

First shown on ITV Network on June 5, 1984 at 9 pm

SECOND SERIES

THE COPPER BEECHES
Dramatized by Bill Craig

The second series of six *Adventures* started with a plaintive cry to Sherlock Holmes from young Violet Hunter, the governess to Mr Jephro Rucastle's small son, to come to her aid as she was at her wits' end. The fact that her employer has made Violet cut off her luxuriant chestnut hair before taking up the post, also intrigued the great detective. Starring as Violet was Natasha Richardson – the daughter of actress Vanessa Redgrave and director Tony Richardson – whose aunt, Lynn Redgrave, had co-starred with Jeremy Brett on Broadway during his summer break from the series. It was Natasha's first time before the cameras, and during filming she said, 'I just hope I can measure up to the achievements of my family – but they never pushed me into acting and I think my mother would rather I had been a doctor or something like that'. For the part she had to dye her hair red, but so enjoyed the role she said afterwards she was 'avidly reading all the other Sherlock Holmes stories'. The role of Jephro Rucastle was played by Joss Ackland.

Sherlock Holmes .. JEREMY BRETT
Doctor Watson .... DAVID BURKE
Violet Hunter
    NATASHA RICHARDSON
Jephro Rucastle ... JOSS ACKLAND
Mrs Rucastle ...... LOTTIE WARD
Edward Rucastle
    STUART SHINBERG
Fowler .... MICHAEL LONEY
Toller .... PETER JONFIELD
Mrs Toller .... ANGELA BROWNE
Miss Stoper ... PATIENCE COLLIER
Alice .... RACHEL AMBLER

Designer   MICHAEL GRIMES
Director .... PAUL ANNETT

NATASHA RICHARDSON
AS VIOLET HUNTER
IN THE
STRANGE CASE OF
THE COPPER BEECHES.

First shown on ITV Network on August 25, 1985 at 9.45 pm

HOLMES' BROTHER, THE REDOUBTABLE MYCROFT (PLAYED BY CHARLES GRAY), INVITES HIM TO TRY AND SOLVE THE MYSTERY OF *THE GREEK INTERPRETER*.

THE GREEK INTERPRETER
Dramatized by Derek Marlowe

The ninth story introduced Holmes' brother, the redoubtable Mycroft Holmes (played with great panache by Charles Gray) who invites Sherlock to try and solve the extraordinary case of a Greek interpreter and a man he was to cross-examine with sticking plaster all over his face! Cast as the interpreter was Alkis Kritikos who was unable to see himself in the part because he was on holiday when it was screened – in Greece, of course. 'But a friend in Greece did phone me later to say he'd seen the episode there – complete with subtitles,' Alkis said. 'He loved the whole thing, apparently!'

Sherlock Holmes .. JEREMY BRETT
Doctor Watson .... DAVID BURKE
Mycroft Holmes ... CHARLES GRAY
Mr Melas ...... ALKIS KRITIKOS
Wilson Kemp
        GEORGE COSTIGAN
Harold Latimer ...... NICK FIELD
Paul Kratides
        ANTON ALEXANDER

Sophy Kratides
        VICTORIA HARWOOD
Inspector Gregson .... OLIVER
        MAGUIRE
Mrs Stern .... RITA HOWARD
Ticket Inspector ..PETER MacKRIEL

Designer .. MARGARET COOMBES
Director .... ALAN GRINT

First shown on ITV Network on September 1, 1985 at 9.30 pm

210

THE NORWOOD BUILDER
Dramatized by Richard Harris

Enter Inspector Lestrade, the best known of the Scotland Yarders who feature in the stories of Sherlock Holmes. Lestrade (Colin Jeavons) has arrested a young solicitor named John McFarlane (Matthew Solon) who has unwittingly inherited the estate of a mysterious client found dead in a fire at Norwood. While Lestrade believes McFarlane is guilty of murder, Holmes does not – and sets out to prove why. A highlight of this episode was the fire scene and the authentic Shand Mason fire engine used to put it out – actually manned by members of the Manchester Fire Brigade in period costumes. Station Officer Bob Bonner and four of his colleagues enacted the drama complete with London Fire Brigade insignia and fibre-glass 'brass' helmets. The location was not Norwood, though, but Bowden in Cheshire!

A HEAVILY DISGUISED SHERLOCK HOLMES ATTEMPTS TO GET TO THE BOTTOM OF THE CASE OF *THE NORWOOD BUILDER.*

Sherlock Holmes .. JEREMY BRETT	Mrs McFarlane ..... HELEN RYAN
Doctor Watson .... DAVID BURKE	Mrs Hudson . ROSALIE WILLIAMS
Mrs Lexington	Constable ..... ANDY RASHLEIGH
ROSALIE CRUTCHLEY	Tramp .... ANTHONY LANGDON
Lestrade .... COLIN JEAVONS	Seafaring Tramp ... TED CARROLL
John Hector McFarlane	
MATTHEW SOLON	Designer .... TIM WILDING
Jonas Oldacre .. JONATHAN ADAMS	Director .... KEN GRIEVE

First shown on ITV Network on September 8, 1985 at 10.00 pm

THE RESIDENT PATIENT
Dramatized by Derek Marlowe

The eleventh story in the series told of a curious bargain. In return for three-quarters of all his fees, brilliant but impoverished Doctor Percy Trevelyan was given a West End practice by corpulent Mr Blessington. His benefactor also demanded constant attention – which proved no real problem until the poor man began to exhibit all the signs of being frightened out of his life – although he had not been attacked or lost any property. It was obviously a case for 'the best detective in England' – and once again Holmes' marvellous powers of deduction triumphed. Nicholas Clay played Doctor Trevelyan, with Patrick Newell as the terror-stricken benefactor.

Sherlock Holmes .. JEREMY BRETT
Doctor Watson .... DAVID BURKE
Blessington ... PATRICK NEWELL
Doctor Percy Trevelyan .. NICHOLAS CLAY
Mrs Hudson . ROSALIE WILLIAMS
Father (Biddle) ..... TIM BARLOW
Son (Hayward) .. BRETT FORREST
Cartwright ...... CHARLES CORK
Inspector Lanner . JOHN RINGHAM
Nora .... LUCY ANN WILSON
Detective .... NORMAN MILLS
Carpenter .... DUSTY YOUNG

Designer ...... MICHAEL GRIMES
Director .... DAVID CARSON

PATRICK NEWELL AS
MR BLESSINGTON
IN FEAR OF
HIS LIFE IN
THE RESIDENT PATIENT.

First shown on ITV Network on September 15, 1985 at 9.45 pm

JABEZ WILSON (ROGER HAMMOND),
THE MAN AT THE CENTRE OF THE PUZZLE OF *THE RED-HEADED LEAGUE*.

THE RED-HEADED LEAGUE

Dramatized by John Hawkesworth

The advertisement read, 'To the Red-Headed League. There is a vacancy open which entitles a member of the League to a salary of £4 a week for purely nominal services. All red-headed men sound in body and mind are eligible'. It seemed too good an opportunity for Jabez Wilson (Roger Hammond) to miss – but two months later after endlessly copying out the *Encyclopaedia Britannica*, he was so bewildered as to need the services of Sherlock Holmes. Although Roger Hammond has fair hair tinged with red, he required a 'wonderful wig and some cheerfully helpful period clothes' to play Wilson. The story also provided him with a reunion with Jeremy Brett – for he had been an assistant stage manager and actor at the Manchester Library Theatre when Jeremy was first there as a juvenile lead. Eric Porter also made an unexpected – and un-canonical appearance – as Professor Moriarty using his criminal genius to steal some French gold from a London bank. It was, though, merely a prelude to . . .

Sherlock Holmes .. JEREMY BRETT	Doorman .. REGINALD STEWART
Doctor Watson .... DAVID BURKE	Duncan Ross .. RICHARD WILSON
Mr Merryweather	Accountant ..... IAN BLEASDALE
JOHN WOODNUTT	Athelney Jones JOHN LABANOWSKI
Moriarty .... ERIC PORTER	Policeman ..... HARRY GOODIER
Jabez Wilson.. ROGER HAMMOND	
Vincent Spaulding (Clay)	Designer .. MARGARET COOMBES
TIM McINNERNY	Director .... JOHN BRUCE

First shown on ITV Network on September 22, 1985 at 9.45 pm

213

THE FINAL PROBLEM
Dramatized by John Hawkesworth

This famous story in which Conan Doyle originally intended to rid himself of Holmes proved a superb finale to the *Adventures of Sherlock Holmes*. Eric Porter was in outstanding form as 'the Napoleon of Crime' and the climactic duel between him and Holmes at the Reichenbach Falls was filmed for the very first time at the actual location by two highly dexterous and brave stuntmen. (See story elsewhere in this book.) While filming in Switzerland, the Granada team also shot scenes to be included in the new series which was already being planned. As Michael Cox said in a press statement, 'Just as Conan Doyle was forced by public pressure to bring back Holmes after his disappearance at Reichenbach, so we have decided to go ahead and make seven more stories for the viewers'. The only change would prove to be a new Doctor Watson . . .

Sherlock Holmes . . . . JEREMY BRETT
Doctor Watson . . . . DAVID BURKE
Professor Moriarty . . . . ERIC PORTER
Mrs Hudson . . . . ROSALIE WILLIAMS
Director of the Louvre . . . . . OLIVIER PIERRE
Minister of the Interior . . CLAUDE LE SACHÉ
Artist . . . . MICHAEL GOLDIE
Young Expert . . . . PAUL SIRR
American Millionaire . ROBERT HENDERSON
Porter . . . . JIM DUNK
Steiler . . . . PAUL HUMPOLETZ
Swiss Youth . . . . SIMON ADAMS

Designer . . . . TIM WILDING
Director . . . . ALAN GRINT

HOLMES AND HIS ARCH-ENEMY
PROFESSOR MORIARTY (ERIC PORTER)
IN THE FAMOUS CONFRONTATION IN
THE FINAL PROBLEM.

First shown on ITV Network on September 29, 1985 at 9.45 pm

THE RETURN OF SHERLOCK HOLMES

by Sir Arthur Conan Doyle
Developed for television by John Hawkesworth
Executive Producer MICHAEL COX
Producer JUNE WYNDHAM DAVIES
Music PATRICK GOWERS

THIRD SERIES

THE EMPTY HOUSE
Dramatized by John Hawkesworth

The third series of cases which formed *The Return of Sherlock Holmes* opened with the reappearance of the great detective in London after his supposed 'death' at the Reichenbach Falls. John Hawkesworth's adaptation of the famous story of *The Empty House* also introduced the new Doctor Watson in the shape of Edward Hardwicke. He, though, had actually first gone before the cameras as the good Doctor in the story of *The Abbey Grange* which was the first of the series to be filmed in the autumn of 1985. Patrick Allen co-starred as another memorable Holmesian villain, Colonel Sebastian Moran.

Sherlock Holmes .. JEREMY BRETT
Doctor Watson
        EDWARD HARDWICKE
Mrs Hudson . ROSALIE WILLIAMS
Colonel Sebastian Moran
        PATRICK ALLEN
Inspector Lestrade COLIN JEAVONS
The Hon. Ronald Adair
        PAUL LACOUX
Coroner .... JAMES BREE
Mr Murray ...... ROBERT ADDIE
Sir John Hardy ... RICHARD BEBB
The Countess of Maynooth
        NAOMI BUCH

Designer . MARGARET COOMBES
Director .... HOWARD BAKER

A DISGUISED HOLMES KEEPS AN EYE ON COLONEL SEBASTIAN MORAN (PATRICK ALLEN) IN *THE EMPTY HOUSE*.

First shown on ITV Network
on July 9, 1986 at 9.00 pm

HOLMES AND WATSON, WITH INSPECTOR HOPKINS (PAUL WILLIAMSON)
IN THE BACKGROUND, WATCH THERESA WRIGHT (ZULEMA DENE) AS SHE ATTENDS
TO LADY MARY BRACKENSTALL (ANNE LOUISE LAMBERT), IN *THE ABBEY GRANGE*.

THE ABBEY GRANGE
Dramatized by Trevor Bowen

Anne Louise Lambert starred as Lady Mary Brackenstall, the beautiful
Australian woman married to an unpleasant English lord (Conrad Phillips).
When Lord Brackenstall is found brutally murdered, Sherlock Holmes is soon on
the scene along with Inspector Hopkins (Paul Williamson). Also featured in the
story are Oliver Tobias as Captain Crocker and Zulema Dene as Theresa Wright.

Sherlock Holmes .. JEREMY BRETT	Lady Mary Brackenstall		
Doctor Watson		ANNE LOUISE LAMBERT	
EDWARD HARDWICKE	Theresa Wright ... ZULEMA DENE		
Inspector Hopkins	Captain Crocker . OLIVER TOBIAS		
PAUL WILLIAMSON	Mr Viviani ... NICOLAS CHAGRIN		
Sir Eustace Brackenstall	Designer .... TIM WILDING		
CONRAD PHILLIPS	Director ..... PETER HAMMOND		

First shown on ITV Network on August 6, 1986 at 9.00 pm

SHERLOCK HOLMES WITH REGINALD MUSGRAVE (MICHAEL CULVER).

THE MUSGRAVE RITUAL
Dramatized by Jeremy Paul

'This very singular business', as Holmes described the case, featured Michael Culver as the aristocratic Reginald Musgrave who seeks out the detective to get to the bottom of the strange events occurring on his estate at Hurlestone. In particular the goings-on in the manor house, which is believed to be the oldest inhabited building in the country.

Sherlock Holmes .. JEREMY BRETT
Doctor Watson
    EDWARD HARDWICKE
Reginald Musgrave
    MICHAEL CULVER
Richard Brunton
    JAMES HAZELDINE

Rachel Howells... JOHANNA KIRBY
Janet Tregallis .. TERESA BANHAM
Inspector Fereday ... IAN MARTER
Tregallis .. PATRICK BLACKWELL

Designer ...... MICHAEL GRIMES
Director .... DAVID CARSON

First shown on ITV Network on July 30, 1986 at 9.00 pm

218

THE SECOND STAIN
Dramatized by John Hawkesworth

The elegant Patricia Hodge switched roles to play Lady Hilda Trelawney Hope, the wife of a government minister, in this case of a mysterious murder in Westminster and a missing letter which turns up in the most obvious place. For earlier Patricia had scored a considerable success on television playing the sophisticated lady sleuth, Jemima Shore, and was very glad not to be on the hunt for clues yet again.

HOLMES AND WATSON FLANK LORD BELLINGER (HARRY ANDREWS) AND THE RIGHT HONOURABLE TRELAWNEY HOPE (STUART WILSON) IN *THE SECOND STAIN.*

Sherlock Holmes .. JEREMY BRETT
Doctor Watson
     EDWARD HARDWICKE
Lady Hilda Trelawney Hope
     PATRICIA HODGE
Rt. Honourable Trelawney Hope
     STUART WILSON
Lord Bellinger .. HARRY ANDREWS
Lestrade .... COLIN JEAVONS

Dates .... ALAN BENNION
Madame Henri Fournaye
     YVONNE ORENGO
Mrs Hudson . ROSALIE WILLIAMS
MacPherson ..... SEAN SCANLAN
Eduardo Lucas .. YVES BENEYTON

Designer .... TIM WILDING
Director .... JOHN BRUCE

First shown on ITV Network on July 23, 1986 at 10.40 pm

CLIVE FRANCIS AS NEVILLE ST CLAIR
AND ELEANOR DAVID AS HIS WIFE.

THE MAN WITH THE TWISTED LIP
Dramatized by Alan Plater

Another case in which Holmes' mastery of disguise is called upon in the search for clues concerning the mysterious 'disappearance' of Neville St Clair and the dramatic unmasking of the unsavoury beggar-man, Hugh Boone. The story also gave actor Clive Francis the chance to develop his own skill at disguise in the dual role of St Clair/Boone.

A DISGUISED SHERLOCK HOLMES IN THE OPIUM DEN IN THE MAN WITH THE TWISTED LIP.

Sherlock Holmes .. JEREMY BRETT
Doctor Watson
　　　　　　EDWARD HARDWICKE
Mrs Hudson . ROSALIE WILLIAMS
Neville St Clair/Hugh Boone
　　　　　　CLIVE FRANCIS
Mrs St Clair .... ELEANOR DAVID
Isa Whitney . TERENCE LONGDON
Mrs Whitney PATRICIA GARWOOD
Inspector Bradstreet ... DENIS LILL
Lascar .... ALBERT MOSES
Constable .... DUDLEY JAMES

Designer .... TIM WILDING
Director .... PATRICK LAU

First shown on ITV Network on August 13, 1986 at 9.00 pm

221

THE PRIORY SCHOOL

Dramatized by T R Bowen

When Doctor Thorneycroft Huxtable (played by Christopher Benjamin) arrives at 221B and immediately falls unconscious on the floor, it is the prelude to an extraordinary case whose unusual setting is a select preparatory school in the Peak District. Ten-year-old Lord Saltire, the only son and heir to the fabulously wealthy and hugely influential Duke of Holdernesse (played by Alan Howard), has mysteriously disappeared from the school – as has a silent and morose master. Holmes is immediately attracted to the case, which seems initially to bear all the hallmarks of a kidnapping. However, at the bottom of the mystery lies the remarkable secret of the Holdernesse family which leads Holmes and Watson to a dramatic confrontation in an underground cavern.

HOLMES AND WATSON STAND WITH
MR AVELING (MICHAEL BERTENSHAW) AND
DOCTOR HUXTABLE (CHRISTOPHER BENJAMIN)
OUTSIDE *THE PRIORY SCHOOL*.

Sherlock Holmes .. JEREMY BRETT
Doctor Watson
        EDWARD HARDWICKE
Doctor Huxtable
        CHRISTOPHER BENJAMIN
Mr Aveling MICHAL BERTENSHAW
James Wilder .. NICHOLAS GECKS
Duke of Holdernesse ALAN HOWARD
Rivers .... WILLIAM ABNEY
Reuben Hayes .... JACK CARR
Mrs Hayes .... BRENDER ELDER
Mrs Hudson . ROSALIE WILLIAMS
Lord Arthur Saltire . NISSAR MOTI
Caunter .... MARK TURIN

Designer . MARGARET COOMBES
Director .... JOHN MADDEN

First shown on ITV Network on
July 16, 1986 at 9.00 pm

HOLMES WITH HARKER (ERIC SYKES) AND INSPECTOR LESTRADE (COLIN JEAVONS).

THE SIX NAPOLEONS
Dramatized by John Kane

This, the last story in the third series to have been filmed, is described by Holmes as 'absolutely original in the history of crime'. It concerns a strange series of burglaries in which it seems the criminal's sole purpose is to destroy busts of Napoleon. Is this a case of a burglar with a fanatical hatred of the French Emperor, or something far more sinister? Holmes is put on the trail by the first victim of these strange crimes, Morse Hudson (played by Gerald Campion, forever remembered as the television Billy Bunter), but an even stranger robbery serves to deepen the mystery. For after a similar entry to the home of Mr Horace Harker of the Central News Agency (played by top comedian Eric Sykes) the body of an unknown man with his throat cut is found in the grounds not far from the remains of yet another bust of Napoleon . . .

Sherlock Holmes .. JEREMY BRETT
Doctor Watson
      EDWARD HARDWICKE
Harker .... ERIC SYKES
Inspector Lestrade COLIN JEAVONS
Lucretia .... MARINA SIRTIS
Venucci .... STEVE PLYTAS
Beppo .... EMILE WOLK
Morse Hudson GERALD CAMPION

Beppo's Cousin.. NADIO FORTUNE
Mr Sandeford JEFFREY GARDINER
Mr Brown .... MICHAEL LOGAN
Pietro ...... VINCENZO NICOLI
Mandelstam VERNON DOBTCHEFF

Designer .... TIM WILDING
Director .... DAVID CARSON

First shown on ITV Network on August 20, 1986 at 9.00 pm

223

FOURTH SERIES

THE DEVIL'S FOOT
Dramatized by Gary Hopkins

While on a recuperative holiday in Cornwall, Holmes is plunged into the terrible tragedy of the Tregennis family, in which a young woman is frightened to death and two strong men driven out of their senses by an unknown and ancient terror. Starring Denis Quilley as Doctor Leon Sterndale, a famous African explorer and friend of the family, the case also provided a special challenge for the production designer, Michael Grimes, who lives in Cornwall and was specially assigned to the story by producer June Wyndham Davies because of his local knowledge.

HOLMES INVESTIGATES THE MYSTERIOUS
CASE OF *THE DEVIL'S FOOT*.

Sherlock Holmes .. JEREMY BRETT
Doctor Watson
　　　　　　　EDWARD HARDWICKE
Mortimer Tregennis
　　　　　　　DAMIEN THOMAS
Leon Sterndale .. DENIS QUILLEY
Reverend Roundhay
　　　　　　　MICHAEL AITKEN
Mrs Porter .... FREDA DOWIE
Brenda Tregennis
　　　　　　　CHRISTINE COLLINS
George Tregennis ... PETER SHAW
Owen Tregennis NORMAN BOWLER
Doctor Richards . JOHN SAUNDERS
Police Inspector . FRANK MOOREY

Designer .... MIKE GRIMES
Director .... KEN HANNAM

First shown on ITV Network
on April 6, 1988 at 9.00 pm

224

COLONEL ROSS (PETER BARKWORTH), OWNER OF THE KIDNAPPED 'SILVER BLAZE'.

SILVER BLAZE
Dramatized by John Hawkesworth

This story of the kidnapping of the racehorse, 'Silver Blaze', and Holmes' solution of the cunning deception, featured Peter Barkworth as the horse's owner, Colonel Ross, with Malcolm Storry as Inspector Gregory. The Victorian race-meeting for the Wessex Cup which formed the climax of the case was filmed at Bangor-on-Dee racecourse with 120 extras appearing as tick-tack men, bookmakers, race officials, stewards, jockeys and spectators. Cardiff bookmaker David Parsons was brought in as special adviser to the Granada production team on racecourse 'etiquette'.

Sherlock Holmes .. JEREMY BRETT
Doctor Watson
    EDWARD HARDWICKE
Colonel Ross PETER BARKWORTH
Inspector Gregory
    MALCOLM STORRY
Mrs Hudson . ROSALIE WILLIAMS
Edith Baxter
    AMANDA-JAYNE BEARD
Ned Hunter .... DAVID JOHN
John Straker .... BARRY LOWE

Mrs Straker ... SALLY FAULKNER
Silas Brown ... RUSSELL HUNTER
Fitzroy Simpson . JONATHAN COY
Bookmaker .... MARCUS KIMBER
Race Official .. GEOFFREY BANKS
Mapleton Groom NICHOLAS TEARE
King's Pyland Grooms
    SEAN LEE/KIERON SMITH

Designer .... ALAN PRICE
Director .... BRIAN MILLS

First shown on ITV Network on April 13, 1988 at 9.00 pm

HOLMES FINDS INSPECTOR BAYNES ALREADY ON THE CASE WHEN HE ARRIVES AT
WISTERIA LODGE.

WISTERIA LODGE
Dramatized by Jeremy Paul

Strange things have been occurring at Wisteria Lodge in the Surrey countryside,
as a recent visitor, Mr Scott Eccles (Donald Churchill), informs Sherlock Holmes
on a visit to Baker Street. But when the famous detective and his companion
Doctor Watson visit the tumbledown house they find Inspector Baynes (Freddie
Jones) already there investigating the murder of the owner, Aloysius Garcia – and
very anxious to question Scott Eccles. Also starring in this baffling mystery were
Kika Markham, as Miss Burnet, the governess of a neighbouring house, and Basil
Hoskins as her forbidding employer, Henderson.

Sherlock Holmes ..	JEREMY BRETT	Garcia	ARTURO VENEGAS
Doctor Watson		Luis	GUIDO ADORNI
	EDWARD HARDWICKE	The Mulatto ..	SONNY CALDINEZ
Inspector Baynes ..	FREDDIE JONES	Henderson's Daughters	
Scott Eccles	DONALD CHURCHILL		ABIGAIL MELIA/LORNA ROSSI
Miss Burnet	KIKA MARKHAM		
Henderson	BASIL HOSKINS	Designer	TIM WILDING
Lucas	TRADER FAULKNER	Director	PETER HAMMOND

First shown on ITV Network on April 20, 1988 at 9.00 pm

THE BRUCE-PARTINGTON PLANS
Dramatized by John Hawkesworth

A return to the series for Mycroft Holmes (again elegantly played by Charles Gray), who enlists his brother's help in the hunt to find the plans for a top secret submarine which have gone missing and threaten to cause an international crisis. Also on the case which comes to light after the discovery of a young clerk's body in a London Underground tunnel are Violet Westbury (Amanda Waring), the dead man's fiancée and the last person to see him alive, and the redoubtable Inspector Bradstreet (Denis Lill).

Sherlock Holmes .. JEREMY BRETT
Doctor Watson
       EDWARD HARDWICKE
Mycroft Holmes .. CHARLES GRAY
Inspector Bradstreet ... DENIS LILL
Mrs Hudson . ROSALIE WILLIAMS
Colonel Valentine Walter
       JONATHAN NEWTH
Violet Westbury AMANDA WARING
Cadogan West SEBASTIAN STRIDE
Sidney Johnson
       GEOFFREY BAYLDON
Underground Official JOHN RAPLEY
Clerk at Woolwich Station
       ROBERT FYFE
Butler to Sir James Walter
       SIMON CARTER
Hugo Oberstein ..... DEREK WARE
First Platelayer .. STEPHEN CRANE
Second Platelayer .... JOHN LAING

Designer .... ALAN PICKFORD
Director .... JOHN GORRIE

HOLMES AND WATSON SEARCH FOR CLUES
IN THE LONDON UNDERGROUND WITH
INSPECTOR BRADSTREET (DENIS LILL).

First shown on ITV Network on April 27, 1988 at 10.35 pm

THE SIGN OF FOUR

by Sir Arthur Conan Doyle
Dramatized by John Hawkesworth
Executive Producer MICHAEL COX
Producer JUNE WYNDHAM DAVIES
Music PATRICK GOWERS

JOHN THAW AS THE VILLAINOUS JONATHAN SMALL, WITH HIS ACCOMPLICE, TONGA
(KIRAN SHAH).

The two-hour centenary celebration adaptation of the dramatic story of Holmes and Watson's search for the answers to the problems of a mysterious treasure trove of pearls, and some even more mysterious deaths, that are besetting the lovely Mary Morstan (Jenny Seagrove). Shot using 35-millimetre film for the first time, the adventure was made on location in Manchester, Liverpool, Yorkshire, Malta and London – with the finale, Holmes' pursuit of the villainous Jonathan Small (played by John Thaw, star of the ITV series, *Inspector Morse*) down the River Thames to its lower reaches, actually being recreated on the River Yare in Norfolk! Ronald Lacey appeared as Thaddeus Sholto, the important link in solving the mystery . . .

Sherlock Holmes .. JEREMY BRETT
Doctor Watson
           EDWARD HARDWICKE
Small . . . . JOHN THAW
Mary Morstan . JENNY SEAGROVE
Thaddeus Sholto . RONALD LACEY
Athelney Jones . . . . . EMRYS JAMES
Tonga . . . . KIRAN SHAH
Wiggins
         COURTNEY ROPER-KNIGHT
Lal Chowder . . . . ISHAQ BUX
Mr Smith . . . . DAVE ATKINS
McMurdo . . . . ALF JOINT
Major Sholto . . . . ROBIN HUNTER
Mrs Smith . . . . LILA KAYE
Khartar Singh . . . BADI UZZAMAN
Sherman . . . GORDON GOSTELOW
Captain Morstan
              TERENCE SKELTON
Williams . . . . . . DEREK DEADMAN
Inderjit Singh
       RAVINDER SINGH REYATT
Achmet . . . . RENU SETNA

Designer . . . . TIM WILDING
Director . . . . . . PETER HAMMOND

First shown on ITV Network on December 29, 1987 at 8.00 pm

THE HOUND OF THE BASKERVILLES

by Sir Arthur Conan Doyle
Dramatized by Trevor Bowen
Executive Producer MICHAEL COX
Producer JUNE WYNDHAM DAVIES
Music PATRICK GOWERS

A lavish, two-hour adaptation of the most famous of all Sherlock Holmes' cases, which required the building of a huge set representing the Grimpen Mire in Granada's Manchester studios. Yorkshire and Staffordshire locations were also used to represent the wilds of Dartmoor and Holmes' dangerous mission to track down the huge, demonic hound that is the curse of the Baskerville family. Co-starring in the production were Kristoffer Tabori as Sir Henry Baskerville, the latest in the line, and an 11-stone, two-year-old Great Dane named Khan. Jeremy Brett found the animal lovable and initially wondered how it could possibly send shivers down viewers' spines. Then he saw the ferocious robot head with flashing teeth and horrible eyes used in close-ups and commented, 'I was much more scared of the mechanised monster than of Khan!'

SIR HENRY BASKERVILLE (KRISTOFFER TABORI) ENLISTS SHERLOCK HOLMES' HELP IN *THE HOUND OF THE BASKERVILLES.*

Sherlock Holmes .. JEREMY BRETT
Doctor Watson
        EDWARD HARDWICKE
Sir Charles Baskerville
        RAYMOND ADAMSON
Doctor Mortimer ... NEIL DUNCAN
Barrymore ..... RONALD PICKUP
Mrs Barrymore
        ROSEMARY McHALE
Sir Henry Baskerville
        KRISTOFFER TABORI
Purser .... EDWARD ROMFOURT
Stapleton ..... JAMES FAULKNER
Pageboy .... PHILIP DETTMER
Perkins .... STEPHEN TOMLIN
Beryl Stapleton ... FIONA GILLIES
Frankland . BERNARD HORSFALL
Vicar of Grimpen
        DONALD McKILLOP
Selden .... WILLIAM ILKLEY
Countrywoman
        MYRTLE DEVENISH
Laura Lyons
        ELIZABETH SPENDER
Manservant ..... DONALD BISSET
Stuntman .... GARETH MILNE

Designers ... JAMES WEATHERUP
        AND CHRIS BRADSHAW
Director .... BRIAN MILLS

First shown on ITV Network on August 31, 1988 at 8.00 pm

231

THE CASEBOOK OF SHERLOCK HOLMES

by Sir Arthur Conan Doyle
Producer MICHAEL COX
Music PATRICK GOWERS

FIFTH SERIES

THE DISAPPEARANCE OF LADY FRANCES CARFAX

Dramatized by Trevor Bowen

Holmes described this case as 'an example of that temporary eclipse to which even the best-balanced mind may be exposed' when he wrestled with the puzzle of the mysterious wanderings about Europe of the beautiful Lady Frances (played by Cheryl Campbell) and the part in all this of the enigmatic Albert Schlessinger (Julian Curry) and the Earl of Rufton (Michael Jayston).

Sherlock Holmes	JEREMY BRETT
Doctor Watson	EDWARD HARDWICKE
Mrs Hudson	ROSALIE WILLIAMS
Albert Schlessinger/Henry Peters	JULIAN CURRY
Miss Calder/Mrs Peters	MARY CUNNINGHAM
Lady Frances Carfax	CHERYL CAMPBELL
Vicar	ANTHONY BENSON
The Hon. Philip Green	JACK KLAFF
The Earl of Rufton	MICHAEL JAYSTON
Hotel Manager	NICHOLAS FRY
Liveried Official	ANTHONY SCHAEFFER
Woman at Undertakers'	MARGOT STANLEY
Designer	CHRIS WILKINSON
Director	JOHN MADDEN

CHERYL CAMPBELL AS THE 'DISAPPEARING' LADY FRANCES CARFAX, WITH MICHAEL JAYSTON.

First shown on ITV Network on February 21, 1991 at 9.00 pm

THE PROBLEM OF THOR BRIDGE
Dramatized by Jeremy Paul

The mysterious death of the wife of wealthy J. Neil Gibson (Daniel Massey), and the subsequent suspicion which is thrown upon the couple's governess, Grace Dunbar (Catherine Russell) – whom the magnate loves and believes to be innocent – takes Holmes to the suspect's picturesque country estate. Here, while indulging in a little archery as he searches for clues to what at first seems a case of murder, the detective uncovers some extraordinary clues on Thor Bridge. The case also introduces Holmes' Baker Street helpmate, Billy, played by Dean Magri.

Sherlock Holmes .. JEREMY BRETT
Doctor Watson
    EDWARD HARDWICKE
J. Neil Gibson ... DANIEL MASSEY
Grace Dunbar
    CATHERINE RUSSELL
Maria Gibson ·.. CELIA GREGORY
Marlow Bates ..... NIVEN BOYD
Sergeant Coventry
    ANDREW WILDE

Mr Ferguson
    STEPHEN MACDONALD
Mr Joyce Cummings QC
    PHILIP BRETHERTON
Billy .... DEAN MAGRI

Designer .... PAUL ROWAN
Director ...∴ MICHAEL SIMPSON

First shown on ITV Network on February 28, 1991 at 9.00 pm

HOLMES RECEIVES ARCHERY INSTRUCTION FROM WEALTHY MAGNATE J. NEIL GIBSON (DANIEL MASSEY) IN *THE PROBLEM OF THOR BRIDGE*.

HOLMES AND WATSON HEAR THE BACKGROUND TO *THE BOSCOMBE VALLEY MYSTERY*
FROM THE OLD AUSTRALIAN HIGHWAY ROBBER, TURNER (PETER VAUGHAN).

THE BOSCOMBE VALLEY MYSTERY

Dramatized by John Hawkesworth

Bromley Cross Quarry near Bolton doubled as the Australian outback for a flashback recalling the ambush of a gold wagon in this story of Holmes' investigation into a brutal murder in Cheshire. The murdered man, William McCarthy (Leslie Schofield), was Australian by birth and it is his son, James (James Purefoy) who is accused of the murder – until the intervention of Holmes, who learns all about the hardships of life Down Under from a Mr Turner (Peter Vaughan), himself once a highway robber in the 1860s . . .

Sherlock Holmes .. JEREMY BRETT	James McCarthy . JAMES PUREFOY
Doctor Watson	Crowder .... CLIFF HOWELLS
EDWARD HARDWICKE	George/Groom ... MARK JORDAN
Inspector Summerby	Coroner .... WILL TACEY
JONATHAN BARLOW	Patience Crowder
Mr Turner ..... PETER VAUGHAN	MAKALA SAUNDERS
Alice Turner ...... JOANNA ROTH	
William McCarthy	Designer .... STEVE FINEREN
LESLIE SCHOFIELD	Director .... JUNE HOWSON

First shown on ITV Network on March 14, 1991 at 9.00 pm

THE ILLUSTRIOUS CLIENT
Dramatized by Robin Chapman

Baron Gruner (Anthony Valentine), the unscrupulous man described by Holmes as the 'Austrian murderer', has so beguiled the beautiful Violet Merville (Abigail Cruttenden) that she can see nothing sinister in his plans to marry her. But a family friend, Colonel Sir James Damery (David Langton), understandably worries for her future, and recruits the aid of the Baker Street detective to thwart the Baron's plans as well as bring him to justice for all his crimes – a case which produces a murderous attack upon Holmes as well as an unexpected finale . . .

Sherlock Holmes .. JEREMY BRETT
Doctor Watson
    EDWARD HARDWICKE
Baron Gruner
    ANTHONY VALENTINE
Baroness Gruner . CAROL NOAKES
Colonel Sir James Damery
    DAVID LANGTON
Violet Merville
    ABIGAIL CRUTTENDEN
Mrs Hudson . ROSALIE WILLIAMS

Cabman . . . . KEITH LADD
Jarvis . . . . JOHN PICKLES
Kitty Winter . . . . . KIM THOMSON
Shinwell Johnson . . . . ROY HOLDER
First Man . . . . . . ANDY BRADFORD
Sir Leslie Oakshott
    WILFRED HARRISON

Designer . . . . ALAN PRICE
Director . . . . TIM SULLIVAN

First shown on ITV Network on March 21, 1991 at 9.00 pm

JEREMY BRETT AS HOLMES, AND ANDY BRADFORD AS HIS ASSAILANT.

SHOSCOMBE OLD PLACE

Dramatized by Gary Hopkins

Sir Robert Norberton of Shoscombe Old Place (Robin Ellis), known far and wide as a 'daredevil rider', is desperately trying to avoid financial ruin by secretly preparing a horse he hopes will win the Championship Stakes. But his plans begin to founder with the dramatic discovery of a corpse and the reappearance of his chief creditor and old enemy, the rascally moneylender Sam Brewer (James Coyle), whom he once horsewhipped at Newmarket. Into this intrigue plunges Holmes to tackle a case of, as he puts it, 'deep and rather dirty waters'.

Sherlock Holmes .. JEREMY BRETT
Doctor Watson
    EDWARD HARDWICKE
Sir Robert Norberton   ROBIN ELLIS
Lady Beatrice Falder
    ELIZABETH WEAVER
John Mason ...... FRANK GRIMES
Carrie Evans ..... DENISE BLACK
Sandy Bain ...... MARTIN STONE
Josiah Barnes .. MICHAEL WYNNE
Stephens ...... MICHAEL BILTON
Sam Brewer .... JAMES COYLE
Mrs Hudson . ROSALIE WILLIAMS
Joe Barnes .... JUDE LAW
Harvey .... ALAN PATTISON

Designer .... STEVE FINEREN
Director .... PATRICK LAU

First shown on ITV Network
on March 7, 1991 at 9.00 pm

ROBIN ELLIS AS SIR ROBERT, AND ELIZABETH WEAVER AS LADY BEATRICE, IN *SHOSCOMBE OLD PLACE*.

HOLMES AND WATSON INVESTIGATE THE MYSTERY OF *THE CREEPING MAN*.

THE CREEPING MAN
Dramatized by Robin Chapman

The last episode of the Casebook recounts the terrifying experience of Professor Presbury's daughter Edith (Sarah Woodward), who wakes to find a strange figure at her bedroom window – which her father (Charles Kay) nevertheless dismisses as a bad dream. But her fiancé, Jack Bennett (Adrian Lukis), thinks otherwise and asks Holmes to solve the mystery. Holmes spots a link between the girl's nightmare and the disappearance of a great ape from London Zoo, and soon he and Watson and their old adversary, Inspector Lestrade, are involved in an investigation which leads into some dark and dangerous byways . . .

Sherlock Holmes . . JEREMY BRETT
Doctor Watson
EDWARD HARDWICKE
Professor Presbury . CHARLES KAY
Edith Presbury
SARAH WOODWARD
Jack Bennett . . . . . ADRIAN LUKIS
Inspector Lestrade COLIN JEAVONS

Designer . . . . PAUL ROWAN
Director . . . . TIM SULLIVAN

First shown on ITV Network on March 28, 1991 at 9.00 pm

237

THE MASTER BLACKMAILER

Adapted from 'Charles Augustus Milverton'
by Sir Arthur Conan Doyle
Screenplay by Jeremy Paul
Producer JUNE WYNDHAM DAVIES
Music PATRICK GOWERS

HOLMES AND WATSON RALLY ROUND THE ANXIOUS LADY EVA BLACKWELL (SERENA GORDON) IN *THE MASTER BLACKMAILER*.

238

The third two-hour special made newspaper headlines because of the scene in which Holmes, disguised as a plumber to infiltrate the villain's home, has to win the affections of a serving girl Agatha (Sophie Thompson) by kissing her. Jeremy said later, 'I was concerned about the scene because I thought we might be infringing on Sherlock's sexuality given that he is such a private man.'

After this episode was screened in the USA, June Wyndham Davies says the production office received a number of letters from viewers there who had found the kissing sequence very therapeutic. 'They were from people who were also having trouble in making intimate contact with others,' says June, 'and they could relate Holmes' evident reluctance to their own. They all said that watching the scene had helped them in facing up to their own problems.'

Co-starring as the evil and treacherous Charles Augustus Milverton, who emerges from the London underworld intent on destroying the society wedding of the year, was Robert Hardy – a very different part from his then-current role in *All Creatures Great and Small*. He said of Milverton – actually based on a notorious Victorian blackmailer – 'He is a sod of the worst quality, totally heartless. It's interesting to try and find sympathy for such an odious creature – but, of course, all actors love playing villains – it's such a good outlet!'

Sherlock Holmes .. JEREMY BRETT
Doctor Watson
     EDWARD HARDWICKE
Charles Augustus Milverton
     ROBERT HARDY
Diana, Lady Swinstead
     NORMA WEST
The Dowager
     GWEN FFRANGCON-DAVIES
Lady Eva Blackwell
     SERENA GORDON
The Hon. Charlotte Miles
     SARAH McVICAR
Colonel Dorking
     DAVID MALLINSON
Harry, Earl of Dovercourt
     BRIAN MITCHELL
Inspector Lestrade
     COLIN JEAVONS

Agatha ..... SOPHIE THOMPSON
Mrs Hudson . ROSALIE WILLIAMS
Hebworth (alias Veitch)
     HANS MEYER
Stokes .... STEPHEN SIMMS
Bertrand ...... NICKOLAS GRACE
Lillie .... BELINDA PETERS
Daphne
     HENRIETTA WHITSON-JONES
Tronson (Butler)
     ALAN ROTHWELL
Lewis (Batman) .... HOWARD GAY
Gallery Owner ...... DAVID SCASE
Hobbs .... JIMMY HIBBERT
Auctioneer .. TONY BROUGHTON

Designer
     CHRISTOPHER TRUELOVE
Director ...... PETER HAMMOND

First shown on ITV Network on January 2, 1992 at 8.30 pm

THE LAST VAMPYRE

Adapted from 'The Sussex Vampire' by Sir Arthur Conan Doyle
Screenplay by Jeremy Paul
Producer JUNE WYNDHAM DAVIES
Music PATRICK GOWERS

The dramatic fire scene in the opening minutes of this two-hour special was not a special effects creation but an actual blaze. Explained designer Christopher Bradshaw, 'It looked so spectacular that I think many people believed it must have been a model – but the "mansion" which burnt down was actually a wooden one which we built at a cost of more than £30,000 on the remnants of an old ruin in Warwickshire . . . and then set fire to!' The family home where much of the action took place was 400-year-old Pitchford Hall in Shropshire which Bradshaw says was 'an exact match to the house Conan Doyle described in his story – with a dark timber exterior and tall chimneys. There was even lichen on the roof as he'd mentioned.'

Roy Marsden, familiar to many viewers as Commander Adam Dalgliesh in the P. D. James crime stories, played a very different role as John Stockton, a mysterious figure whose arrival in a sleepy Sussex village immediately creates fear among the local people. A hundred years earlier, it transpires, some of his ancestors had been burned to death by terrified villagers who believed them to be vampires, and the present inhabitants are convinced that Stockton is also a vampire and has returned to avenge their deaths. As a result, Holmes and Watson soon find themselves in an atmosphere of superstition where garlic, crosses and wooden stakes are in danger of taking over from law and order . . .

Sherlock Holmes .. JEREMY BRETT
Doctor Watson
    EDWARD HARDWICKE
John Stockton .... ROY MARSDEN
Bob Ferguson .... KEITH BARRON
Carlotta .... YOLANDA VAZQUEZ
Reverend Merridew
    MAURICE DENHAM
Jack .... RICHARD DEMPSEY
Dolores .... JULIET AUBREY
Michael .JASON HETHERINGTON
Mrs Mason . ELIZABETH SPRIGGS
Vera/Janet Burrows
    MARIA REDMOND

Billy (the pageboy) .. PAUL PARRIS
Pedlar .... FREDDIE JONES
Mr Gresty .... PETER GEDDIS
Mrs Gresty ..... KATE LANSBURY
Miss Ruddock ... HILARY MASON
PC Ware ...... STEPHEN TOMLIN
Mrs Carter .... EILEEN O'BRIEN
Mr Carter ..... ANDY ABRAHAMS
Tom Carter
    MARCELLO MARASCALCHI

Designer
    CHRISTOPHER J. BRADSHAW
Director .... TIM SULLIVAN

ROY MARSDEN AS THE SINISTER JOHN STOCKTON IN *THE LAST VAMPYRE*.

First shown on ITV Network on January 27, 1993 at 8.00 pm

THE ELIGIBLE BACHELOR

Adapted from 'The Noble Bachelor'
by Sir Arthur Conan Doyle
Screenplay by T. R. Bowen
Producer JUNE WYNDHAM DAVIES
Music PATRICK GOWERS

The fifth two-hour special, shown in the spring of 1993, co-starred the debonair Simon Williams as Lord Robert St Simon, the scion of an aristocratic British family whose wife-to-be, an American heiress (Paris Jefferson) has disappeared on the morning of their wedding. Called in to investigate, Holmes finds himself uninterested in the case when he compares it to some of the past adversaries he has faced – like Moriarty, for instance. 'He was a giant of evil,' he muses at one stage. 'Without him, I'm obliged to deal with the pygmies of triviality.' But as the great detective begins to dig a little deeper into the affair he finds that the clean-cut Lord Robert is actually a man full of dark secrets. . .

For Mary Ellis, the 93-year-old actress who played the Dowager Duchess, Lady Florence, the film evoked memories of the first stage Sherlock Holmes, William Gillette, whom she had met as a young girl of twelve in 1912. Later, in the 1920s, when she, too, had entered the acting profession, their paths crossed again and she sent Gillette a box of flowers in the hope he might have remembered her. 'The reply came quickly, he had not forgotten,' Mary Ellis says, still cherishing the letter. 'Everything comes full circle, it seems, and by appearing in the TV series I felt somehow that I had thanked William Gillette for his kindness.'

Sherlock Holmes .. JEREMY BRETT
Doctor Watson
    EDWARD HARDWICKE
Mrs Hudson . ROSALIE WILLIAMS
Inspector Montgomery
    GEOFFREY BEEVERS
Helena/Agnes Northcote
    ANNA CALDER-MARSHALL
Lord St Simon . SIMON WILLIAMS
Henrietta Doran
    PARIS JEFFERSON
Flora Miller .JOANNA McCALLUM
Hon Amelia St Simon
    HEATHER CHASEN
Lady Florence ...... MARY ELLIS

Lady Mary ... PHILLADA SEWELL
Lady Blanche ... ELSPETH MARCH
Aloysius Doran .... BOB SESSIONS
Francis Moulton
    PETER WARNOCK
George Tidy ...... PETER GRAVES
Thomas Floutier ... MILES HOYLE
Alice .... TRES HANLEY
Gallagher .... BRUCE MYERS
Esther .... JOYCE GRUNDY
Oswald .... ROBIN HART

Designer
    CHRISTOPHER TRUELOVE
Director ...... PETER HAMMOND

LORD ROBERT ST SIMON (PLAYED BY SIMON WILLIAMS) AND HIS BRIDE-TO-BE (PARIS JEFFERSON) BEFORE HER MYSTERIOUS DISAPPEARANCE IN *THE ELIGIBLE BACHELOR*.

First shown on ITV Network on February 3, 1993 at 8.00 pm

THE MEMOIRS OF SHERLOCK HOLMES

by Sir Arthur Conan Doyle
Producer JUNE WYNDHAM DAVIES
Music PATRICK GOWERS

SIXTH SERIES

THE THREE GABLES
Screenplay by Jeremy Paul

When Holmes and Watson investigate a strange attempt to purchase an old lady's house and possessions, Holmes soon becomes far more interested in the recent death of her beloved grandson. He concludes that the culprits are thugs hired by the victim's former lover, a notorious Spanish society beauty, now betrothed to a young Duke.

With the ducal line in danger of being drawn into a shameful alliance, Holmes has to use all his powers of detection and persuasion to avert disaster. And in so doing, he is also able to let his client fulfil one of her greatest dreams. . .

Peter Wyngarde, famous for his role as the flamboyant Jason King in the cult TV series, *Department S*, gave a stylish performance as Langdale Pike. Leading players were Claudine Auger, Mary Ellis and Caroline Blakiston. Edward Hardwicke's daughter Emma continued the Hardwicke dynasty started by Sir Cedric by playing the role of Dora.

Sherlock Holmes . . JEREMY BRETT
Doctor Watson
    EDWARD HARDWICKE
Mrs Hudson . ROSALIE WILLIAMS
Isadora Klein . . CLAUDINE AUGER
Mary Maberley . . . . . . MARY ELLIS
Langdale Pike . PETER WYNGARDE
Duke of Lomond
    BENJAMIN PULLEN
Douglas Maberley . . . . . GARY CADY

Dowager Duchess of Lomond
    CAROLINE BLAKISTON
Haines-Johnson
    MICHAEL GRAHAM
Susan . . . . BARBARA YOUNG
Steve Dixie . . . STEVE TOUSSAINT
Mr Sutro . . . . JOHN GILL
Dora . . . . EMMA HARDWICKE

Designer . . . . . MICHAEL YOUNG
Director . . . . . . PETER HAMMOND

244

PETER WYNGARDE AS LANGDALE PIKE WITH JEREMY BRETT IN *THE THREE GABLES*.

HOLMES AND WATSON CONFER WITH A WORRIED JOHN GEDGRAVE (PLAYED BY
ROY HUDD).

THE DYING DETECTIVE
Screenplay by T. R. Bowen

When an eminent young banker, Victor Savage, dies suddenly from a rare tropical disease, the family estate passes to a scientist cousin, Culverton Smith, and leaves Savage's beautiful young widow and four children homeless. Holmes' suspicions of foul play are confirmed when a poisoned pack of tobacco from Culverton Smith arrives at Baker Street. Feigning death, the great detective summons Culverton Smith to his bedside, where, convinced that Holmes is dying from the poisoned tobacco, the scientist makes no effort to deny Savage's murder. But Watson over-hears the conversation and a sudden 'miraculous recovery' leads to the successful conclusion of yet another case for Sherlock Holmes.

Trevor Bowen, who played Charles Damant, achieved a unique double for the series – having written the episode, he also acted in it!

Sherlock Holmes .. JEREMY BRETT	Mrs Carnac ..... CAROLINE JOHN
Doctor Watson	Penrose Fisher
EDWARD HARDWICKE	SHUGHAN SEYMOUR
Mrs Hudson . ROSALIE WILLIAMS	Inspector Morton
Victor Savage	JOHN LABANOWSKI
RICHARD BONNEVILLE	Sergeant .... COLIN STEVENS
Adelaide Savage	Mariana .... RACHEL RICE
SUSANNAH HARKER	Chinese Lady .... MARY TEN POW
Culverton Smith	Staples ..... MALCOLM HEBDEN
JONATHAN HYDE	Benson .... KIERAN FLYNN
John Gedgrave .... ROY HUDD	
Charles Damant . TREVOR BOWEN	Designer
Colonel Carnac	CHRISTOPHER TRUELOVE
ROWLAND DAVIES	Director ...... SARAH HELLINGS

THE GOLDEN PINCE-NEZ
Screenplay by Gary Hopkins

Edward Hardwicke was unavailable to film this episode of the sixth series, so Sherlock Holmes' brother Mycroft (played by Charles Gray) was written in to assist the detective.

The case begins with the discovery of a dead body, with no apparent clue except a pair of golden pince-nez glasses clutched in the corpse's hand. Scotland Yard seeks the assistance of Sherlock Holmes to solve a mystery which stretches as far as the war-torn city St Petersburg. . .

Also helping the great detective were Nigel Planer, Anna Carteret, the star of the modern crime series, *Juliet Bravo*, and the veteran Frank Finlay, whose son Daniel also appeared as the Russian Vladimir.

Sherlock Holmes .. JEREMY BRETT
Mycroft Holmes .. CHARLES GRAY
Professor Coram/Sergius
         FRANK FINLAY
Inspector Hopkins . NIGEL PLANER
Susan Tarlton .. NATALIE MORSE
Abigail Crosby
         PATRICIA KERRIGAN
Willoughby Smith
         CHRISTOPHER GUARD
Anna . . . . ANNA CARTERET
Mrs Marker .. KATHLEEN BYRON
Mrs Hudson . ROSALIE WILLIAMS
Alexis . . . . ROGER RINGROSE
Vladimir . . . . DANIEL FINLAY

Designer . . . . . MICHAEL YOUNG
Director . . . . . . PETER HAMMOND

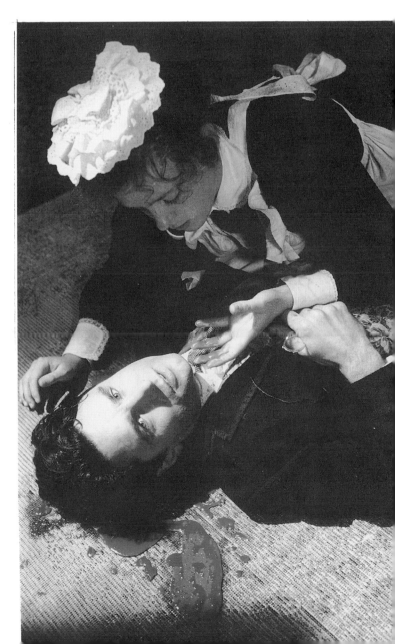

SUSAN TARLTON (PLAYED BY NATALIE MORSE) WITH A VERY DEAD WILLOUGHBY SMITH (CHRISTOPHER GUARD).

THE RED CIRCLE
Screenplay by Jeremy Paul

Another case with international connections for Sherlock Holmes – now rejoined by Watson – with clues to be unearthed in Europe as well as America. A friend of the faithful Mrs Hudson implores Holmes to investigate the strange business of an Italian lodger who has not left his room at the top of her house for two weeks.

Holmes and Watson soon find themselves embroiled in the dangerous web of the Red Circle, a secret political society whose evil claws stretch to Italy and New York. Holmes has to tread a precarious path between murder and violence – but is finally able to save the lives of two courageous young Italians.

The versatile Betty Marsden co-starred as Mrs Warren, the friend of Mrs Hudson, and the evergreen comedy star Kenneth Connor made a rare straight appearance as her husband.

Sherlock Holmes	JEREMY BRETT
Doctor Watson	EDWARD HARDWICKE
Mrs Hudson	ROSALIE WILLIAMS
Mrs Warren	BETTY MARSDEN
Mr Warren	KENNETH CONNOR
Giorgiano	JOHN HALLAM
Vera	LOUISE HEANEY
Firmani	JOSEPH LONG
Leverton	KERRY SHALE
Emilia Lucca	SOPHIE DIAZ
Gennaro Lucca	JAMES COOMBES
Inspector Gregson	TOM CHADBON
Designer	CHRISTOPHER PEMSEL
Director	SARAH HELLINGS

HOLMES AND WATSON WITH MRS HUDSON (PLAYED BY ROSALIE WILLIAMS) AND HER FRIEND MRS WARREN (BETTY MARSDEN).

HOLMES AND WATSON TACKLE THE DOUBLE MYSTERY OF *THE MAZARIN STONE*.

THE MAZARIN STONE
(Incorporating 'The Three Garridebs')
Screenplay by Gary Hopkins

This was the first mystery to combine elements of two stories by Sir Arthur Conan Doyle, offering dedicated Sherlockians an interesting puzzle in separating the various incidents.

The case opens with Holmes being requested on behalf of the Prime Minister to find the stolen crown jewel, the Mazarin Stone. While Holmes pursues his prime suspect, the infamous Count Sylvius, Watson undertakes a case on behalf of the elderly Nathan Garrideb, who has been contacted by an American named John Garrideb.

It is only when Holmes spots John Garrideb's true identity and links his name with Count Sylvius that the two cases are joined together. Holmes and his faithful chronicler have to survive a dramatic confrontation in which Watson comes close to death before they can resolve the tangled web of crime and intrigue.

Sherlock Holmes .. JEREMY BRETT
Doctor Watson
      EDWARD HARDWICKE
Count Sylvius .... JON FINCH
John Garrideb
      GAVAN O'HERLIHY
Agnes Garrideb
      PHYLLIS CALVERT

Nathan Garrideb
      SEBASTIAN SHAW

Designer
      CHRISTOPHER TRUELOVE
Director ...... PETER HAMMOND

THE CARDBOARD BOX
Screenplay by William Humble

Holmes is asked by the police to comment on a grisly package which has been delivered to a spinster lady living in Croydon. When he sees that it contains two severed human ears, Holmes suspects murder, and as soon as he has interviewed the old lady and her sister, he immediately dismisses the police opinion that it was all just a prank – and instead begins to piece together a tale of sibling jealousy and betrayal.

The clues lead Holmes and Watson to Liverpool, where the detective discovers the brutal killing of a third sister and her lover. As Holmes closes in on the killer, a man apparently driven mad with jealousy, he puts his own life in jeopardy to bring an end to the terrible killings.

Cast includes:

Sherlock Holmes .. JEREMY BRETT
Doctor Watson
EDWARD HARDWICKE

Designer . . . . . . MICHAEL YOUNG
Director . . . . . . SARAH HELLINGS

THE HORROR OF *THE CARDBOARD BOX* LEADS HOLMES ALONG A DANGEROUS TRAIL.

AFTERWORD:
❦ III ❦

Television producers are often asked to define exactly what they do and it is not an easy question to answer. They certainly worry a great deal because they hold the purse strings and, on a project as big as this one, the purse is measured in millions of pounds.

The series was originally planned to be thirteen films, ending with the death of Sherlock Holmes in *The Final Problem*. If it proved to be successful, there was the possibility of resurrecting our hero – just as Sir Arthur Conan Doyle did – in a further series of adventures, six or seven perhaps if we were very lucky.

Faced with that challenge on such a cherished project, the only solution was to go for the best: the best writers, actors, directors and designers – and miraculously we got them. Not just the best Holmes of his generation, but also the two best Watsons and the best Mrs Hudson, Moriarty, Lestrade, Mycroft . . . And behind that cast list is a production team on which any producer would willingly risk a million or two.

June Wyndham Davies joined the team in 1986 to produce *The Return of Sherlock Holmes*. She has been responsible for 27 hours (including all the two-hour films) out of the 46 hours made so far. There are now more than 40 films in the series, still a few short of the whole canon, but I shall not be surprised if the final score reaches Sir Arthur's 60 not out before the end of the decade. And whoever sees it through will have, as June and I have had in the 1980s and 1990s, the best job in television.

MICHAEL S. COX
Cheshire, 1993

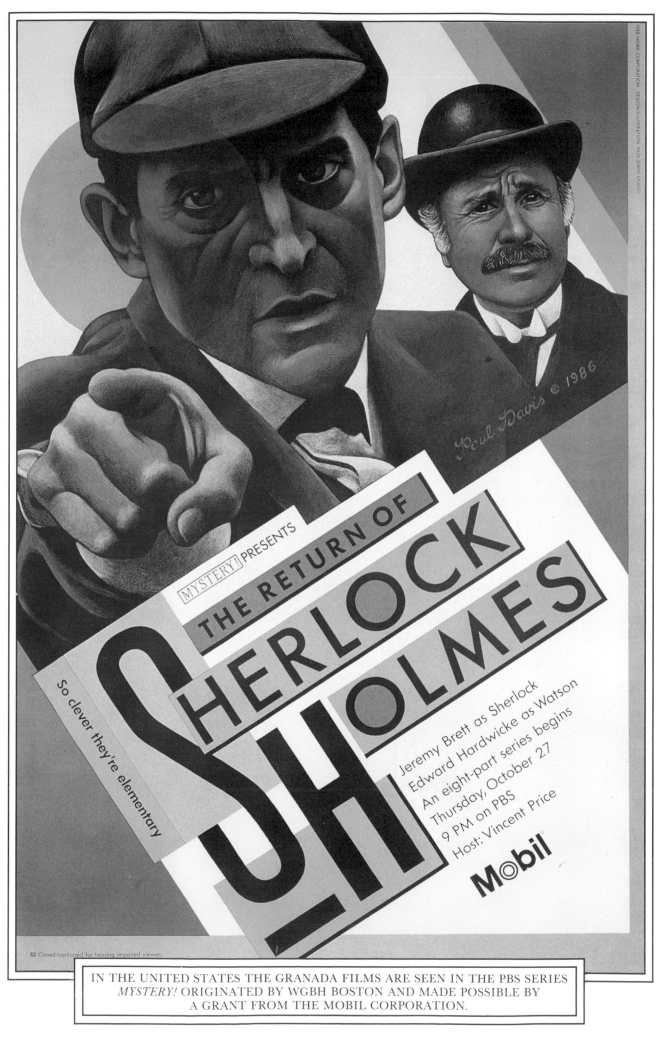

'Watson here will tell you
that I can never resist
a touch of the dramatic.'
SHERLOCK HOLMES
The Naval Treaty

❧ ACKNOWLEDGEMENTS ❧

I owe my sincere thanks to a number of people who helped me in the writing of this book – in particular Michael Cox of Granada Television who made it all possible in the first place, and my good friend John Bennett Shaw in America whose knowledge of the Holmesian canon is encyclopaedic and who helped locate much of the historical information about Holmes on television. To the three actors who have made the Granada production such a world-wide success, Jeremy Brett, David Burke and Edward Hardwicke, my thanks for their co-operation and enthusiasm. Also those splendid 'back-room boys' in Manchester, Stuart Doughty and Peter Mares, for advice and assistance, Sally Bleddyn in London, and the charming producer of the subsequent series, June Wyndham Davies. I must also acknowledge the splendid support and encouragement of my publishers, in particular Bob Tanner, Mike Bailey, Paul Forty and Cecil Smith. In addition to Granada Television, I should also like to thank the following for supplying pictures: The British Film Institute, the BBC, NBC, ABC, Universal Pictures, John Paul, the *Daily Mail*, the *Guardian* and *Punch* magazine. The remaining illustrations are all from my own collection of Holmesiana.

PETER HAINING
October 1993